539134

029.6STE
IWL

Studying Psychology

Southampton
SOLENT
University

D0533298

WITHDRAWN FROM LIBRARY STOCK

7593651

Visit our free study skills resource at **www.skills4study.com**

Palgrave Study Guides

Authoring a PhD
Career Skills
e-Learning Skills
Effective Communication for
   Arts and Humanities Students
Effective Communication for
   Science and Technology
The Exam Skills Handbook
The Foundations of Research
The Good Supervisor
How to Manage your Arts, Humanities and
   Social Science Degree
How to Manage your Distance and
   Open Learning Course
How to Manage your Postgraduate Course
How to Manage your Science and
   Technology Degree
How to Study Foreign Languages
How to Write Better Essays
IT Skills for Successful Study
Making Sense of Statistics
The Mature Student's Guide to Writing (2nd edn)
The Palgrave Student Planner
The Personal Tutor's Handbook
The Postgraduate Research Handbook (2nd edn)
Presentation Skills for Students

The Principles of Writing in Psychology
Professional Writing (2nd edn)
Research Using IT
Skills for Success
The Student Life Handbook
The Palgrave Student Planner
The Student's Guide to Writing (2nd edn)
The Study Abroad Handbook
The Study Skills Handbook (2nd edn)
Study Skills for Speakers of English as
   a Second Language
Studying the Built Environment
Studying Economics
Studying History (2nd edn)
Studying Law
Studying Mathematics and its Applications
Studying Modern Drama (2nd edn)
Studying Physics
Studying Programming
Studying Psychology (2nd edn)
Teaching Study Skills and Supporting Learning
Work Placements – a Survival Guide for Students
Write it Right
Writing for Engineers (3rd edn)
Writing for Nursing and Midwifery Students

Palgrave Study Guides: Literature
General Editors: John Peck and Martin Coyle

How to Begin Studying English Literature
   (3rd edn)
How to Study a Jane Austen Novel (2nd edn)
How to Study a Charles Dickens Novel
How to Study Chaucer (2nd edn)
How to Study an E. M. Forster Novel
How to Study James Joyce
How to Study Linguistics (2nd edn)

How to Study Modern Poetry
How to Study a Novel (2nd edn)
How to Study a Poet
How to Study a Renaissance Play
How to Study Romantic Poetry (2nd edn)
How to Study a Shakespeare Play (2nd edn)
How to Study Television
Practical Criticism

Studying Psychology

Second Edition

Andrew Stevenson

© Andrew Stevenson 2001, 2007

Foreword © Philip Banyard 2007

All rights reserved. No reproduction, copy or transmission of this publication may be made without written permission.

No paragraph of this publication may be reproduced, copied or transmitted save with written permission or in accordance with the provisions of the Copyright, Designs and Patents Act 1988, or under the terms of any licence permitting limited copying issued by the Copyright Licensing Agency, 90 Tottenham Court Road, London W1T 4LP.

Any person who does any unauthorised act in relation to this publication may be liable to criminal prosecution and civil claims for damages.

The author has asserted his right to be identified as the author of this work in accordance with the Copyright, Designs and Patents Act 1988.

First published 2001
Second edition published 2007 by
PALGRAVE MACMILLAN
Houndmills, Basingstoke, Hampshire RG21 6XS and
175 Fifth Avenue, New York, N.Y. 10010
Companies and representatives throughout the world

PALGRAVE MACMILLAN is the global academic imprint of the Palgrave Macmillan division of St. Martin's Press, LLC and of Palgrave Macmillan Ltd. Macmillan® is a registered trademark in the United States, United Kingdom and other countries. Palgrave is a registered trademark in the European Union and other countries.

ISBN-13: 978–0–230–51782–0
ISBN-10: 0–230–51782–X

This book is printed on paper suitable for recycling and made from fully managed and sustained forest sources. Logging, pulping and manufacturing processes are expected to conform to the environmental regulations of the country of origin.

A catalogue record for this book is available from the British Library.

A catalog record for this book is available from the Library of Congress

10   9   8   7   6   5   4   3   2   1
16   15   14   13   12   11   10   09   08   07

Printed and bound in China

SOUTHAMPTON SOLENT
UNIVERSITY LIBRARY
SUPPLIER DAWSONL
ORDER No
DATE 16/4/2008

Contents

List of Boxes

Foreword

This book gives you precisely what it says in the title – a guide to studying psychology. This is an excellent way to advance your studies, and much better than just learning the contents of a massive textbook. You see, there is a lot more to success in psychology examinations than just being able to describe loads of psychological studies and theories. In fact, if you know too much psychological evidence then it can become quite difficult to figure out which bits to use and which bits to reject when you come to answer questions in the examination. You can end up spending half your time dithering over what to put in and what to leave out, and end up with no time to finish the essay.

This guide gives you some clear strategies for making the best of what you know. To do this you need to show the skills, other than knowledge, that are an important part of learning. These skills include analysis and evaluation; the skills of selecting the most important features of any argument, and of being able to comment on the value of the evidence. I have to say that these skills are difficult to develop, but when you learn the tricks of the trade you can demonstrate these skills at will, amaze your friends and dazzle the examiners.

This text is written in an engaging and readable style, and takes you through many of the important analytical and evaluative issues in psychology. It also gives you some handy hints on how to use these skills in examinations. If you want, you can read the text from start to finish, but that is not the only way to use the book. You can also pick out the bits you need when you need them. Maybe, for example, you need to write up a practical report very soon (i.e. yesterday), in which case, you don't need to read the first two chapters just yet. Go straight to Chapter 3 and sift through to the bits you want.

When you get the chance you might like to go to Chapter 5 to figure out what kind of learner you are. We all have our own styles of learning and the best way to be successful is to be honest with yourself and plan your work according to your strengths. Some people work best when they are under pressure and if you are one of them it is probably not worth starting a piece of work a month in advance because you will still end up doing the bulk of it the night before the deadline. Figure out your learning style and play to your strengths.

If you have an essay to write, then before you start have a look at Chapter 2 to check out the do's and don'ts of essay writing. It is surprising how many good students do not make the best of their knowledge and ability because they have not followed the basic rules of essay writing. You can also look in this chapter to see how your DRREEEEEAAAMSS can help you.

So, there you have it. Use this text to help you make the best use of your psychological knowledge. I think you'll find it is very helpful.

Philip Banyard
Nottingham Trent University

Preface: What *isn't* this?

What this *isn't* is a comprehensive psychology textbook, crammed to its rafters with information about all the key studies, theories and concepts you'll ever need to know to succeed as a psychology student. True, it *does* detail some pretty famous, pretty notorious research – Stanley Milgram's study of obedience, Sigmund Freud's case study of the horse-phobic Little Hans. Also true, it does take a detailed look at the nature of psychology and the questionable status of psychology as a 'proper science'. It even gives you a detailed guide to all the main research methods in psychology. But by and large the aim here *isn't* to fill you full of factual *knowledge* about *the study of behaviour*. Rather, what you're holding in your hand is designed to help you develop the necessary *skills* and *strategies* for studying psychology. The question being addressed here isn't 'How much should I *know* about psychology?' but 'What should I *do* to study psychology effectively?'

Whether you're studying psychology at A-level, Access, IB or first-year undergraduate level, sooner or later your tutor will present you with a series of hoops. If you want to jump through them with confidence and style it won't be enough for you to simply to *know an awful lot* about what you've covered on your course. You'll also need to be skilled in:

> understanding the terminology of psychology
> writing psychology essays
> planning and carrying out research
> using statistics
> preparing for assessments
> monitoring your own progress
> making the most of your own style of learning.

All of these skills receive plenty of attention in this book. There's even a chapter assessing your career choices once you've gained a higher psychology qualification. Add to this the *knowledge* you accumulate on your course, and your experience of studying psychology should be twice as enjoyable, twice as effective.

Acknowledgements

Thanks to Dr Louise Walker, University of Manchester, for help with the writing of this book, especially with the statistical content. Many thanks also to Andrea Joseph for her help with producing the illustrations. Also, Jeremy Hopper of Aquinas College, Stockport, for feeding Harry. Thanks too to Sam Walters for help with the presentation.

1 Learning the Language of Psychology

Learning about psychology is a bit like learning a new language. As your course starts you'll encounter a sackful of new words, plus some new meanings for old words. This opening chapter will prepare you for these changes to your vocabulary. It will help you 'get by' in the first few weeks of your course. It will also explain how some of these key words have helped psychology fight for its status as a 'proper science'.

User's Guide to Chapter 1

• 1 Ideas and activities to help you cope with terminology

Terminology in psychology can be a good thing
How to make a glossary of terminology
Words to be wary of when writing about psychology

• 2 Proof, theories, hypotheses and the scientific method

Why we don't use the word 'proof' in psychology
Key study: *Festinger and Carlsmith (1957)*

• 3 Causal links, controlled experiments and correlation

Why we rarely use the word 'cause' in psychology
Key study: *Milgram (1963)*

• 4 Right or wrong: the perspectives in psychology

Do we use the words 'right' and 'wrong' in psychology
Key study: *Freud (1909)*
'Analysis of a phobia in a five-year-old boy'

● 1 Ideas and activities to help you cope with terminology

What to look for in this section
● Terminology in psychology can be a good thing
● How to keep a glossary of psychological terminology
● Words to be wary of when writing about psychology

Terminology in psychology can be a good thing

Psychology is no different from any other academic subject, or any other field of endeavour. Like sociology, skateboarding, philosophy and football, the science of mind and behaviour brings with it a lexicon of terms that can sometimes put newcomers off before they've mastered the basics. Don't be put off though. In psychology, as in every other field, technical terms have their uses. They are there for a reason.

It is often said that the Inuit have 27 different words for snow. Similarly, meteorologists have many words for what most laypeople label indiscriminately as 'clouds'. Such extended, specialist vocabularies are not just about showing off. They facilitate a deeper understanding of an area of interest. Therefore, mastery of some of psychology's key terms early on in a course can give a real impetus to your understanding. Indeed, it is difficult to get to grips with a new subject without the specialised words and terms which enable you to write and talk about it. Learning the language can act as a spur to understanding the concepts. This process is nicely articulated by this famous quote from the philosopher Ludwig Wittgenstein (1922):

> The limits of my language mean the limits of my world.

Technical terminology enables people with a shared interest to communicate effectively and economically about their chosen field. By 'economically' I mean they can talk and write about quite complex ideas without using so many words. When you're writing psychology assessments and striving to stay within a word limit, this is very good news.

Still not convinced about the value of terminology in psychology? Well, imagine what the world would be like without it. In **Boxes 1A**, **1B** and **1C** are three extracts of text that are written without the use of technical terminology. The first comes from the terminology-laden world of football. The other two are examples from psychology. The first thing to say about these extracts is that they are pretty horrid to read. To make them more readable, try to replace the emboldened terms with technical terminology. More readable versions of all three examples (with added terminology) are included in **Box 1D**. Notice the reduction in the word count with the advent of terminology.

Box 1A

Terminology can be a good thing: example 1

Replace the emboldened terms with technical terminology

A beautiful game spoiled

Though potentially a tightly fought contest, this encounter between two top **groups of people playing on the same side as each other** was, sadly, spoiled by the **person who runs up and down the side of the playing field waving a flag**. Time after time attacking players were penalised for being caught **standing with only one opposition player between them and the goal posts**, even though very often this was not the case. Consequently the game remained goalless, even after **another thirty minutes at the end of the game to see if anyone could score**. They couldn't score, and the issue was settled with **a situation where five players from each group tried to score goals one after the other from a spot located ten yards from the goal**. All in all it was a long evening.   [136 words]

Box 1B

Terminology can be a good thing: example 2

Replace the emboldened terms with technical terminology

Who was Sigmund Freud?

Born in Monrovia (now part of the Czech Republic), Freud practised in Vienna, treating his clients using **a set of techniques for exploring the underlying motivations of human behaviour**. Central to Freud's theory is his idea that much of what we say or do is explained by delving into our **influential level of the mind of which we are not aware**. Furthermore, he argued that much of our behaviour could be explained by a raging inner conflict between the **instinctive, libidinous part of our personality which demands immediate gratification** and the **internalised code of morals and ethics which punishes transgressions with feelings of guilt**. Freud claimed that this ongoing conflict is managed by the **cluster of conscious perceptual processes and unconscious defence mechanisms that serve to mediate between instinctual demands and moral inhibitions**. He used a variety of methods for getting in touch with inner conflicts and behavioural motivations, including analysis of **imagery during sleep**.   [155 words]

Box 1C

Terminology can be a good thing: example 3

Replace the emboldened terms with technical terminology

Who was Burrhus Frederic Skinner?

B. F. Skinner (1904–90) was a leading light in the school of
thought known as **the approach to psychology which
argues that the only appropriate subject matter for the
subject is observable, measurable behaviour**. Doing
most of his research at the University of Minnesota,
Skinner experimented on rats and pigeons before
developing his theory of **a type of learning in which an
organism's response is contingent upon the production
of a reinforcement**. As well as experimenting on **animals**, he used his infant
daughter as a participant in his research. Skinner also put forward the principles
of his theory in a **story book** called Walden II. His theory is still used today in
clinical practice as a means of changing dysfunctional behaviour, in what is
known as **a form of behaviour therapy in which a therapeutic environment
is established based on the use of tokens**. [143 words]

Box 1D

Examples 1, 2 and 3, with terminology added

A beautiful game spoiled
Though potentially a tightly fought contest, this encounter between two top
teams was, sadly, spoiled by the **referee's assistant**. Time after time attacking
players were penalised for being caught **offside**, even though very often this
was not the case. Consequently the game remained goalless, even after **extra
time**. They couldn't score, and the issue was settled with a **penalty shoot-out**.
All in all, it was a long evening. [68 words]

Who was Sigmund Freud?
Born in Monrovia (now part of the Czech Republic), Freud practised in Vienna,
treating his clients using **psychoanalysis**. Central to Freud's theory is his idea
that much of what we say or do is explained by delving into our **unconscious**.
Furthermore, he argued that much of our behaviour could be explained by a
raging inner conflict between the **id** and the **super-ego**. This ongoing conflict is
said to be managed by the **ego**. Freud used a variety of methods forgetting in
touch with inner conflicts and behavioural motivations, including analysis of
dreams. [92 words]

Who was Burrhus Frederic Skinner?
B. F. Skinner (1904–90) was a leading light in the school of thought known as
behaviourism. Doing most of his research at the University of Minnesota,
Skinner experimented on rats and pigeons before developing his theory of
operant conditioning. As well as experimenting on **non-humans**, he used his
infant daughter as a participant in his research. He also supplemented his
academic writing by putting forward the principles of his theory in a **novel** called
Walden II. His theory is still used today in clinical settings, as a means of changing
dysfunctional behaviour, in what are known as **token economies**. [98 words]

How to make a glossary of terminology

Now that you're a little more convinced of the value of terminology in psychology, the next challenge is to devise some methods for coping with the new terms and words you'll encounter during the first phase of your psychology course. Perhaps the most important strategy of all is the same one you'd use whatever new skill you were learning (playing the piano, speaking Mandarin, juggling). In a word, practice. In this context practice means using newly acquired terminology whenever you're writing or talking about psychology. After a while it will begin to feel like part of your own language, not someone else's. So when you're answering a question in class and the opportunity arises to use a piece of psychological terminology (for example, *confederate*, instead of *researcher pretending to be a participant*), take it. The more you do so the more convincing your language will become. Chapter 3 includes a number of strategies to help you deal with terminology. **Box 3A** will help you crack the language code in which assignment and essay questions are often phrased. **Box 3D** marks the start of a comprehensive guide to the terminology you need for evaluating research in psychology.

For now though, here's an idea to try during the first few weeks of your course, to help you get to grips with two different types of terminology. Take a look at **Box 1E**. It shows numerous examples of terms from psychology. Without being too concerned about the meaning of each term for now, see if you can work out what the difference between the 'A-list' and 'B-list' is.

Box 1E

Double meanings:
two types of psychological terminology

A-list	B-list
Sample	Social facilitation
Population	Horizontal décalage
Attrition	Operant conditioning
Culture	Conditioned stimuli
Confederate	Oedipus complex
Theory	De-individuation
Method	Ecological validity
Variable	Sampling error
Reinforcement	Cognitive dissonance
Validity	Id
Representative	Super-ego
Opportunistic	Aphasia

Did you spot the difference? The 'A-list' is made up of everyday words which have a second, specialised meaning in psychology. The 'B-list' comprises words which are fairly meaningless outside the study of mind and behaviour. When you study psychology you'll come across both 'A' words (old words with new meanings) and 'B' words (new words with new meanings). It may be that you'll find the 'A-list' type of words the most difficult to get to grips with, since you'll have the inconvenience of learning a second meaning for them. This can be more confusing than starting with a blank slate, as in the case of 'B-list' words.

To help with both 'A' and 'B' words a useful strategy for easing the learning process is to compile a glossary of psychological terminology (see **Box 1F**), to which you can add new terms as you learn them. Keeping your glossary separate from your notes will enable you to consult it when you need a reminder of the meaning of a particular term.

Box 1F

A glossary of psychological terminology

A-list: old words with new meanings in psychology		B-list: new words, meaningless outside psychology	
Sample	Those who actually take part in research	**Social facilitation**	Behaviour influenced by the presence of others
Population	Group to whom research findings are applied	**Horizontal décalage**	In Piaget's theory of cognitive development, when abilities that are associated with a certain developmental stage only appear selectively; not – as it were – across the board
Attrition	Decrease in a research sample over time	**Operant conditioning**	Behaviourist theory of learning in which responses are contingent upon reinforcements
Culture	Set of rules, beliefs and norms within a group	**Conditioned stimuli**	In classical behaviourism, any response which is learned or altered by conditioning
Confederate	Ally of the researcher, posing as a participant	**Oedipus complex**	In Freud's theory of psycho-sexual development, the unconscious desire to compete with the same-sex parent for the affections of the opposite-sex parent
Theory	Series of interrelated statements which attempts to explain certain observed phenomena	**De-individuation**	Where personality markers are hidden, such as in a crowd, often leading to less inhibited behaviour

Words to be wary of when writing about psychology

Like all languages, the language of psychology evolves over time. Words pass in and out of usage according to fashion, the development of new theories and the changing political climate. Flick through a textbook from the early twentieth century and terms such as *mental hospital* and *primitive cultures* will strike you as being out of step with modern psychology. Partly because of the evolving nature of the language of the subject, and partly for more complex reasons having to do with accuracy, there are certain words which are best treated with caution when writing about psychology.

Box 1F (continued)

A glossary of psychological terminology

A-list: old words with new meanings in psychology		B-list: new words, meaningless outside psychology	
Method	Way of carrying out research	**Ecological validity**	Index of the degree to which results from research can be generalised from group to group
Variable	Something whose value changes over time (noun)	**Sampling error**	When findings derived from a sample differ from those prevalent amongst the population to which the results are applied
Reinforcement	A reward, or an event that reduces a drive	**Cognitive dissonance**	A feeling of anxiety associated with the incompatibility of two cognitions
Validity	Index of how much a measuring instrument – such as an IQ test – measures what it means to measure	**Id**	In Freud's theory, the instinctive, libidinous part of our personality, which demands immediate gratification
Representative	Of a sample, which includes examples of all those groups to which results are meant to apply	**Super-ego**	In Freud's theory, the internalised code of morals and ethics which punishes transgressions with feelings of guilt
Opportunistic	Of research, conducted in unique circumstances which are hard to replicate	**Aphasia**	Partial or total loss of language abilities

Box 1G

Top 10 words to be wary of when writing about psychology – and some suggested replacements

1 **Prove** Unlike mathematicians and 'hard' scientists (e.g. physicists), psychologists generally accept that their theories cannot be proven, merely supported by evidence gained from testing hypotheses. Replace with **'support'**. (See later in this chapter for a longer discussion of this controversy.)

2 **Cause** Although we can often observe a consistent relationship between two variables, we needn't assume one is causing the other. Extraneous variables often interfere with causal conclusions. This word 'causes' can sometimes be replaced with 'correlates with'. (See later in this chapter for a longer discussion of this controversy).

3 **Right** This word can be used of directly testable hypotheses. However, theories (and statements taken from them) cannot be shown to be 'right' because they're not directly testable. Replace with **'supported'**. (See later in this chapter for a longer discussion of this controversy.)

4 **Believe** Strictly speaking, when writing about researchers' conclusions and theories you're not referring simply to beliefs but to states of mind arrived at in the light of research. Whilst the use of this word may not be entirely inappropriate, avoid overdoing phrases such as 'Festinger believes'. It sounds too much like idle speculation. Replace with 'argues', 'concludes', 'states', 'suggests' . . .

5 **Man** Phrases like 'mankind' and 'the history of man' belong to a bygone age seemingly before women had been recognised by social science. Replace with **'human'**.

6 **Tribe** When writing about research from different cultures, this word should be treated with caution as it is often applied indiscriminately to cultures in non-industrialised nations. Most social scientists regard this as an imprecise word these days. Avoid writing ' African tribes'. **Appendix 1** has a further discussion of the use of this word. Replace with **'culture'** or **'community'**.

7 **Animals** When writing about psychological research that relates to species other than humans, terms like 'research on animals' comes across as vague, as distinctions between humans and animals are hotly disputed. Replace with **'non-humans'**.

8 **Sub-conscious** When discussing Freudian psychoanalysis this word is often (mistakenly) used instead of 'unconscious' or 'pre-conscious', both of which are Freudian terms. 'Subconscious' isn't. Replace with **'unconscious'** or **'pre-conscious'** depending on which you mean.

9 **Mental** In discussions about atypical behaviour terms like 'mental problems' or 'mental institutions' are to be avoided. 'Mental' is an imprecise, outmoded word in psychology, though for cognitive psychologists it has a more modern feel (as in 'mental processes'). Goodish replacements are **'psychological'** or **'psychiatric'**.

10 **Subject** When referring to those who are being studied in psychological research, this word gives the impression of passive subservience. Whilst this may be close to the truth in some cases, most social scientists prefer to use the word **'participant'**.

What follows is my top ten such words, along with an explanation and a suggested replacement. As **Box 1G** explains, when talking or writing about psychology these are all words which should either be treated with extreme caution, or avoided altogether. Be warned though, if you're reading this in the year 2075 some of the suggested replacements may themselves have dropped out of usage.

● 2 Proof, theories, hypotheses and the scientific method

What to look for in this section
- ● Why we don't use the word 'proof' in psychology
- ● Definitions of and distinctions between **theories** and **hypotheses**
- ● Using the **scientific method** in psychology
- ● Key study: Festinger and Carlsmith on cognitive dissonance

Why we don't use the word 'proof' in psychology

A sure way of getting a frosty response from your psychology tutor is to claim that you've *proved* a theory or that you've *proved* your experimental hypothesis. As soon as you say you've *proved* anything in psychology, whether it's a theory or a hypothesis, you've dropped a clanger. You'll get blank looks all round, but you might not get a satisfactory explanation why. So let's try and sort out the confusion.

We'll begin by looking at how psychology research gets started. Where do researchers get their ideas from? Well, more often than not things start with an existing **theory**, part of which is in need of investigation. In psychology, as in the so-called 'natural sciences' (physics, chemistry, biology), a theory is **a series of interrelated statements which attempts to explain certain observed phenomena**. In order to test a theory a researcher will set about testing any one of these interrelated statements by carrying out a piece of research. But before s/he carries out any research s/he'll probably have an idea about what the results of the study will be. S/he'll make a prediction, or **hypothesis**. A hypothesis is a **testable prediction relating to a statement taken from a theory**. Then s/he goes ahead and tests the hypothesis by carrying out the study.

Let's play that back in stages.

1   Find an existing theory.
2   Find a statement from it that requires investigation.
3   Construct a testable hypothesis relating to the selected statement.
4   Carry out research to test your hypothesis.

These are the first four stages of what's generally called **the Scientific Method** in psychology, and it's in stage 5 of this method that the confusion about proof generally arises. Let's say our researcher has carried out a study and obtained a set of results. What does she do next? Well, she's got two options.

Either her hypothesis was incorrect. It was not borne out in her results. In which case she has to conclude that her hypothesis, along with the theory from which it was taken, is false. She has to *reject* her hypothesis. This isn't the end of the world. She doesn't lose any brownie points for this. All that happens is that her theory has to be *modified*, updated to accommodate these new findings. Alternatively, she may want to modify the method of investigation and carry out the study again, just to check the incorrectness of her hypothesis.

Or she may find that her hypothesis was correct. So what? Has she *proved* the theory correct? Not at all. Because someone else could come along tomorrow and test another statement from the same theory (or even another hypothesis related to the same statement) and find their hypothesis to be incorrect, thus falsifying the theory. So let's keep calm.

Our researcher hasn't *proved* anything. She's *accepted* her hypothesis. She's *supported* the theory. But she hasn't *proved* anything.

So the final stage of the Scientific Method looks like this:

5   Support or modify existing theory.

In fact you could say that rejected hypotheses are more useful than accepted ones. After all, a rejected hypothesis leads to a change or modification in a theory. An accepted hypothesis produces no such change. Hence the following statement from the philosopher of science Karl Popper:

Science progresses by a process of falsification.

Now you've come to terms with the way psychology progresses, practise your language skills by replacing the emboldened text in the exercise in **Box 1H** with the appropriate terminology. You'll find the answers in **Box 1I**.

Box 1H

Terminology can be a good thing: example 4

How does psychological research progress?

You may wonder where researchers get their ideas from. Well, usually from an existing **series of interrelated statements attempting to explain a certain observed phenomenon**. In other words, they don't just 'think up' ideas. Next, the researcher will form a **testable prediction** relating to one of these statements. Research is then carried out. Following this, the **testable prediction** is

> *either* shown to be correct, and the **series of interrelated statements** is **proven**;
>
> *or* shown to be incorrect, and the **series of interrelated statements** is **wrong**.

[87 words]

Key study: Festinger and Carlsmith on cognitive dissonance

To demonstrate how all this works in practice we'll look at an existing theory. Let's use Festinger's theory of **cognitive dissonance** from 1957. Like all theories it's a series of interrelated statements about an observed phenomenon. The theory of cognitive dissonance is about what happens when we have to deal with two conflicting cognitions at the same time. Festinger defines a **cognition** as **an idea we have about ourselves or our environment**. At any one time we may be holding a number of cognitions. Like *I'm a married man* as well as *marriage is a wonderful institution* as well as *I think it's going to rain*. Not especially engaging cognitions but it is quite conceivable that I could think all these three things at the same time. They don't get in each other's way. But what happens when two or more cognitions *do* get in each other's way? What happens if I have to cope simultaneously with the belief that *smoking is bad for my health* and the knowledge that *I've just smoked ten Bensons one after the other*?

Festinger is particularly interested in how we feel when something we believe is in conflict with something we've said or done. Anyone who's worked in retail will probably identify with this kind of dilemma. How often, during the course of a working day, would you find yourself saying (of a ugly blouse) *Yes madam, this is just what you're looking for* or (of a preposterous tie) *Oh yes, it suits you sir*. And how does it feel? Bad, says Festinger. It makes you feel anxious. And the name he gives to this particular type of anxiety is **cognitive dissonance**, defined precisely as **a state of psychological discomfort experienced when an individual simultaneously holds two inconsistent cognitions**.

Box 1I

Example 4 with added terminology

How does psychological research progress?

You may wonder where researchers get their ideas from. Well, usually from an existing **theory**. In other words, they don't just 'think up' ideas. Next, the researcher will form a **hypothesis** relating to one of these statements. Research is then carried out. Following this, the **hypothesis** is

  either shown to be correct, and the **theory** is **supported**;

  or shown to be incorrect, and the **theory** is **rejected/modified**.

[71 words]

So what do I do with cognitive dissonance when I've got it? Naturally I try to get rid of it. And a good way of reducing the unpleasant effects of two conflicting cognitions is to change one of them. Get it to agree with the other one. And if one cognition is something I've *said* and one is something I *think*, the most convenient one to change is the one I *think*. After all, I can't *unsay* what I've already said. So an effective method of reducing my feelings of dissonance is to *change my beliefs to fit in with my behav-*

iour. Hence, my new belief might well become: *Well, my uncle lived 'till he was a hundred and ten and he smoked three packets a day*, or *I look cool with a Benson*.

So that's how Festinger's theory looks, in a couple of paragraphs. Let's see how it looks as a series of interrelated statements.

A   Inconsistency between cognitions produces feelings of discomfort.
B   Dissonance is unpleasant and the individual will try to remove it.
C   The individual will try to avoid situations that might produce dissonance.
D   The greater the conflict between two cognitions, the more pronounced the avoidance strategies will be.

This isn't an exhaustive list, but these four statements are a good summary of Festinger's theory. Now that we've got an existing theory we can use it to illustrate the Scientific Method in psychology – a method which progresses according to five well established stages. Stage1 is now complete. We've got the existing theory. Next we have to select one of the statements related to the theory – preferably one which we feel requires some investigation. I'm going to select

> **Statement B**   *Dissonance is unpleasant and the individual will try to remove it.*

Actually, I didn't select it at all. In 1959 Leon Festinger himself and his research associate James Carlsmith selected *Statement B* and constructed a testable research hypothesis related to it, in line with stage 3 of the Scientific Method. To test their hypothesis they constructed an ingenious and now famous experiment, which I'm about to describe. But you'll have to wait a little longer to find out precisely what their hypothesis was.

It's fairly common for psychological researchers to design studies in which they deceive their participants. A popular deception is to have **a member of the research team pretending to be a participant**. These 'pretenders' are called **confederates** or stooges.

Festinger and Carlsmith's employed precisely this kind of deception. The unsuspecting participants in their study were a group of male undergraduates who were each given a thirty-minute task to complete. This involved turning wooden pegs that were set out in a tray. Sounds boring? Well, that was the idea – to induce a feeling of tedium in the participants. Next, each participant was asked to tell a 'fellow participant' (actually a confederate) that the task was 'interesting, intriguing and exciting'. In other words they were asked to make a statement which was in conflict with their belief that the task was boring. The aim of this was to produce a feeling of anxiety or cognitive dissonance in the participants, since they now had *two incompatible cognitions*. As a reward for doing this the participants were paid. One group received $1, another group $20.

We call the **different groups in psychology experiments – conditions**. So here we've got a $1 condition and a $20 condition.

How about that hypothesis?

Don't worry, it's on its way. The researchers thought that both the $1 condition and the $20 condition would experience feelings of dissonance. But which group would feel it most? The conflict between thinking *it was boring* and saying *it was interesting* would cause a high level of anxiety in the $1 condition, certainly. But in the $20 condition it was predicted that the feeling would be reduced because this group could tell themselves, *Don't worry, it's not so bad, I only lied because I was being well paid.* It was therefore predicted that this group would feel a *lesser* degree of dissonance.

So that's the hypothesis?

Sort of, yes, but here it comes in more precise terms. In the final phase of the study Festinger and Carlsmith asked the participants to tell *them* how enjoyable they'd found the peg-turning task. They asked them to rate their enjoyment level on a scale of 1 to 10. The higher the rating, the greater their feeling of enjoyment.

They wanted to know if either of the two groups had changed their belief about the task to fit in with what they had said to the confederate – as a method of removing their dissonance. After all, *Statement B* says *dissonance is unpleasant and individuals will try to remove it.* And Festinger and Carlsmith say that the $1 condition will be feeling the greatest degree of dissonance. Consequently they predict that of the two groups, this $1 condition will be more likely to alter their belief about the boring task. They will therefore rate it as being more interesting, on a 1 to 10 scale, in this final phase of the study. And that's the experimental hypothesis. Put precisely, it looks like this:

The $1 condition will rate the task as more interesting than will the $20 condition.

To sum up then, the researchers had created a situation in which there was a high level of dissonance in one group and a lower level of dissonance in another group, since both groups had a *belief* which is incompatible with something they've *said*. The researchers then tried to find out if the high dissonance condition would be more likely to alter their belief to fit in with what they had said, in order to reduce their anxiety levels.

And that's just what happened. The $1 condition rated the peg-turning task as being 'not so bad', compared with the $20 condition, which stuck to their guns and rated it as 'extremely boring'. A situation which is roughly equivalent to the shop assistant who finishes up liking the ening telling her customers. Hence the belief that *Well, it's not such a bad blouse after all*.

So it's good news for Festinger and Carlsmith. Well, fairly good news anyhow. They've *accepted* their experimental hypothesis. As for their theory, they've *supported* it. Their theory remains *intact*. It lives to fight another day. Until someone else comes along and finds one of its statements to be false. Then they'll have to alter the theory. Or, to put it more positively, they'll have the opportunity to develop their theory.

So here's how Festinger and Carlsmith's research fits in with the five stages of the Scientific Method.

1   The existing theory of cognitive dissonance   (*theory*).
2   Dissonance is unpleasant and the individual will try to remove it   (*statement*).
3   The $1 condition will rate the peg task as more interesting that will the $20 condition   (*hypothesis*).
4   The experiment is carried out to test the hypothesis   (*research*).
5   Cognitive dissonance theory is supported   (*support*).

Before we leave the subject of proving theories it might be worth pointing out that Festinger's is one of the more complicated theories in psychology. And his study is one of the most complicated experimental designs in psychology. So if you've coped with things so far you shouldn't have too much to worry about with what's to come.

● 3 Causal links, controlled experiments and correlation

What to look out for in this section
● Why we rarely use the word 'cause' in psychology
● Using **controlled experiments** in psychology
● Definition and discussion of **ecological validity** and **correlation**
● Key study: Milgram on **obedience**

Why we rarely use the word 'cause' in psychology

Your days of claiming proof of theories and hypotheses now behind you, it's time to open another can of worms; the use of the word *cause* in psychology, as in

Increased crowding causes increased violent behaviour in female mice.

Statements like this should be made with caution. I won't say you should never make them but I do recommend that you think very carefully about a number of issues before you do. And it wouldn't surprise me if, after thinking about these issues, you decide to keep the word *cause* out of your vocabulary on the grounds that it's more trouble than it's worth. It's your decision. And it's a tough one. So to help you make it, this section will look at the reasons why this word is such a troublesome one for psychologists.

Let's take the claim that *increased crowding causes increased violent behaviour in female mice*. Exactly what's being said here? I'm suggesting a *causal* relationship between two variables. A **variable** is **something whose value changes over time**. So actually I'm claiming that *an increase in Variable A, crowding, causes an increase in Variable B, violent behaviour in female mice*. But what does it mean, to say that a change in one thing causes a change in another? Well, for generations psychologists have been unable to agree about the precise meaning of the word 'cause'. At different times it has meant different things to different psychologists, which is not especially helpful. So let's consider the two most common meanings that have been attached to it and see if we can clear up some of the confusion.

> **Meaning 1** *To say that A causes B means that A is **necessary** for B to happen.* In other words, unless you have a change in *Variable A*, you won't see a change in *Variable B*. And you won't sec a change in *B* unless you have a change in *A*. So in order to produce an increase in the number of fights amongst your female mice you'll *have* to increase the crowding level.

> **Meaning 2** *To say that A causes B means that A is **sufficient** for B to happen.* This means that a change in *Variable A*, on its own, will produce a change in *Variable B*. You won't need anything else. So all you need to do to increase the amount of violence is to crank up the crowding level. You don't need to do anything else.

Do these meanings work?

Well, there are certainly problems with them. Take Meaning 1e to begin with. It may be possible to demonstrate that under certain experimental conditions increased crowding will produce an increase in violent behaviour. But then again, increased temperature may have the same effect. Also, the time of the year. For example, female mice may become more aggressive in June. So to say that increased crowding is *necessary* for increased violence is clearly wide of the mark. A change in *A* may well produce a change in *B*, but it isn't *necessary* for that change. Other things could do it too. For the moment then, we can agree with many contemporary psychologists when they say that Meaning 1 is not always reliable.

How about Meaning 2? If an increase in *A* is *sufficient* for an increase in *B*, I should be able to *control* the level of violent behaviour in female mice simply by varying the level of crowding. Variations in crowding alone should be sufficient to produce these changes. But there is a problem here. Let's say I *can* control the level of crowding in a community of female mice. And let's say I *do* observe changes in levels of violent behaviour. What about those other variables that are varying at the same time? I mean those variables that aren't being controlled. Things like room temperature, season, the diet and age of the mice. It may be that fluctuations in any of these so-called *extraneous variables* might be influencing violence levels as well as the level of crowding. This will interfere with my causal claim. I will have less confidence in my causal statement. So clearly there are problems with Meaning 2 as well.

So now what? Do we give up hope of using the word cause in psychology?

No, wait. There may be a solution. After all, lots of reputable psychologists do look for causal relationships in their research, so presumably they must have found a way around the problems with the two meanings of the word 'cause'. How do they do it? Do they simply ignore them and plough on regardless? Well, no. Their way of dealing with the problems with the two meanings of the word 'cause' is to do all their research in one particular way and in one particular place.

When they carry out their research they use one particular research method. A **research method** is **a way of carrying out research**. The chosen method for anyone who is trying to establish causal relationships in psychology is the controlled experiment. The place they use to conduct them is the laboratory. In a controlled experiment the researcher observes the effect of a change in one variable on the value of another, whilst attempting to control all other extraneous variables. To be more specific, they typically create two conditions (groups) of participants and treat them identically in all but one respect. This single difference between the conditions is known as the *independent variable*. They then seek to assess the effect of this variable on some particular aspect of behaviour which is being measured – known as the *dependent variable*. For instance, they might try to measure the effect of alcohol (independent variable) on short-term memory (dependent variable). They also try to control all other (extraneous) variables which may be present in one condition but not in another, such as trying to make sure the average age or IQ are the same in both conditions.

In a laboratory setting experimenters use this type of method to try to bring all extraneous variables which they would otherwise be unable to control, under their control. So, for example, if I were to set up a controlled experiment to investigate the relationship between overcrowding and the violent behaviour of female mice my design could be written out like this:

Step 1   Select a sample of 40 female mice.
Step 2   Record the age of each mouse.
Step 3   Create two conditions, *X* and *Y*, with 20 mice in each condition.
Step 4   Allocate an equal number of old and young mice to each condition.
Step 5   House *Condition X* together in a small cage.
Step 6   House *Condition Y* together in a large cage.
Step 7   Record the number of violent acts per hour for each mouse for 48 hours.
Step 8   Test both conditions in June.
Step 9   Maintain the temperature in the two cages at an equal level.

The hypothesis for this experiment states that *Condition X will display more violent acts than Condition Y*. For the purpose of this discussion it is especially important to notice how many *extraneous* variables I've taken control of in the design of this experiment. These are variables that would be beyond my control if I were to conduct the study in a **naturalistic** setting. That means **outside the laboratory**, where participants are studied in their natural environment.

There are four such variables in my experiment. Age, season, temperature, number of mice in each condition. Did you spot them? I've kept these variables equal, or constant, for the two conditions, *X* and *Y*. So if there does turn out to be an increase in violent behaviour in *Condition Y* I'll be in a stronger position to claim that it's due to the increase in crowding. Rather than, for example, the fact that the average age for one condition was higher.

So what would be the outcome of an experiment like this? Well, for the sake of argument let's say that there *was* an increase in the level of violent acts in *Condition Y*. Just as I predicted. So now I can propose a *causal* relationship between an increase in *Variable A* and an increase in *Variable B*. I can go ahead and claim that a change in *A* caused a change in *B*. In doing so, remember, I'll be claiming that the change in *A* was *necessary* and *sufficient* for the change in *B*.

Necessary because *in my experiment* no other variables were allowed to have any influence on the level of violent behaviour. After all, I had all those extraneous variables, like age, season, temperature and number of mice in each condition, under my control. I held them constant for the two conditions. So, in my experiment, in order to increase these violence levels, an increase in the crowding level was *necessary*.

Sufficient because in my controlled experiment crowding was the only variable that was allowed to have any effect on the level of violence. As I've just said, all the others were under my control. So in order to vary the level of violence all I had to do was vary the crowding levels. It was enough on its own.

Therefore, in my experiment, changes in Variable A were necessary and sufficient to produce changes in Variable B. To put it bluntly, they caused them.

> *So it looks like we can use the word 'cause' in psychology.*

Well, not exactly. Whilst I hate to pour cold water on these enthusiastic claims about the apparent causal link between two variables, *A* and *B*, I'm afraid there are a couple of problems here. Problems which illustrate the reason why this word *cause* is so sparingly used in psychology.

Problem 1   *You can't control everything in controlled experiments*
Even though I made a fairly good attempt at controlling the extraneous variables of age, temperature, season and the number of mice in each condition in my experiment, there were some other extraneous variables I didn't control. In all controlled experiments, despite the meticulous efforts of researchers, there are always variables that *should have been controlled but weren't*. Not simply because of carelessness, although this is sometimes the reason. More often it's because it is extremely difficult to create a truly controlled environment. For example, in my experiment what if *Condition X* had been selected from particularly violent colonies? Or what if a *Condition Y* developed an epidemic of flu, or some other lethargy-inducing disease, during the course of the experiment? Or what if a high number of participants of *Condition X* had an unusually high metabolism? The point is that any of these uncontrolled extraneous variables might well have influenced one of my conditions more than the other, thus reducing the amount of control in my experiment. It is extremely difficult for researchers to control all possible extraneous variables in their experiments. And the ones they overlook will interfere with any causal relationships that may arise out of their work. This makes their use of the word *cause* less convincing.

Problem 2   *Ecological Validity*

In my experiment I'm observing and recording the behaviour of the mice in their newly acquired cramped – or spacious – cages, depending on which condition they're in. I discover that the mice in the cramped cages are more violent than the ones in the spacious cages. I accept my hypothesis. But at the back of my mind I have the feeling that I'm studying mice under *unusual circumstances*. They're in a new environment, with new peers and a number of new tests have been run on them. Consequently it occurs to me that if they're anything like you or me they might behave unusually in such circumstances. This makes it harder for me to make generalisations from the results of my study about the natural, everyday behaviour of other mice, or indeed humans. And if mice behave unusually under controlled conditions I'm pretty sure that you or I would. So when humans are used as participants in controlled experiments it is even more difficult to translate the behaviour they exhibit in the laboratory into theories about everyday human behaviour and experience. Another way of putting this is that the results from controlled experiments lack **ecological validity**. Meaning they lack **applicability to real life settings**. So, many psychologists are wary of claiming causal links between variables when these variables have been observed and tested under controlled settings. That is, in controlled experiments. This makes these causal claims less convincing.

In summary then, you could say that psychologists face two problems when using the word *cause*. First, there are so many extraneous variables that have to be consid-

---

Box 1J

Terminology can be a good thing: example 5

What happens in controlled experiments?

Controlled experiments are one of many **ways of carrying out research** in psychology. They often involve the researcher setting up two or more **different groups in psychology experiments**. The researcher often treats these groups slightly differently and this so-called **way in which the two groups are treated differently** may be crucial in determining the **aspect of the participants' behaviour which is being observed and recorded during the experiment**. Though the groups are treated slightly differently, a number of other **things whose values change over time** are controlled, or held constant, by the experimenter. These are often called **things whose values change over time that are present in one group but absent in the other (other than the way in which the two groups are treated differently by the experimenter)**. Another common feature of controlled experiments sees researchers employ **members of research teams who pretend to be participants**. This is quite unethical and has prompted some researchers to abandon the controlled experiment in favour of research which takes place in settings which are **outside the laboratory**.

[174 words]

ered when designing a controlled experiment that some are likely to be overlooked. And secondly, the more extraneous variables they *do* manage to control, the more difficult it is for them to draw conclusions about everyday behaviour and experience from their research. These problems reduce the validity of psychologists' claims about causal relationships.

Clearly, this 'c-word' is a difficult one. Is it best to avoid it? Is there another word that should be used in its place? Before we answer these questions and see how one particular researcher dealt with the problems of *causing* in psychology, try replacing the emboldened text in **Box 1J** with the appropriate terminology from the controlled-experiment scenario. You'll find the answers in **Box 1K**.

Key study: Milgram on Obedience

Stanley Milgram's 1963 study of obedience is famous for producing a surprising set of results and for sparking off a debate about whether researchers are within their rights to subject their participants to stressful situations in the interests of finding out more about human behaviour.

Milgram wanted to find out if people would obey an instruction even if it resulted in fatally injuring a colleague. Participants were drawn from a range of skilled and unskilled occupations. They responded to a newspaper advertisement requesting volunteers 'for a study of memory'. On the day of the experiment each participant reported to Yale University Psychology Department where they were greeted by a lab-coated man in his thirties who then introduced them to Mr Wallace. Mr Wallace was a mild-mannered forty-something confederate who, in traditional style, was playing the role of another participant. The participant and Mr Wallace were informed that they would be working together on an investigation into 'punishment and learning' and that one of them would be assigned the role of 'learner' and the other one would be assigned the role of 'teacher'. Milgram saw to it that the participant always got the role of 'teacher'. What followed were unpleasant or titillating scenes, depending on your tastes.

Box 1K

Example 5 with added terminology

What happens in controlled experiments?

Controlled experiments are one of many **methods** in psychology. They often involve the researcher setting up two or more **conditions**. The researcher often treats these groups slightly differently and this so-called **independent variable** may be crucial in determining the value of the **dependent variable**. Though the groups are treated slightly differently, a number of other **variables** are controlled, or held constant, by the experimenter. These are often called **extraneous variables**. Another common feature of controlled experiments sees researchers employ **confederates**. This is quite unethical and has prompted some researchers to abandon the controlled experiment in favour of research which takes place in settings which are **naturalistic**.   [105 words]

Mr Wallace, by now strapped into a (fake) electric chair, was given a (fake) memory test in which he had to demonstrate to the 'teacher' that he had learned a sequence of words. The participant was instructed to give MrWallace progressively more intense (fake) electric shocks after each mistake he made. And Mr Wallace, obligingly, made plenty of mistakes. Each time a shock was administered the participant would hear (fake) screams of pain coming from the adjoining room, where Mr Wallace was sitting. Each time the teacher got squeamish and complained of not wanting to continue, the lab-coated official, who was standing only a few feet away from him, would issue verbal prods like 'please continue' or 'you must go on'.

Milgram wanted to find out how many of the 40 participants would follow the instructions up to the maximum reading on the (fake) voltage board, by which point Mr. Wallace's screams had, rather ominously, faded to silence. The answer was 26. A disturbingly high number, which doesn't inspire a lot of confidence in your fellow man (or woman, since not all of Milgram's participants were male). But it's what happened next that is of particular interest to us.

Clearly the participants who took part in this experiment had been shown to be an obedient lot. But *why*? What interested Milgram now was: *What variable in the design of his experiment was the crucial one in producing such a high level of obedience?* He had a few ideas. So he made a shortlist list of them.

1   Was it the prestigious, academic nature of the Yale University setting?
2   Was it the fact that the 'teacher' couldn't see Mr Wallace during the experiment?
3   Was it the proximity of the lab-coated experimenter, who was right next to him, urging him on?
4   Was it that the 'teacher' was alone, with no-one present to encourage him to quit?

To find out which of these four ideas was most accurate Milgram designed a number of controlled experiments. For example, in order to investigate *idea 1* he replicated his experiment in a run-down office block whilst keeping all the other variables the same as in the original study. Under these circumstances the obedience level fell from 65% to 48%; still an alarmingly high number, suggesting that the so-called 'Yale factor' was not the crucial one.

In fact, the variable which seemed most responsible for the high level of obedience was the one associated with *idea 4*. The obedience level fell to 10% when there was a second confederate in the room next to the participant, urging him to quit delivering the shocks. Milgram concluded that the absence of peer pressure, someone to look to for guidance (a so-called 'dissenting peer'), was particularly influential in producing a high level of obedience in his original experiment.

Using the results of these four follow-up experiments we can rank the four possible reasons for a high level of obedience from the most influential one to the least influential one:

Experimental design	Obedience level
original experiment	65%
when the experiment took place in a run-down office block setting	48%
when the 'learner' was in full view of the 'teacher'	40%
when the 'prodder' was moved away from the 'teacher', into the next room	21%
when the 'teacher' was accompanied by a 'dissenting peer'	10%

Summarising the results for Milgram's four follow-up experiments

First – the absence of a dissenting peer.
Second – the presence of a lab-coated official standing in close proximity urging the participant to continue.
Third – Mr Wallace being in the next room and therefore invisible.
Fourth – the academic setting of Yale University.

Milgram's work shows that all four of these variables had some effect on the level of obedience. We can say this with confidence because in each of the four follow-up studies the level of obedience changed as each of the four variables was manipulated. For instance, when Mr Wallace was placed next to the 'teacher' and all other variables were kept the same as they were in the original experiment, the obedience level changed from 65% to 40%. But we *can't* say that any one of these four factors *caused* the increase in obedience levels. Why not? For the two reasons we discussed earlier. To illustrate these two reasons, let's take the follow-up study which dealt with the variable that was ranked as the *most influential*, the absence of a 'dissenting peer'.

Reason 1   *You can't control everything in controlled experiments*
When Milgram conducted his experiment with a 'dissenting peer' standing next to the 'teacher', whilst keeping everything else the same as in his original experiment, obedience fell to 10%. This suggests that the presence or absence of the peer *influences* the obedience level. But it would be too much to claim a *causal* relationship here. After all, there may have been other, uncontrolled extraneous variables also having an influence. For example, the original study and the follow-up study may have been held during different seasons. Or they may have been held at different times of day. Or during different political climates. Extraneous variables such as these, which were not held at a constant level over the two experiments, would make any causal claim less convincing.

Reason 2   *Ecological Validity*
Although it appears that the absence or presence of the dissenting peer is an influential factor in this experimental demonstration of obedience, the fact remains that this demonstration took place under unusually controlled conditions – conditions that were far removed from the naturalistic, everyday conditions we are used to. It is difficult to confidently apply the findings gathered under such unusually controlled conditions to our everyday experience. This makes the claim that there is a *causal* relationship between the two variables less convincing.

All this suggests that to claim that the change in one variable (the appearance of the 'dissenting peer') *caused* the change in another variable (obedience) would be unwise and inaccurate. Nevertheless, it is clear from Milgram's experiments that there is some sort of connection between these two variables. Maybe not a causal one, but a relationship which is more than just a *random* one. So if we can't be confident in calling it *causal*, what *can* we call it?

Well, the good news is that for those psychologists who have decided to avoid 'the c-word' when drawing their conclusions, there is an alternative. A word you can use without upsetting anyone. And it's another c-word. And the word is **correlation**.

Correlation

The outcome of psychological research often leads researchers to conclude that **two variables alter their value at the same time**. In other words, they go up and down together. This is called a **correlation**. In one experiment I observed that an increase in crowding was consistently associated with an increase in violence. The two varied together. Milgram observed that the absence of a dissenting peer was consistently associated with an increase in obedience. Again, the two varied together. We have suggested that in both of these cases it is dangerous to assume these variables are *causally* related. So let's ease off a little. Let us say instead that these are *correlational* relationships. In other words, they are relationships where one variable is seen as varying reliably, predictably and consistently at the same time as another. So that when a change in variable X is observed you can bet you'll observe a change in variable Y too (Chapter 4 has a longer discussion of correlation and Chapter 5 will tell you more about the statistics associated with it).

After all, in a world where we can't control all the extraneous variables in our experiments, there's no *need* for us to suggest that the change in variable X is actually *causing* the change in variable Y.

● 4 Right or wrong: the perspectives in psychology

What to look out for in this section
● Do we use the words 'right' and 'wrong' in psychology
● Explanations and definitions of **empiricism**
● Testing **hypotheses** and drawing conclusions
● The **perspectives: psychoanalysis, behaviourism, cognitive psychology**
● Key study: Freud on **phobias**

Do we use the words 'right' and 'wrong' in psychology?

Another good way of giving your psychology tutor a fright is to point to a theory (or a statement taken from a theory) and ask if it's right. You'll get the same reaction if you ask whether the conclusions arrived at by a particular researcher are right. Was Milgram right about obedience? Was Festinger right about cognitive dissonance? And what about a statement like 'Women are more intelligent than men' – is that right?

Well the truth is that when you use the word 'right' in psychology you open up another can of worms that can be just as unpleasant as the ones you open up when you use the words *proving* and *causing*. Suggesting that a statement or conclusion is right is something psychologists do very cautiously. But there are circumstances under which they will do it. In this section we'll look at two sets of circumstances under which it's alright to point at something and say that it's right. But before we look at the first of these we're going to consider something beginning with 'E'.

Explanations and definitions of Empiricism

If you were to argue that **psychology should base its theories on *observable data* which have been gathered from research**, rather than on discussions and arguments, you'd be arguing an empiricist's viewpoint. Empiricism is a philosophy which concerns itself with how psychology should conduct its research and draw its conclusions. Empiricists argue that support for all theories (and all statements taken from theories) should be demonstrated for all to see, in research settings like laboratories, for example. In fact, they regard theories (and statements) that have no such support as *unscientific*. Theories that arise out of discussions and arguments alone are described by empiricists as 'armchair theories' and aren't taken seriously. The *Scientific Method* – discussed earlier in this chapter – is central to the *empirical* approach to psychology.

So how does this help us?

Well, it may be that we can use the concept of empiricism to help us answer some of our queries about the rightness of theories and conclusions in psychology. To figure out how, let's take a closer look at the statement that made a brief appearance in an earlier paragraph

Women are more intelligent than men.

Let's call this *Statement A*. Let's say that Statement A is one of a number of statements that collectively form *Theory A*, which states that

> *Intelligence is determined by gender.*

Naturally, being psychologists, we'd like to test this theory. But because we've read the first part of this chapter we know that theories (and statements taken from theories) cannot be tested directly. We need a testable *hypothesis* relating to statement A. One possibility would be

> *A sample of 20 women will outscore 20 men on the Evans Intelligence Test.*

Now we have the full set. A *theory*, a *statement* taken from it and a testable *hypothesis* relating to the statement.

> **Theory A**   *Intelligence is determined by gender.*
> **Statement A**   *Women are more intelligent than men.*
> **Hypothesis**   *A sample of 20 women will outscore a sample of 20 men.*

Here we have a theory, a statement and a testable hypothesis and there you are in your psychology class with your hand in the air demanding an answer to your question 'Are any of these "three As" *right*?' If your psychology tutor is in the mood to produce an informed, carefully thought out answer, it will go along these lines. She'll begin by reminding you that neither theories, nor statements taken from them, can be *proved* in psychology. They can be *supported* by the results of research, in which case they live to fight another day. It only takes one set of research findings to *oppose* a theory (or statement) and it is *falsified*, leading to it having to be modified in some way. Therefore, according to the terms of the scientific method, we can say that theories and statements cannot be proved but they can be shown to be false. In other words, they can be *wrong* but not *right*.

Pausing momentarily to allow this to sink in, she'll then go on to remind you that hypotheses have something that theories (and statements taken from them) don't have. Namely, testability. After reading a hypothesis a researcher should be able to go away and design a piece of research to test it. Hypotheses also predict the outcome of research. The accuracy of such predictions is demonstrated for all to see by the results of the ensuing study. If a hypothesis predicts the results accurately, the theory from which it was derived is supported and will live to fight another day. If it doesn't predict the results accurately the theory will have to be modified.

The key point here is that the accuracy, or *rightness*, of the hypothesis can be demonstrated observably. It can be demonstrated empirically, before your very eyes. Another way of putting this is to say that hypotheses can be clearly shown to be right or wrong.

> *How does this relate to our 'three As'?*

In the case of *Hypothesis A*, if the sample of 20 women does outscore the sample of 20 men, the hypothesis is *accepted* as *right*. *Theory A* and *Statement A* are then supported and live to fight another day. But if the female sample doesn't outscore the male sample, the hypothesis is rejected as wrong and Theory A has to be modified.

So there you have it. One circumstance in which psychologists will say that something is right is when they're talking about testable hypotheses. **Box 1L** sums this up.

Box 1L

Can theories, statements and hypotheses be right or wrong?

	Can they be right?	Can they be wrong?
Theories	**No**. But they can be **supported** by research findings.	**Yes**. It only takes one research finding to oppose a theory and that will show it to be false and in need of some modification.
Statements	**No**. But they can be **supported** by research findings. This produces support for the theory from which the statement has been taken.	**Yes**. One piece of evidence will show a statement to be false, along with the theory from which it has been taken. Modification will be required.
Hypotheses	**Yes**. Because they are **empirically testable**. They predict events that are observable. If hypotheses are right, the statements and theories they derive from are supported.	**Yes**. If the event a hypothesis predicts does not transpire, it is wrong. So we reject it, along with the theory it comes from.

Are there any other circumstances in which psychologists will say something is 'right'?

Yes. But before we consider these we're going to consider something beginning with 'P'.

The Perspectives: psychoanalysis, behaviourism, cognitive psychology

'So what is psychology then?' 'And what do you do actually *do* in psychology?'

If you enrol on a psychology course you'll have to get used to coming home from college and facing these two questions from your family, friends, lodgers, landlord etc. If you'd chosen pharmacy, economics or aerobics you wouldn't have had this to cope with. The fact is, even professional psychologists can't agree on the answers to these two questions.

For the past hundred years there's been debate about what the subject matter of psychology is and about how to conduct research into it. To put it another way, psychology has lacked a **perspective**: **an agreed definition of what is to be studied and how to go about studying it**. Instead, different groups of psychologists have co-existed, researching, forming theories, whilst having different ideas about *what* psychology is and *how* it should be studied. These groups are sometimes referred to as 'schools of thought'.

How does all this help us?

Well, it may be that we can use this concept of perspectives to help us discover another one of those rare circumstances under which psychologists are prepared to use the word *right*.

We'll return to this presently. First, take a look at **Box 1M**, which tells you more about some of the more influential perspectives in psychology.

Box 1M

Different perspectives have different ideas about what psychologists study and how to go about studying it

Perspectives include . . .	Famous names include . . .	Psychology's subject matters are . . .	Psychology should be studied using . . .
Psychoanalysis	Freud Jung Erikson	. . . the **emotional** or affective aspects of human personality. In particular, how these aspects develop and how they are influenced by unconscious motives.	. . . **case studies** involving detailed, prolonged analysis often of an individual participant's ideas and memories.
Behaviourism	Pavlov Skinner Watson	. . . how **behaviours** are learned. The effect of the environment on this learning process. How we can control behaviour by controlling the environment.	. . . **experimental research** in controlled settings, such as laboratories. Such experiments often use non-humans as participants.
Cognitive psychology	Piaget Gregory Broadbent	. . . **thinking**. In particular, memory, problem solving and visual perception. Also, how we develop and use our capacity for language.	. . . **experimental research** in controlled settings, such as laboratories. These experiments predominantly use humans as participants.

These aren't all the schools of thought in psychology. There are seven or eight main ones.

At different times over the last hundred years particular schools have been more popular than others. During the 1920s, for example, behaviourism had its heyday. More recently the cognitive approach has been in favour. It comes and goes in cycles. The one constant factor is that no single school of thought has ever dominated psychology so much that the others have thrown in the towel and abandoned their own preferred ideas about what to study and how to study it. There's never been a single, dominant paradigm.

If you look closely at these three schools of thought you'll see that each of them has an interest in a different aspect of 'the whole person'. They all have an interest in people, but for different reasons. If, for instance, you were to be studied by a psychoanalyst, s/he would pay particular attention to your *emotional* (sometimes called *affective*) life. A behaviourist, on the other hand, would focus on your *actions* rather than your feelings. That is, what you do rather than how you feel about what you do. And just to be different again, a cognitive psychologist would concentrate on your powers of reasoning and problem solving. S/he'd want to know about the *thinking* part of you, rather than the *feeling* and *doing* parts. Because of their special areas of interest these three approaches are sometimes referred to as the A (*affective*) B (*behavioural*) C (*cognitive*) of psychology.

But let's get back to our central question. *Are any of these schools of thought right?* Well, it depends who you talk to. This might seem like a confusing answer, so let me try to explain it.

Put yourself in the position of a psychologist who has carried out a piece of research and drawn conclusions from the results. For the sake of argument, let's say you're a psychoanalyst. In other words you're from the psychoanalytic school of thought. You regard psychology as the study of affective aspects of 'the whole person'. You carry out research using individual case studies rather than large-scale surveys or experiments. In short, you use the psychoanalytic perspective.

Now let's try that question again. Are the conclusions you've drawn from the results of your research right? Well, if you talk to another psychoanalyst your conclusions may well be regarded as right. If, on the other hand, you talk to a behaviourist (or a cognitive psychologist) your conclusions will almost certainly not be. In other words, if you talk to someone who shares your ideas about what psychology is and how it should be studied they're likely to agree with the conclusions you've drawn and they may well regard them as right. Mind you, this isn't guaranteed. It's quite likely that even a fellow psychoanalyst will still disagree with your conclusions. Nevertheless, when you're talking to someone from your own school of thought there's a reasonable chance they will agree with you because they share your ideas about what psychology is and how it should be studied.

If, on the other hand, you talk to someone who doesn't share your perspective (a behaviourist, for example) you'll find them reluctant to agree with your conclusions. Not only will they be unlikely to regard them as right, they may even draw their own, different conclusions from your results. Conclusions that fit more closely with their own school of thought, their own perspective.

To summarise, psychologists will be far more likely to regard the conclusions drawn from research data as being right if they share the perspective of whoever carried out the research. To illustrate how this works in practice we'll look at Freud's 1909 case study of 'Little Hans', famously known as the 'Analysis of a Phobia of a Five-Year-Old Boy'.

Key study: Freud on phobias

Freud was the founder of the psychoanalytic school of thought. He carried out his research using individual case studies rather than large-scale surveys or experiments. But his research into the case of Little Hans was unusual in that the two only ever met twice. Consequently he gathered all his data by talking to and exchanging letters with the boy's father.

When Hans was four years old his father reported that his son had developed a fear of horses. In particular, he was afraid of 'horses falling down in the street'. This isn't as strange as it sounds. Horses were a common feature of street life in 1900s. They were the traffic of the day, used for pulling buses and carriages. So being afraid of horses was the equivalent of our being afraid of cars or trucks. Even so, the intensity of Hans's fear was fairly extreme and Freud diagnosed a **phobia: an irrational fear of some object or situation**.

The psychoanalytic school of thought comes complete with suitcases full of fairly complex ideas about the affective aspects of the 'the whole person'. It's impossible to summarise all these ideas here, but one of them is especially important for our understanding of Hans's case. Freud argues that the troublesome anxieties and neuroses we experience as adults originate in our childhood experiences and interactions. So, for example, if you are excessively mean or stubborn or addicted as an adult, this may be a kind of delayed reaction to some relationship or event you experienced as a child. So since phobias are a kind of neurosis, psychoanalysts argue that these 'irrational fear reactions' can be explained by talking about our earliest memories and interactions. Of course, adults often find this process of sifting through the past difficult and painful. For Hans though it was relatively easy since he didn't have to go so far back.

Freud met and corresponded with Hans's father regularly. Together they examined the boy's statements and reactions to various domestic situations, always looking for clues that might lead to an explanation for his fear of horses. Freud maintained that if he could find the origin of Hans's phobia, he could then set about treating its symptoms. Here's what he came up with

Why Hans was scared of horses: a psychoanalytic explanation

Hans was competing with this father for the affection of his mother. As a result of this rivalry Hans was frightened of what his father would do to him. He was so small and weak and his father was so big and strong and he was scared that his father would attack him and punish him by chopping his penis off. But

*because expressing feelings of fear and hatred towards his father was socially
and domestically unacceptable, Hans unconsciously displaced his feelings onto
horses, as they had a great many of the characteristics his father had. They
were big and strong, they had whiskers and wore glasses (blinkers). So Hans
was using horses as a scapegoat for his fear towards his father.*

A fascinating explanation. But is it right? Well, it depends who you talk to. It has
plenty of supporters, especially from within the psychoanalytic school of thought. If
you talk to psychologists who use this perspective you'll find a lot of them will regard
Freud's explanation of Hans's phobia as being right.

But if you talk to people from other schools of thought you'll get a different
response. If you talk to behaviourists you'll find they'll tend to regard Freud's interpretation as wide of the mark. If you talk to enough of them you'll probably find one or
two who'll replace Freud's explanation with their own, alternative explanation for
Hans's phobia; one that fits more closely with their own school of thought. Here's an
example.

Why Hans was scared of horses: a behaviourist explanation
*Hans exhibited a fear response whenever he came in contact with horses, or
with any object associated with horses, like muzzles and bridles. His response
goes back to an incident he witnessed where a horse-drawn van collapsed in
the street. This frightened him at the time and thereafter he generalised his fear
response from that particular horse-drawn vehicle to all such vehicles, all
horses and all horse accessories.*

This explanation is less complex than Freud's. It was put forward by Wolpe and
Rachman in 1960. They see phobias as fear responses that are associated with particular phobic objects. In Hans's case the phobic object was horses and he generalised
his fear response to anything connected with horses – carts, bridles, muzzles and so
on. Notice that Wolpe and Rachman don't mention emotions or unconscious motives
in their explanation. This is because they are using a behaviourist perspective, which
means that they concentrate on observable actions and responses rather than inner
feelings and motives.

So is Wolpe and Rachman's explanation right? Other behaviourists may well think
that it is. Psychoanalysts, though, would be unlikely to. In other words, it depends
who you talk to.

Freud's research into the case of Little Hans was carried out using a psychoanalytic
approach. Many other researchers from the psychoanalytic school of thought agree
with his explanations of Hans's phobia, whilst behaviourists (and cognitive psychologists) are more likely to disagree with him. Some behaviourists, like Wolpe and
Rachman, have even replaced Freud's conclusions with conclusions of their own. This
illustrates one of those rare circumstances under which psychologists are prepared to
use this troublesome 'r' word. They may regard conclusions drawn from research
data as *right* if they share the perspective of whoever carried out the research.

The word *right* is a hot potato in psychology. Ask your tutor if a theory or a conclusion is right and she'll surely squirm a little. In this section I've tried to explain why she reacts

as she does. 'Right' is a word that's rarely used by psychologists, probably because there are so many contradictory and competing theories about every aspect of human behaviour.

But there are some circumstances under which psychologists may be tempted to say that something is right. One is when they're talking about testable hypotheses. Another is when they're talking about research that is carried out by someone who shares their perspective. Now before you finish this chapter, try your hand at replacing the emboldened text in **Box 1N** with the appropriate terminology. Answers can be found in **Box 1P**.

Box 1N

Terminology can be a good thing: example 6

The ABC of psychology

Psychologists can often be distinguished from each other in terms of their **approach which is defined by their definitions of psychology's subject matter and views about how it should be studied**. For example, Freud's work typifies **the approach to psychology which concentrates on affective aspects of personality**. Skinner meanwhile advocates **that approach to psychology which argues that the only appropriate subject matter for the subject is observable, measurable behaviour**. A third researcher, Broadbent, represents **the approach to psychology which focuses on thinking**. These approaches also differ in terms of their preferred **way of carrying out research**. Freud used **detailed studies of individuals**, whereas Skinner and Piaget preferred to use **a situation in which the effect of an independent variable on a dependent variable is measured under laboratory conditions**. The three approaches – one *affective*, one *behavioural*, one *cognitive* – are often referred to as *the ABC of psychology*.   [146 words]

Box 1P

Example 6 with added terminology

The ABC of psychology

Psychologists can often be distinguished from each other in terms of their **perspective**. For example Freud's work typifies **psychoanalysis**. Skinner meanwhile advocates **behaviourism**. A third researcher, Broadbent, represents **cognitive psychology**. These approaches also differ in terms of their preferred **research method**. Freud used **case studies**, whereas Skinner and Piaget preferred to use **controlled experiments**. The three approaches – one *affective*, one *behavioural*, one *cognitive* – are often referred to as *the ABC of psychology*.
[72 words]

2 Studying Psychology in Ways that Maximise your Learning Style

Look around your psychology class. You'll see people with quite a bit in common and with plenty to distinguish them as individuals. Different tastes in clothes, books, films and crisps, different social and emotional needs. Most importantly for this chapter, they'll all have different styles of learning. Each individual will have their own preferences and needs when it comes to how they learn most effectively. Some like lectures. Some like discussions. Some like playing games. This chapter will help you identify your own style of learning and suggest some ways to use that knowledge to become more effective when studying psychology.

User's Guide to Chapter 2

• 1 Learning styles: What's it all about?

Eating at Frank's Place
The basics of the learning-styles approach

• 2 The Wholist–Analyst theory

Know your profile: wholist or analyst?
Play to your strengths: wholist or analyst?
Chip away at your weaknesses: wholist or analyst?

• 3 The Listening, Looking and Doing theory

Know your profile: auditory, visual or tactile-kinaesthetic?
Play to your strengths: visual, auditory or tactile-kinaesthetic?
Chip away at your weaknesses: visual, auditory or tactile-kinaesthetic?

- **1 Learning styles: what's it all about?**

Eating at Frank's Place

Students and tutors at our college could learn a lot from Frank. Frank runs the restaurant on the first floor. He puts on a lovely spread. More importantly, he puts on a different spread for different people. When you enrol at our college Frank gives you a form to fill in, asking for details of the kind of foods you prefer, the kind of nutrients you're lacking, what you try to avoid for religious, ethical and medical reasons and so on. Frank takes the completed forms away and devises a 'diet profile' for every one of his customers, guaranteeing that every meal you eat at **Frank's Place** will combine 'a little bit of what you fancy' with 'a little bit of what does you good'. The result? Happy, healthy students and tutors. If only they themselves would apply Frank's motto – '**different people like and need different things**' – to their own studying and teaching, there really would be a few improvements around here.

The basics of the learning-styles approach

Not everyone studies psychology (or anything, for that matter) in the same way. We each have a different **style of learning**. Partly because we all have **individual *preferences* for learning in certain ways** and partly because we all have **individual needs that have to be attended to when we're taking in new material**. Some of us prefer to be told what to study and how to go about it. Others prefer to develop our own pathways through our learning. Some of us need silence to be able to concentrate. Others need some background noise. No two learners are quite the same. Just like when we're eating at Frank's Place, when we're learning we're happiest and most effective when we're combining a little bit of what we fancy with a little bit of what does us good.

Though this sounds like common sense, it isn't very common for tutors and students to pay much attention to individual styles of learning. Take tutors, for example. Few of them spend time exploring students' individual learning needs and preferences with a view to altering their teaching methods to cater for everyone. In their defence, perhaps this is because of the sheer size of their classes. So if tutors haven't the time to read every single student's 'learning fingerprint', maybe it's up to students themselves to take matters into their own hands. Yes, that means you. This chapter offers you a guide to identifying your own individual needs and preferences, so you can devise your own learning profile and answer questions such as

What kind of psychology student am I?
Why do I excel in some areas of my course and not others?
Could I prepare for assessments more effectively?

Furnished with answers to these questions, your performance ought to improve, however good it already is.

Before proceeding any further though, let's take a quick look at how three sets of researchers have tried to complete the sentence *Different people have different styles of learning in terms of* . . .

Carbo, Dunn and Dunn (1986) suggest that: *Different people have different styles of learning in terms of how they concentrate when learning new material and skills* A key influence here is **the learning environment**. To be more specific, different levels of sound, light and temperature suit different people, as does the chair they choose to sit in. For example, you may work best with some background noise to block out the noise of your own breathing or rustling papers. Alternatively, you may work well with subdued lighting. Or you may prefer to lounge on the floor rather than sit at a table. It's a matter of personal style. There's no one right way.

Honey and Mumford (1993) say that: *Different people have different styles of learning in terms of how they acquire new skills and information*. For them, learning takes place at different stages of a **learning cycle**. This cycle incorporates a number of processes that are ongoing during all kinds of learning. Processes such as *reflection, planning, experiencing*. For Honey and Mumford, *different people learn most effectively at different stages of the learning cycle*. Some of us are by nature *reflectors*, who like to stand back, observe, and stroke our chins as we learn. Others are *activists*, best employed when engrossed in 'here and now' activities. A third group, *pragmatists*, like to be shown how something is done according to an established model. Fourthly, *theorists* are happy to acquire abstract ideas that have no immediately obvious practical application. Whilst some people are in the happy position of being able to thrive at more than one stage of the learning cycle, no single style is superior to any other; though you could argue that some courses attract people who thrive at particular stages of the learning cycle. For example, pure maths might attract *theorists*.

Sadler-Smith (1996) says that: *Different people have different styles of learning in terms of the kind of learning activities they prefer to take part in*. This relates to **how much power and influence we have over our learning**. Some of us are *dependent learners*, who like tutors to give us instructions in structured scenarios like lectures and seminars, preferably with deadlines imposed. Some of us are *independent learners*, who like to exert some influence over (negotiate with our tutor) the options we take, the assignments we do. Here, the tutor is seen as a resource to be used, not an authority whose word is taken as law. Thirdly, *collaborative learners* are social animals who work best on group projects. All three of these styles of learning can be effective, although they're not all equally catered for in the typical college setting.

You'd be right to conclude from these three models that plenty has been said and written about individual styles of learning. In fact, there are shelves full of research on the subject. To narrow things down a little the rest of this chapter will focus on two models that have plenty to offer undergraduate psychologists who are on a mission to find out more about the strengths and weaknesses of their own learning, about how to make the most of their strengths and about how to iron out their weaknesses. With all this in mind, over the next few pages you'll be encouraged to take three significant steps towards being better at studying psychology.

Step 1   **Know your profile** – Find out your individual style of learning.
Step 2   **Play to your strengths** – Organise your learning to make the most of areas you excel in.
Step 3   **Chip away at your weaknesses** – Organise your learning to improve in areas you don't excel in.

● 2 The Wholist–Analyst theory

When you describe a film you saw the previous day to your mother or your neighbour do you find yourself remembering the grand themes or the minutiae? Do you dwell on the overall feel of the film – what film students call its 'mise-en-scène' – or do you come up with accurate – yet often disjointed – details, word-for-word one liners and intricate plot details? Which are you, the 'big picture' film critic or the stickler for 'fine detail'? If you're the former, chances are you're what Eugene Sadler-Smith (1996) has called a *wholist learner*. If you're the latter, you may be one of Sadler-Smith's *analytic learners*.

The difference between the two refers to how we organise and process new material. In effect, we're talking about two styles of thinking. Wholist learners excel at learning and remembering the big themes in new material. They prioritise these at the expense of the 'small change' of detail and factual accuracy, both of which they're happy to sort out later or ignore altogether. For the analytic learner, fine detail is a top priority. They're happiest concentrating on analysing facts, rather than considering global themes. Indeed, an overall understanding of major themes rarely dawns on analytics until all the facts and details have been accumulated. You could say wholist learners think 'top–down', analytics think 'bottom up'.

Know Your Profile: Wholist or Analyst? You may already have a pretty shrewd idea of which of these thinking styles is most applicable to you. If not, or if you're on the lookout for confirmation, here are a couple of methods for sorting out the wholists from the analytics

Method One   The 'Field-Dependency' Test

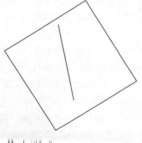

Picture A

This test relates to a theory put forward by Witkin (1959), who suggests that people who are *field dependent* have personalities that give them 'heightened social aware- ness'. In other words, they have a strong sense of what other people are thinking and expecting from them. *Field-independent* people, on the other hand, tend to take less notice of the thoughts and feelings of those around them. Witkin argues that these broad personality types also show up in how we perform on certain perceptual tests. These tests focus on how well we pick out or detach objects from their contexts or backgrounds. One of Witkin's most famous perceptual tests is this field-dependency test.

To take the test, first cover up **picture B** and **picture C**. Next, place a 'POST-IT note' (or any thin piece of paper) over **picture A**, the so-called 'rod and frame' drawing. Next, trace the *frame* in the drawing through your 'POST-IT note'. Next, keeping your 'POST-IT note' in position, re-draw the *rod* in such a way as to make it vertical, rather than tilted (as it is in **picture A**).

Now look at the drawing you've made. If it resembles **picture B** you may well be a field-independent or analytic learner. You're someone who is relatively unaffected by overall contexts. If your drawing resembles **picture C** you may well be a field- dependent or wholist learner. In other words, you may be someone who is affected by contexts. You may even have heightened social awareness.

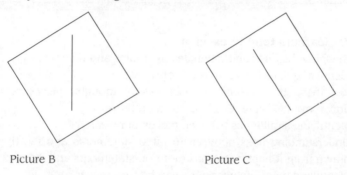

Picture B   Picture C

Try the 'Milgram-Memory' test in **Box 2A**. Did you find **Set A** or **Set B** harder? If you struggled more with **Set A** but faired reasonably well on **Set B** there's a good chance you're an *analytic* learner. If it was the other way around you may well be a *wholist* learner.

The *Field-Dependency* and *Milgram-Memory* tests will give you some indication of the strengths and weaknesses of your thinking style. If you want to try a more rigor- ous wholist-analytic test, have a look at Riding's *Cognitive Styles Analysis (1991)*.

Play to your strengths: wholist or analyst?

Knowing whether you tend towards the wholist or analytic style of thinking should help you explain a few things. Knowing how you process new material should help you work out why you excel in some areas of your psychology course and not others.

> ## Box 2A
>
> ### Method Two: The 'Milgram-Memory' Test
>
> Base your responses to this test on what you know about Milgram's experiment on obedience (1963). If you're already familiar with the study, go ahead and answer the questions in **Sets A** and **B** below. If not, read the summary in Chapter One, then try the questions.
>
> **Set A**
>   What's the aim of this study?
>   What's the use of this study to society as a whole?
>   Write down one similarity between Milgram's study and any other piece of research.
>   Suggest four problems with this kind of research.
>
> **Set B**
>   How did Milgram get his sample?
>   What was the 'learner's' surname?
>   What percentage of participants obeyed to the maximum voltage in the original study?
>   Name the four variables Milgram manipulated in his follow-up studies.

Wholist learners tend to excel at . . .

1 Grasping the aims and rationales of studies and theories;
2 Identifying links between pieces of research;
3 Identifying the perspectives (schools of thought) pieces of research are drawn from (Chapter One has more on these);
4 Identifying similarities between pieces of research;
5 Understanding links between testable statements and the theories they're drawn from (Chapter One has more on statements and theories);
6 Identifying the usefulness of research to society as a whole.

Analytic learners tend to excel at . . .

1 Recalling procedural details of research;
2 Recognising important design and control features of studies;
3 Summarising and identifying important findings from studies;
4 Identifying weaknesses in research;
5 Recalling names and dates associated with research.

Chip away at your weaknesses: wholist or analyst?

Riding (1991) suggests that once you know which thinking style you prefer you should focus on the *other* one – the one you like least. I call this *the jugglers' method of learning to learn*, based on that well known circus maxim that jugglers devote most of their practice time to training their subordinate hand (Finnigan 1992) up to the standard of their superior hand. What we're talking about here is a balanced approach to learning: a flexible style of thinking that enables you to process material efficiently whether it comes to you in the form of 'the big global themes' or the 'flotsam and jetsam of factual detail'. A logical step towards achieving this balance is to organise your learning in a way that compensates for your weaker, least preferred style of thinking. So wholists, be more analytic; analysts, vice versa. Here are some practical suggestions.

Wholists, be more analytic by . . .
1   Organising your **note-taking** by setting out topics and research in ways that highlight the component parts and substantive facts of the material. Drawing attention to them like this will make you less likely to gloss over them.
2   Adopting an approach to **essay writing** that's 'grounded in detail'. Habitually illustrate your arguments and conclusions with supporting facts, figures, findings and other relevant details.
3   Testing yourself on the little facts from the relevant research when you're **preparing for assessments**.
4   Drawing attention to the **differences** between different pieces of research.

Analysts, be more wholist by . . .
1   Organising your **note-taking** in a way that highlights the overall aims and rationales of research. Habitually indicate how research is useful for society as a whole.
2   Drawing attention to the **similarities** between different pieces of research.
3   Being aware of **the thinking style of your tutors**, since this may influence the way your class notes are organised. It's worth knowing that the teaching profession tends to attract analytics (Carbo, Dunn and Dunn, 1986), so it may be that you've been attending classes in which global themes were somewhat neglected. With this in mind, you may want to write your notes in a way that redresses this bias. Let your tutors know what you're doing and why you're doing it. They might be glad of the feedback on their teaching style.
4   Adopting an **essay-writing** style that draws out the big themes in the research you're discussing (aims, and applications to society as a whole). Habitually keep in mind the overall requirements of the essay question as you're writing (Chapter 3 has a guide to writing psychology essays).
5   Testing yourself on the aims and usefulness of the relevant research when you're **revising for assessments**.

Neither of these two styles of thinking is superior to the other. *Wholist* learning and *analytic* learning both have their strengths. But the most effective, most desirable style of all is one that's well-balanced – part *wholist*, part *analytical*. So think like a juggler. Make the most of what you do excel at, develop what you don't excel at.

● 3 The Listening, Looking and Doing theory

Are you any good at recalling details from news stories? You're answer to this will probably be 'It depends'. And let's face it, it depends on lots of factors. One of these will be how you came across the story to begin with. In other words, how the story reached you. Did someone tell you it? Did you see the pictures on TV? Were you physically there, taking part, peripherally or otherwise, in the event that later became news?

According to Marie Carbo and Kenneth and Rita Dunn (1986), some of us excel at remembering material we hear, others do better with stories we see pictures of, others excel when we're actively involved in what we're trying to learn and remember. You could say it's a matter of *perceptual preference*. If you prefer learning by hearing about new material you may be what Carbo, Dunn and Dunn call an *auditory* learner. If learning by looking at pictures, images and dramatisations helps you remember, you show signs of being a *visual* learner. If learning by feeling, making and doing is your preference, you're probably a *tactile-kinaesthetic* learner. This last group typically includes 'tinkerers' and 'doodlers' who like their learning to involve some kind of activity that has them moving around, making or manipulating objects, working with different textures.

Being a member of any of these groups doesn't mean you learn using one modality exclusively. Rather, you flit between the three but maintain a preference for one modality in particular. And although these three perceptual preferences are all as

Box 2B

Method One: The 'Figure of Speech' Test

Select a piece of psychological research you're familiar with. I'm using Freud's case of Little Hans as an example. If you're not familiar with the research, see Chapter 1 for a full description. To take the test, cover up the three boxes below. Next, talk about your selected piece of research for two minutes. Record your speech. Play it back and note down any 'figures of speech' that are similar to those in **Groups A**, **B** or **C**.

Group A	Group B	Group C
'from Freud's point of view . . . looking at the case of Hans . . . from the psychoanalytic perspective . . . the problem with this study is clear to see . . . the way I see it . . . a confused picture of a phobia emerges . . . an intimate portrait . . .'	'this theory sounds convincing . . . Freud only heard what he wanted to hear . . . Hans' plea fell on deaf ears . . . listening to Hans' case . . . to Freud, Hans' symptoms sounded like a phobia . . . Freud never heard Hans talk directly about his father . . . I've seldom heard such nonsense . . .'	'Freud wrestled with the facts . . . Freud manipulated the facts . . . a case of square pegs and round holes . . . I don't feel convinced by his argument . . . a cumbersome approach . . . putting myself in his shoes . . . Freud paved the way for future research . . .'

effective as each other, it seems fairly clear that not all of them are catered for equally well on most undergraduate courses.

Know your profile: auditory, visual or tactile-kinaesthetic?

Try the methods in Boxes 2B and 2C for separating 'lookers' from 'listeners' and 'manipulators'.

Your two-minute speech may be littered with figures of speech similar to those in all three groups, but it's likely that one group will feature most prominently. If **Group A**-type statements loom large in your speech you may well be a visual learner. If you use phrases from **Group B**, it sounds to me like you're an auditory learner. If you lean towards **Group C** it feels like you're a visual-kinaesthetic learner.

Read the descriptions in **Box 2C**. If Maurice sounds like you, chances are you're a visual learner. If you're more of a Robin, you could be an auditory learner. If you're a Barry you probably have a perceptual preference for tactile-kinaesthetic learning.

The 'Figure of Speech' and 'Who Are You Most Like?' tests will tell you something about your perceptual preference. For another test of perceptual preference – straight from the horses' mouths – have a look at Dunn, Dunn and Price's *Learning Styles Inventory* (1985).

Box 2C

Method Two: The 'Who Are You Most Like' Test

Here are three people talking about themselves. 'Who Are You Most Like?'

'My name is Maurice and my favourite party game is Pictionary. When I'm trying to spell a word I picture it in my head. I've a good memory for faces, but not names. When I'm studying I get distracted by people moving about in my visual field. At weekends I like to watch TV and go to the cinema. I'd rather visit an art gallery than a concert hall or a gym. In psychology classes I always take note of diagrams, demonstrations and slides.'

'I'm Robin and my favourite party game is Chinese Whispers. When I'm trying to spell a word I say each letter in my head until it sounds right. I'm good at remembering names, but not faces. When I'm reading I get distracted by background noise. In my spare time I enjoy listening to music and chatting on the 'phone. I'd rather go to the 'phone. I'd rather go to or a gym. I enjoy the lectures on this psychology course and appreciate good, clear verbal explanations.'

'Hi, they call me Barry. My favourite party game is Charades. When I'm trying to spell a word I write it down. I've a good memory for things I've done and places I've been, though faces and names often escape me. When I'm reading I can't concentrate properly unless I'm physically comfortable. On my days off I enjoy playing sport, cooking, mending and building things. Maurice says I'm a bit of a "tinkerer". I'd rather visit a gym than an art gallery or a concert hall. In psychology classes I like designing research, playing games, going on visits, doing role-plays.'

Play to your strengths : visual, auditory or tactile-kinaesthetic?

Knowing your perceptual preference should help you explain why you excel in certain areas of your psychology course. It should also help you change the way you learn new material and prepare yourself for assessments to exploit your own individual style. Here are some suggestions

Visual learners

Play to your strengths by paying special attention to what your **notes** look like. With your preference for the visual modality, no doubt you already take care with your presentational style, but you could take things further by using patterned notes. This involves making 'spidergram pictures' to illustrate central and peripheral themes from concepts, studies or theories (or whatever it is you're making notes on). Patterning is fully explained in *Chapter 3* in the section on 'Making a patterned assessment plan'.

Making written text into patterns and pictures plays into the hands of visual learners. Try to do this whenever you plan and prepare for assignments. Why is it so effective?

Because it exploits your natural preference for thinking and remembering in images. **Box 2D** shows a typical example of a visual learner's notes. She's illustrated some positive and negative evaluations of Freud's case of Little Hans by using cartoons that help her remember them. As you'll know if you're one yourself, visual learners are often picture-junkies. Their notes are littered with diagrams, spider-

Box 2D

Evaluating Freud's Little Hans study using words and pictures

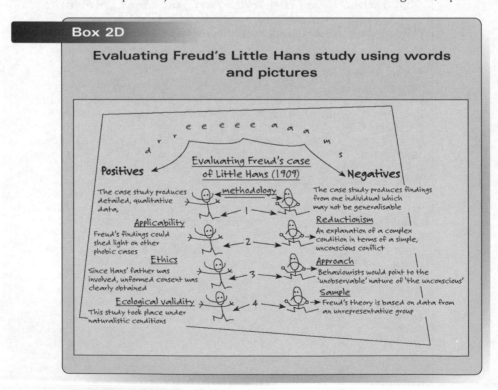

grams, pie-charts and cartoons. To an outsider it may look a bit batty, but it's actually a smart attempt to make the most of a particular style of learning.

One last thought for visual learners. Ask your tutor to recommend **readings** for topics in advance of class. You'll respond better to the material if you're introduced to it by seeing it first, rather than by hearing about it in a lecture (Carbo, Dunn and Dunn, 1986)

Auditory learners

Play to your strengths by finding a cassette recorder, or some other sound-recording device. To you these are a valuable learning aid. In fact, you're a bit of a human cassette recorder yourself. You probably recall a far higher percentage of what you hear in **lectures** than those learners with other styles do (Carbo, Dunn and Dunn, 1986) – much of it word for word. A good set of written **notes** will cement your understanding further. And this is where your recordings come in. As you **prepare for assessments**, supplement your regular revision methods by recording the key points from the material you're revising, then playing it back to yourself regularly in the run-up to the big day (or night). Your memory for the material will be reinforced in precisely the way that suits your perceptual preference.

Another way of turning audio technology to your advantage is to record the **lectures** you attend, again playing them back later to reinforce your understanding. To avoid embarrassing scenes, ask permission first. I'd guess that most lecturers, far from being unnerved by the idea, will probably be flattered. Though these recordings won't replace your written notes, they'll make a handy complement.

Unlike visual learners, auditory learners benefit from doing the **readings** for topics after lectures or classes. This way new material is introduced through the auditory modality first. Your readings will have the greatest impact if you use them as a follow-up to what you've already heard.

Tactile-kinaesthetic learners

Play to your strengths by feeling your way through your course wherever you can. Your style of learning is often undervalued in undergraduate teaching, where the learner's role is traditionally seen as a passive one. But being aware of your preference for feeling, making and doing will help explain why you find yourself twiddling your thumbs and doodling during talks and lectures. Whilst you'll have little influence over the proportion of activity-based classes that crop up on your psychology course, there are some steps you can take to make your learning more tactile-kinaesthetic friendly.

First, you can recognise and make the most of the activities that do figure on psychology courses – **designing and carrying out research, seminar presentations** and **role-plays**. Expect to excel in these activities.

As for **lectures**, rather than regarding them as 'one-way learning traffic', focus on the one thing you can have an influence over – the quality of your written notes.

When **preparing for essays and timed assignments** you have several opportunities to take matters into your own hands. Don your inventor's hat. Make up games and devices to reinforce your learning. I've outlined two activities for feeling, making and doing Psychology' in **Boxes 2E** and **2F**. Both require cardboard, 'POST-IT notes', glue, and laminating facilities, so make friends with your college stationer. These games and devices are designed to improve your learning as you make and use them, so invest some time researching and designing them. See it as a craft, rather than a

Box 2E

Activities for feeling, making and doing psychology 1

The 'POST-IT' ™ Evaluation Board

Cut out a circular card to a size that suits. Divide the circle into segments, as below. Write the names of some evaluation issues from 'the DRREEEEEAAAMS system for evaluating studies' (this features in Chapter 3) in each of the segments. In the middle of the circle leave a blank space. Now you've made your 'evaluation board'. Laminate it, for that wipe-clean finish.

THE POST-IT™ EVALUATION BOARD

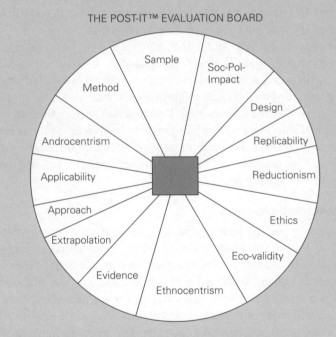

Next, write the name of a study or theory on a POST-IT™ note. Stick this in the middle of your circle. Think of as many positive and negative evaluations as you can for that study or theory. Explain each evaluation on a separate POST-IT™ note. Now stick your evaluations in the appropriate segment on your evaluation board. You could have different colours for positive and negative respectively.

The POST-IT™ board is a good way of formulating detailed evaluations for research. Use it individually or in groups. Attach a coat-hanger to the back of your evaluation board and hang it where your brother's dartboard used to be, for easy access.

chore. These activities can be adapted to use on your own or with other learners. You could even run them by your tutor as potential class activities.

Box 2F

Activities for feeling, making and doing psychology 2

'Top Psychology Trumps'

Top Trumps is a card game that made its name in the 1970s and has recently made a comeback. Make a set of cards with a different card for each study you've covered on your course. On each card include (a) the researcher's name and the date of the study, (b) the title, (c) a short outline of the procedure and findings, (d) a rating of 1–5 (compiled by you, awarding a maximum '5' for a good rating, a minimum '1' for a poor rating) for some appropriate evaluation issues from 'the DRREEEEEAAAMS system for evaluating studies' (see Chapter 3). Laminate your cards for a shower-resistant finish. Once you have your cards you can carry them with you everywhere and flick through them on the bus, in queues and at other opportune moments. Alternatively, you can play 'Top Psychology Trumps'. See Figures 1 to 6 for some examples of completed Top Psychology Trumps cards, and for instructions on how to play the game.

TOP PSYCHOLOGY TRUMPS
A Game for Psychology students aged 8- 108

How to Play

FIRST, MAKE YOUR SET OF CARDS

- Use a separate card for each study you've covered on your course.
- On each card write . . .
  (a) the researcher's name
  (b) the title of the study
  (c) a brief outline of the procedure and findings
  (d) a rating of 1–5 (5 is 'good', 1 'poor') for a selection of evaluation issues
- Laminate your cards.

Now you have your deck of cards you can carry them with you everywhere and flick through them in bus queues and at other opportune moments. Alternatively, you can play 'Top Trumps'.

PLAY THE GAME

- Deal the cards evenly between two players.
- Player 1 next describes the study on her 'top card' and selects one evaluation issue.
- She reads out the 1–5 rating for that evaluation issue, for that particular study. If this value is greater than the corresponding value on Player 2's top card, Player 2 surrenders his top card to Player 1, who then places both cards at the bottom of her pile.
- Player 1 then repeats the sequence by reading from her next 'top card'. This continues – sometimes for days – until one player has no cards left. This player is deemed the loser.

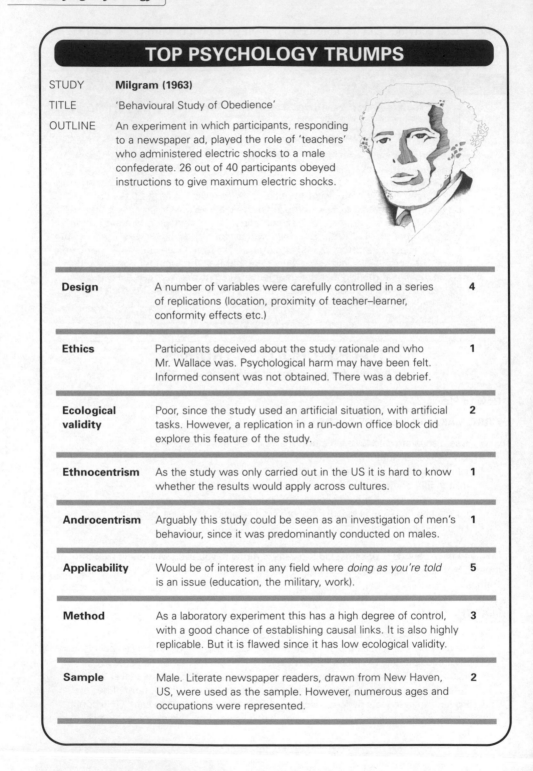

TOP PSYCHOLOGY TRUMPS

STUDY **Milgram (1963)**

TITLE 'Behavioural Study of Obedience'

OUTLINE An experiment in which participants, responding to a newspaper ad, played the role of 'teachers' who administered electric shocks to a male confederate. 26 out of 40 participants obeyed instructions to give maximum electric shocks.

Design	A number of variables were carefully controlled in a series of replications (location, proximity of teacher–learner, conformity effects etc.)	4
Ethics	Participants deceived about the study rationale and who Mr. Wallace was. Psychological harm may have been felt. Informed consent was not obtained. There was a debrief.	1
Ecological validity	Poor, since the study used an artificial situation, with artificial tasks. However, a replication in a run-down office block did explore this feature of the study.	2
Ethnocentrism	As the study was only carried out in the US it is hard to know whether the results would apply across cultures.	1
Androcentrism	Arguably this study could be seen as an investigation of men's behaviour, since it was predominantly conducted on males.	1
Applicability	Would be of interest in any field where *doing as you're told* is an issue (education, the military, work).	5
Method	As a laboratory experiment this has a high degree of control, with a good chance of establishing causal links. It is also highly replicable. But it is flawed since it has low ecological validity.	3
Sample	Male. Literate newspaper readers, drawn from New Haven, US, were used as the sample. However, numerous ages and occupations were represented.	2

TOP PSYCHOLOGY TRUMPS

STUDY   **Zimbardo et al. (1973)**

TITLE   'A study of Prisoners and Guards in a Simulated Prison'

OUTLINE   A simulation in which participants, responding to a
            newspaper ad, were assigned the roles of *prisoners
            and captors* in a purpose-built fake prison. Over the
            period of a week or so, the moods of the two groups
            grew antagonistic and polarised.

Design	A meticulously crafted study, involving the local police. Prisoners and guards were given carefully worded instructions, with enough freedom for them to explore their roles. All were screened before the study began, to see if they were *normal*.	4
Ethics	Participants consented to take part in a study of prison life. Guards were explicitly told not to use violence. All were warned of losing some civil liberties. Prisoners were deceived about the arrest. A right to withdraw was granted, though this was not made entirely clear.	3
Ecological validity	An artificial situation, with artificial tasks. However, the simulated prison did mimic many of the trappings of prison life – shiftwork, uniforms, roles etc.	3
Ethnocentrism	Would the results apply across cultures, beyond the US? Also, these were findings drawn from a middle-class 'culture'. The concept of *playing roles* could also be seen as belonging to western notions of personhood.	1
Androcentrism	Male participants were used exclusively, although the concepts of social roles and prison life are arguably as relevant to males and females.	2
Applicability	Of interest in particular to practitioners in the prison service. Can also help us study how roles we play are used as instruments of power.	5
Method	Simulations have some of the advantages of field experiments, since they mimic real-life settings and have some ecological validity. The researcher has plenty of control over the environment. Yet, since participants know they're being studied, demand characteristics are likely.	3
Sample	24 males were used. They were drawn from a *normal, healthy* sampling frame. They were middle class and white, so not entirely representative of society as a whole.	1

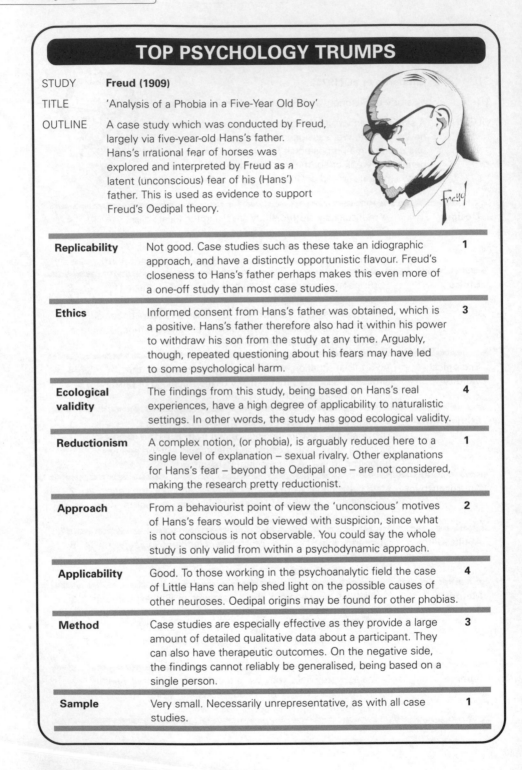

TOP PSYCHOLOGY TRUMPS

STUDY   **Freud (1909)**

TITLE   'Analysis of a Phobia in a Five-Year Old Boy'

OUTLINE   A case study which was conducted by Freud, largely via five-year-old Hans's father. Hans's irrational fear of horses was explored and interpreted by Freud as a latent (unconscious) fear of his (Hans') father. This is used as evidence to support Freud's Oedipal theory.

Replicability	Not good. Case studies such as these take an idiographic approach, and have a distinctly opportunistic flavour. Freud's closeness to Hans's father perhaps makes this even more of a one-off study than most case studies.	1
Ethics	Informed consent from Hans's father was obtained, which is a positive. Hans's father therefore also had it within his power to withdraw his son from the study at any time. Arguably, though, repeated questioning about his fears may have led to some psychological harm.	3
Ecological validity	The findings from this study, being based on Hans's real experiences, have a high degree of applicability to naturalistic settings. In other words, the study has good ecological validity.	4
Reductionism	A complex notion, (or phobia), is arguably reduced here to a single level of explanation – sexual rivalry. Other explanations for Hans's fear – beyond the Oedipal one – are not considered, making the research pretty reductionist.	1
Approach	From a behaviourist point of view the 'unconscious' motives of Hans's fears would be viewed with suspicion, since what is not conscious is not observable. You could say the whole study is only valid from within a psychodynamic approach.	2
Applicability	Good. To those working in the psychoanalytic field the case of Little Hans can help shed light on the possible causes of other neuroses. Oedipal origins may be found for other phobias.	4
Method	Case studies are especially effective as they provide a large amount of detailed qualitative data about a participant. They can also have therapeutic outcomes. On the negative side, the findings cannot reliably be generalised, being based on a single person.	3
Sample	Very small. Necessarily unrepresentative, as with all case studies.	1

TOP PSYCHOLOGY TRUMPS

STUDY   **Sherif et al (1956)**

TITLE   'The Robber's Cave'

OUTLINE   A field study, set in an Oklahoma boys' camp, in which two groups of boys ('rattlers' and 'eagles') developed opposing norms and attitudes, and prejudices. Though extremes of discrimination emerged, in a second phase the boys overcame their oppositions following the pursuit of super-ordinate goals.

Design	An ingenious design, conducted over three phases. In each of the phases group dynamics were observed and assessed using qualitative and quantitative methods, including sociograms. A series of tests, games and tasks were organised in each phase to help measure the development and reduction of prejudice.	4
Ethics	Putting the boys in conflict-ridden situations in the name of research may produce psychological harm (though arguably no more so than regular camp activities). However, the boys were not informed about the aims of the research.	2
Ecological validity	Ecological validity is high in this study since it is conducted in an Oklahoma boys' camp that had, as part of its regular activities, games and entertainments that formed part of the field study itself. Consequently the results from the study can be applied in contexts beyond the research.	4
Applicability	A useful study for anyone who is interested in how prejudice emerges when groups are competing for scarce resources. Also, it shows how those in charge of disparate groups can reduce prejudice by introducing super-ordinate goals. Teachers and social workers take note.	4
Method	Field experiments have the advantage of taking place in naturalistic settings, which yield behaviour which itself is 'natural'. However, it is difficult to observe behaviour reliably, to replicate the study, and to control extraneous variables. Its covert nature also raises ethical problems	3
Sample	Males, aged 11 and 12. All American, white and middle-class. Not a representative sample.	0
Socio-political impact	Research which looks at how prejudice and discrimination arise and can be reduced is of interest in the management of inter-ethnic conflicts. For example, we might learn from this study that wars have been fought in the past largely due to the lack of super-ordinate goals between groups who are competing for scarce materials.	4

TOP PSYCHOLOGY TRUMPS

STUDY   **Elliot (1968)**

TITLE   'Blue eyes, brown eyes'

OUTLINE   This oft-repeated field experiment first took place in
            Jane Elliot's primary school class. She labelled brown-
            eyed pupils as smarter than their blue-eyed fellows
            and rewarded them accordingly. Severe changes in
            esteem and performance ensued, though the debrief
            revealed the dangers of prejudice to the pupils.

Design	A clever design, with the effect of exposing all participants to the effects and dangers of prejudice and discrimination. The two-day nature of the study gave the children plenty of time for reflection. The collars highlighted the effects of labelling, based on superficial characteristics.	5
Replicability	Elliot herself has replicated this study many times in her own classroom over the years. She has also conducted an adult version in a number of workplaces, usually with similar results to the original research. However, a high degree of skill and sensitivity is required by any facilitator attempting such replications.	3
Ethics	Although a detailed debrief was carried out at the end, during the two days of the study there was a likelihood of psychological harm being felt by the participants. Certainly their self-esteem was affected. Until the final debriefing the children were clearly unaware of the purpose of the research.	1
Ecological validity	Being carried out in an ongoing school setting, the results clearly shed light on real life, everyday events. This is a true to life simulation with plenty of applicability to real educational (and other) environments.	5
Applicability	As a consciousness-raising exercise this study holds much interest for a variety of institutions who are in the business of education and training (schools, colleges, prisons, public services). For promoting awareness of multiculturalism and the effects of discrimination the study has much to offer.	5
Androcentrism	Males and females were used, and the experiment deals with issues which apply to both genders.	5
Sample	A fairly small sample of primary school children in one American town was used by Elliot in the original study, although many more have since taken part in replications.	2
Socio-political impact	Raising consciousness about the dangers of prejudice, by giving them a taste of its negative side, should arguably help us to develop policies to reduce prejudice. This study should have a positive impact.	4

The *'POST-IT'*™ *board* (**Box 2E**) and *Top Psychology Trumps* (**Box 2F**) both aim to make preparing for psychology assessments and learning about research more of a *tactile-kinaesthetic friendly* activity than, say, reading and writing notes.

Speaking from personal experience as a tutor, I've found they make lively and useful class activities. Methods like these won't replace your more traditional preparation methods, though they can be a welcome change for doodlers. Use them whenever it is convenient. Better still, make up your own. Other *touchy-feely* activities might include: *asking each member of your group to bring in an object or prop to introduce a piece of research; 'Psychology Charades' using 'classic studies' instead of books, films and so forth; 'Psychology Blockbusters'; 'Psychology Pictionary'* and so on. By the way, many of these activities will also appeal to *visual* learners.

Chip away at your weaknesses: visual, auditory or tactile-kinaesthetic?

Whilst all of us have a perceptual preference for learning and reinforcing new material, a balanced style of learning remains the most desirable one of all. So although it's wise to emphasise your preferred modality as you learn, it's also wise to reinforce your learning by dabbling in a wide variety of the methods that feature in this section. Effective learning should have a lot in common with eating at Frank's Place, where a balanced diet of a little bit of what you fancy combines nicely with a little bit of what does you good.

...ng Psychology ...ssessments and Examination Answers

Whether you're facing end-of-year examinations or modular assignments, it's likely that a hefty proportion of the assessment for your course will involve written assessments. In this chapter we'll look at some typical psychology assessment questions and some devices to help you answer them.

Writing answers to psychology assessments is undoubtedly an art in itself. Plenty of students never learn the art and are left in possession of knowledge and understanding but without the means to express their ideas on paper. This chapter is designed to reduce the number of psychology students who fit this description.

User's Guide to Chapter 3

• 1 Typical psychology assessments

Structured assessments questions and all-in-one assessments

• 2 Reading the words in the question

Decoding instruction words and psychology words in assessment questions
The top 10 instructions in psychology assessment questions

• 3 Planning assessment answers

Dealing with time-limits and word-limits
Making a patterned assessment plan

• 4 Writing in an academic style

Distinguishing between academic writing and non-academic writing
Knowing your audience
Using paragraphs
Using your own opinions in written work
Ending
Quoting, citing and referencing

- **5 Evaluating psychological research**

  The need for evaluation
  The DRREEEEEAAAMSS system for evaluating psychological evidence

- **6 Monitoring – and accelerating – your own progress**

  Five reasons to actively monitor your own progress
  How to evaluate your own assignments
  How to make the most of tutor feedback
  How to set goals for future improvement

- **7 Preparing for – and passing – psychology exams**

  Who likes exams?
  A 10-point plan for passing psychology exams

1 Typical psychology assessments

> *What to look for in this section*
> - Definitions and examples of **structured assessment questions**
> - Definitions and examples of **'all-in-one' assessment questions**

Structured assessment questions and 'all-in-one' assessment questions

Who thinks up psychology assessment questions? Teachers, lecturers, examiners. They may be from different backgrounds and have different tastes and personalities but when it comes to thinking up psychology essay questions they all think along similar lines, since the questions they come up with all fall into similar types.

Before we look at some examples it's worth stopping momentarily to consider what your tutor, lecturer or examiner is interested in when she sets you a question on, for example, the psychology of *memory* or *health promotion*. She's not just trying to find out how much you know about the topic, she's trying to find out how much you know about writing psychology assessments. She wants to assess how well you know the topic *and* how well you express your ideas on paper. She wants to assess both your knowledge of health promotion and your skills at writing. It's these skills for writing psychology assessments that are the focus of this chapter.

So what about these different types of psychology assessment?

Whether you're facing end-of-year examinations or modular assignments you'll find the questions come in distinct flavours: *structured assessments* and *all-in-ones.* Some students prefer one type, others prefer the other. Some examples of each type will help you understand more about the distinction.

Two typical *structured* assessments

(a) Describe what psychologists have learned about health promotion.
                                                                    (8 marks)
(b) Evaluate what psychologists have learned about health promotion.
                                                                    (10 marks)
(c) Using your knowledge of health promotion, suggest a programme that would encourage children to eat more healthily. *(6 marks)*

(a) Describe two models of remembering and forgetting. *(8 marks)*
(b) Evaluate these models. *(10 marks)*
(c) Explain how one of these models might be used to help students prepare for examinations. *(6 marks)*

Two typical *all in one* assessments

Describe and evaluate psychological research into human altruism and bystander intervention. *(24 marks)*

Discuss the nature–nurture debate in relation to visual perception.
                                                                    (24 marks)

So what's the difference between these two types of question?

Typical structured assessments have two characteristics. First, they require you to complete separate tasks for each separate part of the question. In our example on health promotion *Part (a)* requires you to **describe** research, whilst *Part (b)* requires you to evaluate research. As we'll discover later in this chapter these separate, distinct tasks require you to have quite separate, distinct skills. The second characteristic of structured assessments is that you're told how many marks are available for each part of the question. This helps you to decide how much time and space to devote to each part. For example, you should devote a quarter of your time and space to *Part c* of the question on health promotion, since it's worth a quarter of the overall mark (6 out of 24). Structured assessments appeal to a lot of students because of the extra guidance they offer and because they reduce the need for planning and organising, since much of this is done for you.

All-in-one assessments tend to appeal to students who like more freedom to develop their arguments in their own way. They like to plan their answers themselves without the restrictions of the *a–b–c* format. Being a hapless conformist who likes to be told what to do, I prefer structured questions. But that's just a personal preference.

The point is that whichever type of essay question your tutor, lecturer or examiner presents you with you'll need a load of skills for writing psychology assessments if you're going to provide a quality answer. An extensive *knowledge* of the topic you're being asked about won't be enough. You'll need to demonstrate the *skills* necessary for expressing your knowledge in a lively, well-informed, coherent response. The rest of this chapter deals with these necessary skills.

2 Reading the words in the question

> *What to look for in this section*
> - Decoding **instruction words** and **psychology words** in assessment questions
> - The Top Ten **instruction words** in psychology assessment questions

Decoding instruction words and psychology words in assessment questions

It's been said that psychology assessment questions are written in code. In other words, certain words in these questions have special meanings for psychology students, tutors, lecturers and examiners, so they can't just be taken at face value. They have to be read in a certain way. Or, if you prefer, they have to be decoded. Studying psychology enables you to learn how to read these words in a certain way and so to understand what these questions are asking you to do.

There are two types of words in assessment questions that need to be decoded. First there are **the psychology words**. These are the **words that tell you what your answer should be about**. They are technical and psychological terms that don't have a great deal of meaning outside the study of human behaviour. To understand these words you need to have a sound knowledge of your topic. Let's take one of our example questions and pick out the psychology words in it:

> *Describe and evaluate psychological research into human altruism and bystander intervention.*

A good way of identifying the psychology words is to show the question to someone (of reasonable intelligence) who's never studied psychology and wait for them to point at a word and say 'What does that mean?' Try this exercise with your lodger or the woman up the road. In the example we're using they'll probably point to *altruism* and *bystander intervention*. These are the psychology words. Outside of psychology, their meaning is not well known.

So what do you do with them when you've identified them?

Starting an essay

When you're writing your assessment a good way of getting started is to first identify and then define (or, if you prefer, decode) the technical and psychological terms in the question. Beginning your answer with clear, concise definitions of the psychology words immediately puts your reader in the picture. It's a neat way of demonstrating your knowledge of the topic and, importantly, it gets you off the starting blocks. So a possible opening sentence would be

> *Altruism, sometimes called 'pro-social behaviour', means behaviour that is unselfish, performed for the sake of someone else, without any personal gain.*

Earlier I said there are two types of words in essay questions that you need to be on the lookout for. The second type is **the instructions**. Once you've defined the psychology words in the question, you need to know **what you're going to *do* in your essay**. How will you use your knowledge of *altruism* and *bystander intervention*? This is where the instructions come in. Unlike the psychology words, the instructions are everyday words with everyday meanings. But when they appear in psychology essay questions they also have second, more precise, specialised meanings which are well understood by tutors, lecturers and examiners; code meanings, if you like. If you're to produce a quality answer to the question you too need to learn these second, specialised meanings. You need to be able to read these words in a certain way. Sounds like hard work, I know. But the good news is there are only ten or so of these instruction words – an all-time *Top Ten* of classic instructions that crop up again and again in assessment questions.

Box 3A defines and decodes them for you. Unlike most *Top Tens*, there aren't hundreds of other instruction words being released every week and straining to break into the chart. We've had the same top ten for generations.

As you can see, these words are all in common everyday use. But you need to read them in a more precise, specialised manner for the purpose of writing psychology assessments. Let's take a look at the instructions in one of our example questions.

(a) Describe what psychologists have learned about health promotion.

   (8 marks)

(b) Evaluate what psychologists have learned about health promotion.

   (10 marks)

(c) Using your knowledge of health promotion, suggest a programme that would encourage children to eat more healthily.   *(6 marks)*

Clearly this essay is going to be about **health promotion**. These are the psychology words in the question. The World Health Organisation defines **health promotion** as

> *The process of enabling people to increase control over, and to improve, their health habits.*

Defining the psychological, technical terms in the question like this is an effective way of beginning your essay. It demonstrates to your reader, right from the outset, that you know your topic.

Box 3A

Top 10 instructions in assessment questions

In an assessment question, this one's asking you to...

1 **Describe** . . . *provide details of some concept, theory or study, without any opinions. It's a neutral account that has no evaluations of any kind.* (An ever popular all-time favourite, especially for the first part of a structured question.)

2 **Evaluate** . . . *look in detail at the positive and negative features of a concept, theory or study. You'd substantiate this with supporting and critical evidence and maybe some of your own ideas.* (This one always carries a lot of marks. Often appears as *critically evaluate*. *Assess* and *critically assess* mean the same, too. See later in this chapter for a guide to evaluating.)

3 **Identify** . . . *indicate the identity of a concept, theory or study without going into lengthy detail or analyses. This may simply involve giving names, dates and a very basic outline of, say, a particular theory.* (May appear as the first part of a structured question.)

4 **Discuss** . . . *provide details of some concept, theory or study, including supporting and critical arguments that are backed up with evidence and maybe some of your own opinions. More partial than impartial. You may even talk about practical, real-world uses and implications here.* (An all-time favourite. A bit old-fashioned but still very popular. Involves elements of each of the *Top 3*.)

5 **Define** . . . *explain, in precise terms, what a word or phrase means.* (A classic. Often used as a starter in structured questions.)

6 **Explain** . . . *take a concept, theory, study and make it easy for the reader to understand. Give reasons for the existence or development of the concept, theory or study, so that the reader understands how it came about.* (Tricky, due to it's vagueness. Includes elements of *description*, plus a requirement to trace the *origin* of a concept. On its way down the chart, although still pretty common.)

7 **Outline** . . . *run through the most important aspects of a concept, theory or study, leaving out the fine details.* (The skill here is to select the important points and leave out the unnecessary detail. More difficult than it looks.)

8 **Compare** . . . *look at two or more concepts, theories or studies in relation to each other. This involves bringing out their relative good and bad points. So it's a critical, as well as descriptive, exercise.* (Often appears alongside *contrast*, inviting you to bring out similarities *and* differences between two concepts, theories or studies.)

9 **Illustrate** . . . *explain the meaning of a concept, word or phrase, citing examples or even diagrams to support and clarify your explanation.* (This is like *defining*, plus examples.)

10 **Analyse** . . . *take a close-up, detailed look at some concept, theory or study. This may involve dividing something up and examining each of its parts separately.* (Includes elements of *evaluation*, since you'll be looking at the merits and drawbacks of whatever is under your scrutiny. *Examine* and *critically examine* mean more or less the same thing, with more emphasis on evaluation in the latter.)

But what about the instructions?

Alright, I'm coming to that.

In their research into *health promotion* psychologists have learned a number of things about how health professionals attempt to encourage people to behave in ways that maintain good health and to avoid behaviours that lead to ill-health. In *Part (a)* of your essay you'll need to *describe* some examples of this research. You should adopt a neutral, non-evaluative style, whilst looking in detail at the aims of the research, how it was carried out and what the findings were. Here's an example of a pretty good description of Meyerowitz and Chaiken's 1991 study into health promotion . . .

> . . . in which the researchers wanted to find out about the effect of health education messages on breast self-examination. They divided their participants into two conditions, A and B. Condition A was given messages that emphasised the positive benefits of self examination, whilst Condition B was given messages that emphasised the negative outcomes of non-examination. It was found that both messages increased the likelihood of and intention to examine in the short term. But in the long term (four months after the messages) Condition A was more likely to carry out regular examinations. These results suggest that positive health education messages are more effective in the long term than negative, fear-arousing, messages.

In *Part (b)* of your answer you'll move on to look in detail at the positive and negative features of the research into health promotion. You'll probably deal with many of the same studies and theories you'd described in *Part (a)*. See later in this chapter for a guide to evaluating studies and theories.

Although *Part (c)* doesn't feature any of our *Top Ten Instructions*, you're clearly being invited to write about the usefulness, in a real-world setting, of the research into health promotion. So *Part (c)* is about *applying* studies and theories.

Whatever type of psychology assessment question you're answering, it's worth remembering that before you start putting pen to paper (or finger to keyboard) you need to be clear precisely what the instructions are asking you to do with your knowledge. In other words, don't go simply *describing* what you're meant to be *discussing*. A good way of testing yourself on this is to make a list of all ten instruction words, cover up the left-hand column of **Box 3A** and try to identify which word belongs to the appropriate definition in the right-hand column.

● **3 Planning assessment answers**

What to look for in this section
● Dealing with **time-limits** and **word-limits**
● Deciding what to leave out and what to include in your answer
● Making a **patterned assessment plan**

Dealing with time-limits and word-limits

Chances are that by the time you reach the planning stage either you'll be sitting in your room poised to write one of your modular assignments or you'll be in a gymnasium somewhere sitting an end-of-term examination. Wherever you are, you'll be either staring at a structured question or looking down the barrel of an all-in-one question. The knowledge you need for writing your essay will either be at your fingertips (if you're writing a modular assignment) or in your memory store (if you're in the gym) and you'll have thoroughly read and decoded the words in the question. All you need to do now is get started on that first paragraph.

But wait. You can't simply start writing. Not just like that. There are some things you need to sort out first. Some questions you need to ask yourself. Like, for example

QUESTION 1: **How much time do I have?**
QUESTION 2: **What's my word limit?**
QUESTION 3: **What shall I include?**
QUESTION 4: **What shall I leave out?**
QUESTION 5: **What kind of plan shall I make?**

These are the questions that a carefully thought-out, clearly presented plan should answer for you. If you begin your essay without considering them it's unlikely you'll make the most of your knowledge. You'll probably find yourself running out of time, including irrelevant material, answering the wrong question or coming up against a number of other common difficulties. So let's look at each of these questions in turn.

Question 1: How much time do I have?

This is a question you'll ask yourself when you're working under time-constrained conditions. Psychology exam questions usually allow 30, 45 or 60 minutes. Spend the first five minutes working on your plan. If you're working on a structured question be sure to take note of how many marks are up for grabs for each part of the question and allocate your time accordingly. Also, if you finish early, although it's tempting to sit and look at the rope ladders, resist. Use the spare time to proof read your essays. You'll almost certainly be able to claw in a few extra marks.

Question 2: What's my word limit?

This is a question you'll ask yourself if you're working on a modular assignment. These tend to have limits of 1000, 1500 or 2000 words. Your plan should ensure that you fulfil all the requirements of the question, at the appropriate level of detail, without overstepping the word count. Sounds like a tall order. So spend *an hour or so* devising and revising your plan *before* you begin your first paragraph. If you're working on a structured question check the number of marks allocated for each part of the question and divide up your words accordingly. Finally, don't *understep* the word limit. If you think you've answered the question and you've still got 300 words to play with, you've included too little detail.

Question 3: What shall I include?

Anyone planning any kind of psychology assessment answer will ask themselves this question. The answer is **include concepts, studies and theories that relate directly to the** psychology words *and* the instructions *that are in the question*. So if it relates to the appropriate topic and the appropriate skills, you can put it in. A clear plan of what material you're going to include and how you're going to use it will enable you to stick to the question as you're answering it. Never let it out of your sight.

Question 4: What shall I leave out?

Ruthlessness, a quality normally associated with high-flying executives and park-keepers, is one you'll need when you're answering this question. A lot of well-prepared psychology students try to include *all* their knowledge of the topic, even though it means misreading the psychology words and the instructions in the question For example, when answering a social psychology question about *'the dissolution of relationships'* a student might include concepts, studies and theories relating to *'the formation and dissolution of relationships'*. If you ask them why they might say 'because it's what I revised' or 'because it was all one topic when we did it in class'. Use your plan to help you ensure that you leave out superfluous material. Including it wastes times and doesn't gain you any marks. Be ruthless.

Question 5: What kind of plan shall I make?

Your plan should provide you with a carefully thought-out, clearly presented, fingertip guide to what to include in your answer. It should also tell you what order to present your material in. The most common way of ordering your material is to use a *linear* approach, where you simply make a list of what to include, starting at the top with the introduction and finishing at the bottom with the conclusion. Although this approach is widely used and pretty effective, I'm going to suggest an alternative. Instead of *lists*, I'm going to suggest *patterns*.

In his book *Use your Head* (1999) Tony Buzan observes that when most people plan speeches, seminars, meetings and essays they tend to use a linear framework. They make lists. The problem with this method (Buzan suggests) is that it doesn't fit in with the way we think. When we use our heads to plan and solve problems, rather than organising our ideas into lists we organise them into patterns. These patterns take the form of lots of ideas that are *connected* to lots of other ideas in the pattern. This means that when one of these ideas pops into our head it can spark off a connection with any one of a number of other ideas.

This view of thinking differs from the traditional, linear view of the way we plan and solve problems, where one idea inevitably leads on to the next idea, which inevitably leads on to the next and so on. For Buzan our thought processes take the form of *patterns of ideas with interrelated connections, rather than lists of ideas with linear connections.* So because we think in patterns, Buzan says we should plan our seminars, meetings, speeches and assessment answers in the same way.

Making a patterned assessment plan

Imagine you're working on this question

> *Describe and evaluate psychological research into the dissolution of relationships.*

To make a *patterned plan*, find yourself a blank sheet of paper. In the centre of it write down what the essay is going to be about. This will be your central idea. For this essay you could use *'the dissolution of relationships'*. You could say these are *the psychology words*, though they're not especially technical. Even so, social psychologists would certainly regard them as psychological terms.

Next, write the names of the concepts, theories and studies you want to include in your essay around the outside of your central idea. We'll call these your *related ideas*. Now draw some lines connecting the central idea to the related ideas and then from each related idea draw some more lines that point to some extra information about

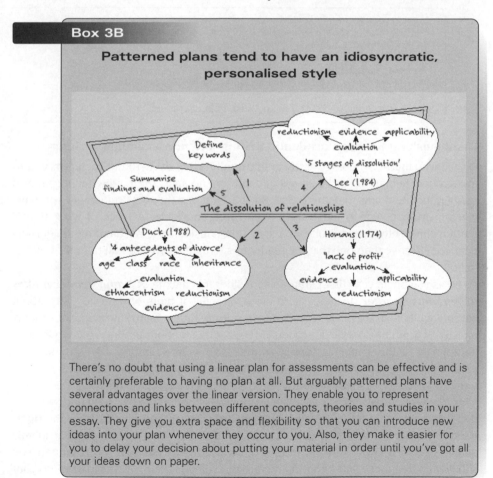

Box 3B

Patterned plans tend to have an idiosyncratic, personalised style

There's no doubt that using a linear plan for assessments can be effective and is certainly preferable to having no plan at all. But arguably patterned plans have several advantages over the linear version. They enable you to represent connections and links between different concepts, theories and studies in your essay. They give you extra space and flexibility so that you can introduce new ideas into your plan whenever they occur to you. Also, they make it easier for you to delay your decision about putting your material in order until you've got all your ideas down on paper.

various aspects of these related ideas. Such aspects would include descriptions and evaluations of the concepts, studies and theories you're dealing with. This anchors your plan firmly to the instructions in the question.

Now you've got a plan showing details of all the ideas you're going to include in your answer. Next you can decide what order you want to present these ideas in. You can do this by numbering your related ideas according to the order you want them to appear in.

Some students who use this method embellish their plan with colours, pictures, symbols etc. This is fine, so long as you're not working under time-constrained conditions. **Box 3B** shows the typical shape of a patterned plan. Notice the swirly, personalised style. This owes much to the fact that it's meant to reflect the shape of its author's thought processes.

● **4 Writing in an academic style**

What to look for in this section
● Distinguishing between academic writing and non-academic writing
● Knowing your audience
● Writing for an intelligent, literate, novice
● Using paragraphs
● Using your own opinions in your work
● Ending
● Giving credit where it's due: quoting, citing, referencing

Distinguishing between academic writing and non-academic writing

People who mark psychology assessments don't have it easy. Tutors, lecturers, examiners routinely mark 60 or 70 essays at a sitting and apart from a few fanatics they'd really rather be doing something else. So spare them a thought. Remember you have it within your power to make their work more enjoyable. A piece of work that is written coherently, purposefully, in a style that considers the needs of the reader will be more effective than one that the reader has to fight tooth and nail to make head or tail of.

So as you begin your first paragraph consider this maxim: *A happy reader makes a generous marker*. Included here are a handful of hints on how to write about psychology in a style which is academic in nature, rather than, say, personal or journalistic. Hitting the so-called 'academic register' is all about producing text which is appropriate to the academic context, rather than to more informal writing, such as emails, letters or journalism. So how does academic writing differ from other types of writing? What are its characteristics? **Box 3C** indicates some of these.

When writing psychology assessment answers the idea is to produce text which displays features in the left-hand column of **Box 3C**, rather than those in the right-hand column. You may find it useful to refer to **Box 3C** when assessing the academic qualities of your own work. After one or two assessments have been written you should find that these 'left-hand' characteristics will find their way habitually into your writing.

Box 3C

Some characteristics of academic and non-academic writing

Academic writing	Non-academic writing
Suitable for essays, research reports, academic journals	*Suitable for email, other personal communication, fiction, journalism*
Relevant *Only text which relates to the title at the top of the page is included.*	**Tangential** *Writer is at liberty to 'go off at a tangent' and stray from the subject.*
Informative *Text is based on facts, arguments and research findings.*	**Entertaining** *Humour, suspense and emotional appeals can all be used to entertain the reader.*
Technical *Terminology which is relevant to the discipline is used.*	**Colloquial** *Non-technical, everyday language is used.*
Supported *Statements and conclusions included in the text are supported by research findings.*	**Unsupported** *Statements and conclusions may be made with only at best anecdotal support.*
Objective *Writer attempts to maintain balance when presenting evidence, not to 'take sides'.*	**Partial** *Text may be used to persuade the reader of his or her own viewpoint.*
Referenced *Writer details all books, articles and websites used.*	**Unreferenced** *Texts and websites used by the writer are not generally provided.*

Know your audience

Another feature of academic writing which needs to be considered is what's known as *audience*. Who are you actually writing for? Text that has the characteristics of academic writing is designed for consumption by tutors, lecturers and examiners. Non-academic text has a different readership altogether – family, friends, pen-pals, local rag readers and so forth. Consider, for example, these three accounts of Stanley Milgram's research into obedience. They all contain similar information but are written with very different audiences in mind.

Behavioural Study of Obedience (written for an academic audience)

Stanley Milgram (1963) wanted to find out if people would obey an instruction even if it resulted in fatally injuring a colleague. Participants were drawn from a range of skilled and unskilled occupations. They responded to a newspaper advertisement requesting volunteers 'for a study of memory'. On the day of the experiment each participant reported to Yale University Psychology Department where they were greeted by a lab-coated man in his thirties who then introduced them to Mr Wallace. Mr Wallace was a confederate playing the role of another participant. The participant and Mr Wallace were informed that they would be working together on an investigation into 'punishment and learning' and that one of them would be assigned the role of 'learner' and the other one would be assigned the role of 'teacher'. Milgram ensured that the participant always got the role of 'teacher'.

Mr Wallace, by now strapped into a (fake) electric chair, was given a (fake) memory test in which he had to demonstrate to the 'teacher' that he had learned a sequence of words. The participant was instructed to give Mr Wallace progressively more intense (fake) electric shocks after each mistake he made. Each time a shock was administered the partici-pant would hear (fake) screams of pain coming from the adjoining room, where Mr Wallace was sitting. Each time the participant complained of not wanting to continue, the lab-coated official, who was standing only a few feet away from him, would issue verbal prods like 'please continue' or 'you must go on'.

Milgram wanted to find out how many of the 40 participants would follow the instructions up to the maximum reading on the (fake) voltage board, by which point Mr Wallace's screams had, rather ominously, faded to silence. The answer was 26, or 65%.

Mad Professor's Shocks 12 Angry Men (written for a local newspaper)

Psychologist Professor Stanley Milgram yesterday scared the living daylights out of a dozen or so men who had innocently responded to an ad in their local newspaper. The men, who had been told they were to be part of an experiment about memory, soon found themselves cast in the torturer's role, giving electric shocks to a complete stranger.

On arrival at the downtown office complex where this bizarre experi-ment into the darker side of human nature took place, the men were introduced to the mild-mannered Mr Wallace. Though claiming to be as naive as the ad-respondents, Wallace was very much on the Professor's payroll. Soon Wallace – playing his role well enough to deserve an Oscar nomination – was being strapped, lamb-like, into an electric chair, where he would be given an IQ test. The by now bewildered respondents were urged by 'mad' Professor Milgram to crank up the voltage each time Wallace made an error, and he made plenty.

Though the electric chair was a fake, only Wallace and Milgram knew this.

Three of the beleaguered ad-respondents collapsed under the pressure with nervous exhaustion. More worryingly, most went along with Milgram's orders, torturing Wallace until his screams could no longer be heard and he faked his own death. 'I couldn't believe how many of these guys went all the way', said Milgram later.

Psycho professor (written for a friend)

To : sally@hotmail.com

subject: psycho

Dear Sally, thx for the e-mail. I'm settling in to my new halls really well and I've met some dead nice folks, though I'm not so sure about this psychology course. I chose psychology because I wanted to renew my faith in human nature but so far we've been studying some pretty twisted stuff. Today we had a lecture about some guy called Milgram from the 1960s who did experiments about how normal everyday guys would torture people they'd hardly met if you put them in the right situation. He put an ad in the local paper and when guys responded he told them he wanted them to help him study memory and then he had them testing this complete stranger on his IQ and giving him electric shocks if he made mistakes. And he made plenty. And guess what, most of the ad-respondents went along with it and did the torture, just 'cos Milgram stood there telling them to. How twisted is that? If that had been me there's no way I'd shock some guy I didn't know, 'cept maybe Milgram himself. I guess it's interesting to see how low people can get but if this course doesn't get more upbeat soon I reckon I might think again. Next week we're doing prison life, so there's no immediate let up it seems. Sorry to be so dark. Mail me soon. Kisses etc . . .

Writing for an intelligent, literate, novice

You will no doubt have noticed that the first of these three accounts adheres more closely to the 'left-hand' characteristics in **Box 3C** than do the others. Now let's think more deeply about your psychology tutor/lecturer, in other words your audience. He or she will no doubt be of above average intelligence, will have a good command of written language and be an expert in psychology. It's this third trait (characteristic) that often gets in the way of good academic writing – *because as a psychology student you're required to disregard it.*

Students who write for the intelligent, literate expert encounter difficulties because they should really be writing for someone who only has the first two of these traits. That is an intelligent, literate novice. The sad thing is that on many psychology courses this convention is never properly pointed out. Tutors often wait for it to dawn on their students, which, in many cases, never happens. So let's have it out in the open.

> Your reader needs to have all psychological and technical terms that don't have a great deal of meaning outside the study of human behaviour (what we've been calling **the psychology words**) defined and clarified for them as they're introduced.

Don't just mention them and move on. Say what they mean. For example, in an essay dealing with Freud's 1909 case study of Little Hans (for a full outline of this study see **Chapter 1**) you might write something like:

> *Freud argued that Hans's irrational fear of horses masked an underlying fear of his father, which had been driven into his **unconscious** by a process of **repression**. Freud regarded the unconscious as a vast store of unpleasant, often socially unacceptable fears, memories and desires that are held out of reach of our conscious thoughts. Repression is a Freudian term that refers to the process of pushing these unpleasant ideas into the unconscious . . .*

Here **the psychology words** (in bold type) are defined and clarified as they're introduced. Notice how this excerpt is written with an intelligent, literate novice in mind. It's clearly meant for someone who isn't familiar with Freud's theory. If it were written for an intelligent, literate expert the first sentence would be enough on its own.

The reason you're required to write for the novice in psychology assessments is so you can demonstrate your knowledge of the subject. Students who write for the expert (and plenty do) lose the chance to pick up marks because they assume too much knowledge on the part of their reader. This is a bit like writing a postcard home and not mentioning the weather, assuming everyone already knows it's raining.

Using paragraphs

A student I know did a little experiment. He handed in copies of one of his psychology essays to two different tutors. Each tutor received the same essay except that *TUTOR A*'s copy had no paragraphs. It was written in uninterrupted dense text. Predictably enough, *TUTOR B* who received the essay with the paragraphs left in, reported significantly higher feelings of satisfaction after reading the essay and awarded a significantly higher grade. It may be that *TUTOR A* was a meaner marker and this contributed to what happened here. But it's also likely that writing with paragraphs increases the effectiveness of writing.

So what do paragraphs do?

They ease the job of the reader by providing a separation between ideas, or aspects of ideas. And for a bog-eyed tutor, lecturer, examiner who's already read fifty scripts before breakfast, writing that is separated into ideas (and aspects of ideas) is a breath of fresh air.

You should use paragraphs to parcel off what you write into sections. For example, if you're asked to *Outline psychological research into phobias*, you'd probably want to write about a number of studies, so you'd devote a separate paragraph to each separate study. Alternatively, if a question asked you to *Discuss Freuds's case study of Little Hans*, you'd be required to look at this study in quite a lot of detail, so you'd devote separate paragraphs to separate aspects of the study. The general rule is that each new idea deserves a new paragraph. For example, I'm going to start another one now because I'm going to make a fresh point.

Here's a final word about paragraphs: links. These are what you use to move from one paragraph to another. In the interests of keeping the reader satisfied and attentive, keep your links smooth. Avoid sudden changes of tack as they can destroy the continuity of your writing. Here's an example of a smooth link between two paragraphs from an essay about the case of Little Hans:

> . . . *On the whole a great many behaviourists have been critical of Freud's work because of his use of the concept of the unconscious mind, which, behaviourists argue, is unobservable and therefore difficult for psychologists to study empirically.*
>
>   **Another school to have criticised Freud** *is cognitive psychology, who denounce his emphasis on the emotional life of the humans. They say he neglects our thinking and problem solving capacities . . .*

Notice how the *linking* phrase (in bold) eases the transition between the two ideas being discussed. Good for continuity. Good for the satisfaction level of the reader.

Using your own opinions in written work

'Can I use my own opinions in my essay?' is one of the *Top Ten Most Common Questions* students ask their tutors before they write psychology assessments. It's a hard one to answer. On the one hand tutors don't want to encourage students to write essays that are overloaded with polemic and personal prejudice. On the other hand they don't want to be accused of clamping down on original thought. Consequently the question is often left dangling. The answer to this prickly question begins something like this. *'Yes, on two conditions . . .'*

Condition 1
Your opinions will only be effective where they're supported with psychological evidence. That is, concepts, studies and theories which back them
up. In this respect, your opinion is just as valid as anyone else's. If you
include Freud's opinions, Piaget's opinions or Milgram's opinions without
any psychological evidence to support them your essay won't be especially
effective. So yes, by all means include your opinions, but back them up with
concepts, studies and theories from psychology'.

Condition 2
Opinions that aren't supported by psychological evidence should only be
used sparingly. For example, they may be included as a supplement to
other ideas that are presented in the light of research. It may be that you
come up with an opinion or idea that hasn't been widely researched by
psychologists, or one that no-one else has thought of. In cases like this
it's fine to include your opinion in your essay but don't overload your
essay with this type of unsupported, anecdotal opinion. If unsupported
opinions are used sparingly and if they're relevant to the question,
include them'.

Here are two examples of personal opinions that have been used effectively in
written work. Both excerpts have been lifted out of an answer to *Part C* of a structured
question on the psychology of stress, where you're asked to *Describe ways in which a
person may prepare in advance for stressful events*.

Example 1
. . . One way of preparing in advance for a stressful event (like a job interview or a driving test) would be to talk to friends and family about your
apprehensions and anxieties. Social support networks can lighten stressful
feelings associated with forthcoming events. **Folkman et al. (1987)**
support this idea with a theory which sets out a variety of strategies for
coping with stress. One of the strategies they recognise is 'seeking social
support', involving asking for advice, talking to friends and family. In their
study they . . .'

Example 2
. . . Another way of reducing the stressful effects of a forthcoming event
would be to attend a course in meditation and breath control at a local
Buddhist Centre for the weeks leading up to the event. Developing ways of
regulating, attending to and controlling our breathing can enhance our
powers of coping . . .'

Note how, in *Example 1* the opinion is supported and made more convincing by the
use of evidence from psychological research. Using personal opinion in this way is the

most effective method. But *Example 2* is a perfectly legitimate use of a personal opinion, since it does relate directly to the question. It's a valid suggestion too, which, to be fair, needs to be researched into. Be careful though, too much of this type of unsupported opinion doesn't go down well.

Here's a final thought on the use of opinions in assessments, related to something called the '**I think**' problem. Look again at the two examples from the essay on stress and you'll notice that even though personal opinions have been included, the student has refrained from using the term *I think*. Whether to encourage students to write I think in their writing is something which different tutors, lecturers, examiners have different ideas about. Some say it sounds too informal, too homespun. Some say it's a good way of encouraging students to have original ideas. Because of this internal division amongst psychologists it's probably best to avoid it. Look at it this way; if you include an idea that isn't credited to anyone else, it's fairly clear that it's yours. Instead of 'I think', try 'it is argued' or something equally neutral or passive.

Ending

There's an art to ending an assignment. A final thought on writing academically: consider the needs of your reader one last time. Leave them with a pleasant aftertaste. End your essay smoothly, not abruptly. Bring things to a close thoughtfully, seamlessly, perhaps by summarising some of the points you've made, perhaps by reiterating an overall conclusion of some sort, perhaps by suggesting some ideas for future research. But whatever you do, don't just stop. Some endings come so suddenly that the reader is left with the idea that the writer has been called away unexpectedly. So when you've finished, re-read your final sentence and ask yourself if it reads like a carefully thought-out ending or like a sudden

Quoting, citing and referencing

Whilst you may include the occasional opinion of your own when writing about psychology, the bulk of your work will inevitably involve discussing the ideas and research of other people – psychologists. When you use other people's ideas, found in books, articles or on the internet, you need to give credit where it's due to the original authors. There are three ways of doing this. Quoting, citing and referencing. There are strict conventions attached to each of these and we'll look at each of them in turn.

Quoting

Quoting other psychologists in written work, especially at length, isn't especially popular with tutors, lecturers or examiners. Better to try and put things in your own words. However, if you do think it necessary to include the odd quote here and there, follow it with the author's name, the date of the publication the quote comes from, as well as the page number of the book where the quote appears. There are two main methods of using quotations, each with its own conventions. These are outlined below, with (fictional) examples to illustrate.

- *Short quotations*
  These are included within the body of the text and are preceded by a colon, as in

  > Flanagan and Allen (2010) argue that: 'The breakdown of relationships is often associated with increased working hours' (p. 444).

  This method is used when quoting entire sentences. For quoting parts of sentences, you can incorporate the quote within one of your own sentences, as in

  > Winters and Winters (2001) later claimed that '...teamwork and trust-worthiness are two of the most under-rated qualities in today's world' (p. 555).

- *Longer quotations*
  These should be kept to a bare minimum. However, if they're considered necessary you include them as separate blocks of text, as in

  > Again and again researchers have uncovered statistical support for the argument that people from opposite ends of the extroversion scale are attracted to each other, especially in the Southern hemisphere. (Dean and Torvill, 1988, p. 14)

Citing

Citing is necessary when you refer to any piece of psychological evidence in your work. You should cite the author and give the date of publication of the research within the body of your work. Various conventions apply here, depending on the nature and scale of the citation. Here are some guidelines, again with some examples to illustrate.

- *Single citations*
  When referring to one author, include his or her name and the date of publication as in

  > Boredom is likely to set in after three hours (Yorke, 2002).

- *Multiple citations*
  Where more than one author is cited, include publication dates in chronological order, as in

  > Egocentrism is not conducive to long-lasting friendship (Baker, 1985; Eccleston, 2005)

- *Multiple authors*
  If there are two authors, include both names, as in (Freeman & Hardy, 2000). For three or more authors, include just the first named author and use 'et al', as in (Freeman et al., 2000).

- *Secondary sources*
  If you don't have the reference for the work you're trying to cite, but you know it was cited in another, secondary, source, refer to it through this secondary source, as in

  It has often been stressed by Willis that the life-long friendship is difficult to find on the internet (cited in Clark, 2004).

- *TV and radio broadcasts*
  Whilst it is not generally as highly regarded as print publications in academia, it is sometimes useful to refer to a broadcast to support an argument. If you do, include the title, channel and date of broadcast, as in

  It has been noted that children find it easier to make friends than adults do (*Newsnight*, BBC2, 2 October 2006)

Referencing

Referencing is necessary when you've written a modular assignment. It isn't expected in exams. Include a reference section at the end of your assignment listing all the books, articles, websites and other sources you've referred to in the text. There are strict conventions for referencing so ensure you go along with them. References should be presented in alphabetical order using authors' surnames. Here are some guidelines, with examples. Note the use of colons and italics.

- *Books*
  The convention for books is

  Author's Name (date), *Title*, City of Publication: Publisher
  Smyth, T. (2004), *The Principles of Writing in Psychology*, London: Palgrave

  When referencing an edited book insert (Ed.) after the editor's name, in order to avoid portraying him/her as the author.

- *Journals or Magazines*
  When referencing a paper from a journal or a magazine article the convention is

  Author's Name (date), Title of Paper, *Title of Journal*, Volume, page numbers
  Asch, S. (1955), Opinions and social pressure, *Scientific American*, 193, 31–5

- *Newspapers*
  The convention here is
  Author (date). Headline. *Publication*, page number
  Flannery, B. (2007, 4 Jan.). Nobody loves psychometrics. *Sydney Examiner*, p. 6

- *Internet sources*

   When referencing internet sources ensure that sufficient information is given for the reader to find the source, as in

   Document title, full website address, date of retrieval
   www.library.manchester.ac.uk/eresources/citerefs [Accessed July 31, 2007]

5 Evaluating psychological research

What to look for in this section
- The need for **evaluation**
- **The DRREEEEEAAAMSS system** for evaluating psychological evidence

The need for evaluation

For assignment questions or research reports your chances of producing a quality answer without a heavy dose of evaluating studies and theories are slim. Look again at our *Top Ten Instructions* in **Box 3A** from the beginning of this chapter and notice how many of them have the skill of evaluating right at their core. Evaluating, applying, discussing, comparing and analysing psychological evidence all involve writing about the positive and negative aspects of studies and theories. It is almost unheard of for tutors, lecturers and examiners to set assignments that don't have any of these words, or their close relatives, in them.

   In the pecking order of skills for writing psychology assignments, evaluating studies and theories is at the front of the queue. True, describing research is important, but this *e-word* is where the big prizes are. So let's work out how to evaluate studies and theories. Better still, let's develop a system for evaluating studies and theories. We'll call it **the DRREEEEEAAAMSS system**, for reasons that will become apparent.

The first thing you need to consider when you're evaluating evidence is that you should be writing about positive *and* negative aspects of studies and theories. Evaluating isn't just criticising. It involves being complimentary as well as critical.

But what about these DRREEEEEAAAMSS?

I'm coming to that.

   The second thing you need to consider is what criteria you're going to use to evaluate psychological evidence. And this is where **the DRREEEEEAAAMSS system** comes in. There's a long list of evaluation criteria you can use to highlight the positive and negative aspects of psychological evidence. As you're planning and writing your assignment you need to be sure to refer to as many of these criteria as you can for each study and theory you include. You can use **the DRREEEEEEAAAMSS system** as a checklist to ensure you don't short-change your reader by leaving out relevant evaluation criteria.

So DRREEEEEAAAMSS basically refers to a list of things to consider when you're doing your evaluations.

Correct. The system is summarised in Box 3D.

Hang on. This looks complicated. Am I supposed to remember all 14 of these big words?

Don't panic. When you're writing your assignment you're not expected to comment on all 14 criteria for every study you evaluate. Nor are you expected to comment on all 7 criteria for every theory you include. Instead, **use** *the DRREEEEEAAAMSS system* **to help you remember the criteria and then for each** *study* **or** *theory* **you evaluate select the criteria you think are most relevant for you to comment on**. So you might end up using a handful of criteria for each *study* you include, or perhaps four criteria (or more, or less) for each *theory* you include.

Box 3D

The DRREEEEEAAAMSS system for evaluating psychological evidence

DRREEEEEAAAMSS gives you 14 criteria for evaluating studies and theories.
For each STUDY you evaluate use as many of the 14 criteria as you can.
For each THEORY, use as many of the 7 asterisked criteria as you can.

D-esign *(the control of extraneous variables)*
R-eplicability *(whether or not a study can be repeated with the same results)*
R-eductionism * *(explaining complex wholes in terms of their component parts)*
E-thics *(whether participants are harmed or deceived during research)*
E-thnocentrism * *(the view that one's own cultural world view is central)*
E-cological validity *(whether research findings can be applied to the wider world)*
E-xtrapolation *(whether data from non-humans help us understand humans)*
E-vidence * *(whether research conclusions are supported by other researchers)*
A-pproach * *(can evidence be evaluated in terms of its perspective?)*
A-pplicability * *(whether or not the evidence can be put to any use in the real world)*
A-ndrocentrism * *(is research written from a masculine standpoint?)*
M-ethod *(evaluating evidence in terms of the research method that is used to gather it)*
S-ample *(whether the participants who took part in the study were representative)*
S-ocio-political impact * *(could this research reduce inequality or oppression?)*

Remember to be complementary as well as critical.

Spelling 'dreams' with two 'R's, five 'E's and three 'A's gives you a convenient way of remembering 14 criteria for evaluating studies. *DRREEEEEAAAMSS* is a good mnemonic (way of remembering) for bringing the 14 big words to mind. But what about evaluating *theories*? This requires a slightly different approach. Some of these evaluation criteria aren't really suitable for the purpose. For example, you can't comment on the design or method of a theory, since they aren't actually pieces of research. So **DRREEEEEAAAMSS** offers you seven evaluation criteria to use for evaluating theories as well as studies. They're the ones with the asterisks:

Applicability, **A**pproach, **A**ndrocentrism, **E**thnocentrism, **R**eductionism, **E**vidence, **S**ocio-political impact.

Now we need a mnemonic to help you remember them. How about, ***Adam And Eve Ran Absolutely Everywhere, Slowly***? Alternatively, perhaps you should make your own up.

Before we look at each of these 14 'big words' in detail, I should point out that this isn't an exhaustive list of evaluation criteria. You might come up with others you yourself use for commenting on the pros and cons of psychological evidence. What **DRREEEEEAAAMSS** does give you is a healthy, balanced diet of evaluation criteria. Feel free to supplement it.

So here goes. What follows is a detailed review of the *meanings* of the 14 big words in *The DRREEEEEAAAMSS System*, along with some suggestions about how to use them in psychology assignments. You probably won't remember all 14 criteria after the first (or second) reading. But when you've used them for evaluating evidence once or twice they'll start to stick. Before too long you should see a change for the better in the structure and quality of your work.

> **Design** refers to the steps researchers take to control extraneous variables in their studies. If a researcher is investigating the influence of *Variable A* on *Variable B* s/he'll try to control or hold constant the effect of any other (extraneous) variable that might have an influence on *B*. The problem of achieving this degree of control is a problem of design. A good ploy for controlling extraneous variables is to divide participants into 'matched' conditions. For instance, if you're studying how background noise (*Variable A*) affects participants' problem-solving abilities (*Variable B*) you might want to ensure that an extraneous variable such as intelligence is held constant across the two conditions (high noise and low noise). To do this you could design your study so that participants with high and low intelligence levels are allocated equally between the high and low noise conditions. This helps you to isolate the proposed link between *A* and *B*.

In an assingment, in (positively) evaluating the *design* of our experiment on *the effect of overcrowding* on *violent behaviour in female mice* (see **Chapter 1** for a full description) you might include a statement like . . .

The researchers have taken a number of steps to control extraneous variables such as temperature, age, season and the number of mice in each condition. These variables are all held constant across the two conditions. This strengthens the proposed link between Variable A, the level of crowding, and Variable B, violent behaviour.

Replicability refers to whether or not a study can be repeated to produce similar findings. Two things are at stake here. First, whether a study can be repeated at all. Second, whether similar results emerge if it is repeated. Some studies can't be repeated at all because they're conducted in unique situations that are hard to replicate; earthquakes, eclipses, coronations etc. Psychologists refer to this type of 'one-off', unrepeatable study as *opportunistic* research. Other studies are repeated but they produce different findings. Psychologists refer to this as *unreliable* research. Studies that are opportunistic or unreliable can both be said to 'lack replicability'. They might have interesting results but if no-one can go out and replicate or verify them they may be seen as flawed.

In an assignment, in (negatively) evaluating the *replicability* of Freud's 1909 case study of Little Hans' (see Chapter 1 for a full discussion), you might include a statement like . . .

This study has low replicability because of Freud's peculiar relationship with Hans's family. Before his acquaintance with Hans's case he had had therapeutic relations with his mother. Also, unusually, the analysis of Hans was carried out by his father, who then passed on his interpretations to Freud 'second hand'. A similar therapeutic situation would be difficult to replicate, making Freud's findings difficult to verify.

Reductionism* refers to the way psychologists sometimes try to explain complex concepts (the list is endless, but some examples are *thinking, aggression, interpersonal attraction*) in simplified terms, without recognising their complexity. A typical *reductionist* ploy is to try and explain a complex concept by focusing only on the characteristics of some of its constituent parts. For example, trying to explain the brain's (complex) capacity for thinking in terms of nothing more than series of chemical processes could be regarded as reductionist. Although neurochemistry is involved in thinking, alone it doesn't do justice to the complexity of how we figure things out. A fuller, more rounded explanation of thinking could include a discussion of developmental, cognitive and cultural factors as well as chemical ones. Critics of reductionism argue that complex concepts need to be understood holistically, recognising the influence of a variety factors. The motto of this approach is 'the whole is greater than the sum of its individual parts'. Unlike most of the other criteria in **DRREEEEEAAMSS**, *reductionism* is pretty much exclusively seen as a negative feature of psychological evidence. You'd hardly congratulate a theorist for being *reductionist*.

In an assignment, reductionism can be used as a criterion for evaluating studies *or* theories. For example, social exchange theory of interpersonal behaviour states that we form friendships on the basis of profit and loss (Homans, 1974; Coleman, 1990). We choose our friends after weighing up how we can benefit from them (affection, protection, status and so on) versus what they'll cost us (time, energy, money). In evaluating (negatively) this idea in terms of reductionism you might include a statement like . . .

> *Interpersonal attraction is a complex issue. Exchange theory highlights only one aspect of the formation and breakdown of friendships – the concept of profit and loss. Whilst this may shed some light on the topic, the theory is reductionist in that it fails to discuss the full array of social, cultural, sexual and emotional factors involved.*

Ethnocentrism* refers to the tendency to regard other cultures (and the people and institutions that make up those cultures) solely from the perspective of one's own culture. It is sometimes referred to a cultural bias. It's a form of prejudice. Like egocentrism, where an individual is unable to appreciate another's point of view, ethnocentrism is a failure to appreciate another culture's viewpoint. An ethnocentric world view is often accompanied by the belief that the customs and products of one's own culture are the norm, or are superior to those of other cultures. In psychology ethnocentrism is especially relevant when discussing transcultural research. As with reductionism, it's generally seen as a negative characteristic of evidence.

In an assignment, as with reductionism, *ethnocentrism* can be used as a criterion to evaluate studies *or* theories. In 1977 Leff, reviewing research by the World Health Organisation into the incidence of schizophrenia across ten nation states, found that schizophrenia was more likely to be diagnosed in some countries (such as the US) than it was in others. However, this major study has recently been criticised on the grounds of ethnocentrism. You might refer to these criticisms as follows . . .

> *In this study psychiatrists from different countries were asked to use a diagnostic instrument (for identifying schizophrenia) which was developed in the UK. Arguably patients from Nigeria, Colombia and India were being diagnosed according to a procedure which was insensitive to local notions of illness and health. Such a procedure carries the assumption that schizophrenia is a universal concept, defined and diagnosed in the west and then applied cross-culturally (Fernando, 2002). This approach risks **ethnocentrism** as it fails to entertain the possibility that psychological abnormality can be understood differently in different cultures.*

Ethics refers to the way psychologists treat (human and non-human) participants during research. At stake here are the safety and dignity of participants. It's up to the researcher to make sure both of these are preserved. Several ethical questions are posed when conducting psychological research. Are participants protected from physical and emotional harm? Do they have the opportunity to withdraw midway through a study? Do they give informed consent to be studied? Are they protected from deception? Do they receive a thorough debriefing after the research? Plenty of researchers are prepared to answer 'not really' to some of these questions in the interests of finding out more about human (and non-human) behaviour. Consequently this is a particularly fruitful criterion for evaluation (*Chapter Five* has a detailed guide to treating participants ethically).

In an assignment, evaluating (negatively) the *ethics* of Milgram's 1963 obedience study (described fully in Chapter 1) you might include a statement like . . .

> *There are a number of ethical problems with Milgram's study. In particular, although Milgram professed not to have expected so many participants to behave so obediently, some were visibly experiencing stress as they increased the voltage level. It could be argued that participants were unnecessarily exposed to an emotionally harmful situation.*

Extrapolation refers to a philosophical debate about the difference between humans and non-humans. Some theorists regard humans as *quantitatively* more advanced than non-humans. They think we (humans) have behavioural and mental capacities that are of the same kind as those of non-humans, but which are more developed. This is sometimes described as the **behavioural continuity** argument. Others regard humans as *qualitatively* different from non-humans. According to this view we're not just more advanced, we're a different *kind* of creature. Theorists who support this view see studies using non-humans as useless for telling us anything about humans, since we can't generalise (or extrapolate) findings from non-humans to humans. Those who favour the behavioural continuity view *do* feel that studies of monkeys and dogs and so forth tell us something about humans. *Extrapolation* is a useful criterion for evaluating studies which have non-human participants

In an assignment, in evaluating (negatively) our study into *the effect of overcrowding on the violent behaviour of female mice* (see Chapter 1 for a full description), you might include a statement like . . .

> *Even though the mice were observed to behave more violently in the crowded condition, this doesn't necessarily tell us anything about human violent behaviour. After all it may be a mistake to extrapolate from the behaviour of such a distantly related species to the behaviour of humans.*

Ecological Validity refers to whether findings gathered in laboratory research can be applied in more naturalistic (real-life) settings. Where researchers put participants in unusual settings and ask them to perform unusual (to them) behaviours research is said to lack ecological validity. This is a criticism often levelled at studies that take place in laboratory settings. True, laboratory research allows researchers to have a lot of control over the variables they're studying, but the downside is that their participants are more likely to behave unnaturally. This is a problem since it doesn't tell us anything about their everyday behaviour. Critics of laboratory research prefer to carry out ecologically valid studies that take place in real-life (*naturalistic*) settings – streets, cafeterias, trains etc. This way they can observe naturally occurring behaviour. Chapter One has a longer discussion of ecological validity.

In an assignment, in evaluating (positively) the *ecological validity* of Milgram's own replication of his 1963 obedience study (described fully in Chapter 1), where he transferred his experiment to a run-down office block, you might include a statement like . . .

When Milgram transferred his experiment from the Yale laboratory and into an office block, the setting was more naturalistic. Although participants were still required to perform unusual behaviours, the setting was at least common-or-garden. Participants' behaviours apparently followed suit. The obedience level fell from 65% to 48%. This exercise demonstrates the researchers' awareness of the importance of ecological validity.

Evidence* refers to whether or not researchers can point to other evidence to support their own. Conclusions from studies and theories are taken more seriously if other researchers have come to similar conclusions from their work. It's a case of strength in numbers.

In an assignment you can use *evidence* to evaluate studies *or* theories. In evaluating the World Health Organisation's 1974 research into the cross-cultural differences in diagnoses of schizophrenia you might include a statement like . . .

Over-diagnosis of schizophrenia in the US was a recurring theme in this research, suggesting that psychiatrists in different places use the 'schizoid' label more with some groups than others. More **evidence** *from Loring and Powell (1988) showed that psychiatrists sometimes apply diagnostic labels differently when treating different racial groups. They presented 290 US psychiatrists with identical case notes for black and for white patients, only to find that blacks were over-diagnosed schizophrenic. There are other examples of over-diagnosis of schizophrenia for black patients (Harrison et al., 1997; Bhugra et al., 1997). Evidently, the term schizophrenia can be applied differ-*

ently by clinicians from different cultures and to patients from different groups.

> **Approach*** refers to the relationship between a piece of evidence and the perspective (school of thought) it's associated with. As Chapter 1 discusses at some length, there are half a dozen or so perspectives in psychology, each one with different ideas about its subject matter and its methods for carrying out research. Some studies and theories are more closely wedded to specific schools of thought than others are. Where there's a clear relation between a piece of research and a perspective you can evaluate the research by evaluating the perspective it's associated with. This is like pulling the rug from beneath the researcher (where the evaluation is negative). Another useful evaluation ploy is to comment on the perspective underlying a piece of evidence from the point of view of another perspective. So you might comment on a study which has emerged out of psychoanalysis from a behaviourist viewpoint. There's an example of this technique coming up.

In an assignment, you can use *approach* as an evaluation criterion for studies *or* theories. In evaluating (negatively) the approach of Erikson's 1980 theory of life-cycle development, where he presents us with a view of human personality based on Freudian psychoanalysis, you might include a statement like . . .

> *Erikson shows how personality matures through a number of challenges that arise at different stages of the life cycle. However, the effectiveness of his theory depends on the effectiveness of a number of Freudian concepts upon which it is built. Like id, ego and super-ego. These components of personality are not observable. Theorists from a behaviourist perspective would therefore argue that Erikson's theory is flawed because it depends upon invisible concepts that can't be measured.*

> **Applicability*** refers to whether the conclusions from studies or theories are of any use to anyone. Can they help us understand any real-life situations, issues or incidents? Can they help educators, childminders, pharmacists, athletes, police, pianists or politicians (and so forth) in their work? As well as a way of evaluating evidence it's increasingly common for assignment questions, or at least parts of *structured* assignments, to ask you to apply the findings of studies and theories. So it's worth getting into the habit of thinking and writing about what use evidence can be put to. It's also refreshing to know that psychologists are providing society with a service.

In an assignment, applicability can be used to evaluate studies *and* theories. In 1999 Burton et al. conducted research into memory for faces. They found participants' abilities to recognise faces and identify people from video footage depended largely on whether the targets were familiar to them or not. In evaluating (positively) the applicability of this research you might include a statement like . . .

> *The research has applicability to eyewitness testimony, since many witness reports hinge on the identification of witnesses from poor quality CCTV footage. Where footage features people who are familiar to witnesses their testimony may be more reliable.*

Androcentrism* refers to gender issues in psychology. Like ethnocentrism, it's a form of prejudice. Research that doesn't recognise the viewpoint of women is seen as *androcentric*. Feminists have criticised psychology because of the high proportion of studies that use only male participants and whose findings are then generalised to all humans. Another manifestation of *androcentrism* is the tendency, amongst some psychologists, to regard issues that are especially relevant to men (perhaps issues relating to war and combat) as more mainstream to psychology, whilst issues that especially concern women (matters relating to pregnancy or female genital mutilation) are seen as more peripheral and feature less often in the literature. Like reductionism and ethnocentrism, androcentrism is regarded as a negative feature of evidence.

In an assignment, *androcentrism* can be used to evaluate studies *and* theories. In evaluating (negatively) Erikson's (1980) theory of life-cycle development, you might include a statement like . . .

> *Erikson's model is based solely on findings drawn from a male sample, yet he applies his theory of personality development to women as well as men. He even suggests that males and females approach the acquisition of 'ego identity' differently – females gaining identity via co-dependent sexual relationships, rather than in the more independent, masculine way (Gross and McIlveen, 1999). Applying a model researched only on men to all humans in this way is an example of androcentrism.*

Method refers to ways researchers carry out studies and collect data. There are a number of popular research methods used by psychologists. Favourites include *controlled experiments, longitudinal studies, case studies, cross-cultural research* and *field experiments*. Some methods are closely associated with specific perspectives. Cognitive psychologists, for example, favour controlled experiments. Some methods are particularly suitable for measuring aspects of participants' behaviour and are referred to as 'quantitative methods' (controlled experiments are an example). Others are better suited to *describing* behaviour and are referred to as 'qualitative methods' (case studies). Still other methods can be either quantitative or qualitative, depending on how the researcher chooses to set up (or design) the study. When using this evaluation criterion bear in mind that no method is better than another. They all have their own strengths and weaknesses. This means that whatever study you're evaluating you should be critical and complimentary. See Chapter 4 for a more comprehensive review of research methods in psychology.

In an assignment, when evaluating (positively) the case study *method* you might include a statement like . . .

> *The case study method provides a great deal of detail about a client. The researcher is able to develop a relationship with and an understanding of 'the whole person'. Studying the same person over a projected period also allows an understanding of developmental aspects of behaviour.*

Sample refers to the participants used in psychological research. Ideally samples used in research should be representative of the population. This means they should represent all the social groups that the results of the study are meant to apply to. So if a study is about aggression in humans, yet it has an all-female sample, we can say it's *unrepresentative*. Representing all societies' groups (twins, eccentrics, geniuses etc.) in psychological research is an unrealistic aim, but researchers who cast their nets wide do produce more effective data. As well as representativeness, researchers should also go for size. A study that has a large sample will produce results that can be generalised to the rest of society with more confidence.

In an assignment, in evaluating (positively and negatively) the *sample* Burton et al. (1999) used in their study into memory for faces you might include a statement like . . .

> *On the positive side the sample for this study was drawn from three different backgrounds, including undergraduates and police officers. However, although this meant that the sample was representative of different groups in society, only 60 participants were used overall, making the sample somewhat limited in size.*

Socio-political impact* refers to whether the research could be used to affect situations of inequality, exploitation or oppression. It may be that the results of a study could be taken up by a group in society who have experienced unfair treatment at the hands of those in power – oppressive regimes, tyrannical bosses. Alternatively, psychological evidence may be used by powerful groups to maintain unequal, exploitative states of affairs.

In an assignment, when evaluating (negatively) the *socio-political impact* of Milgram's (1963) work on obedience, you might say . . .

> *Whilst this experiment tells us much about the human tendency towards 'doing as we're told', this is a worrying study in that its findings could be used by those who are in a position to elicit obedience in employees and prisoners. The socio-political impact of this could be to sustain oppressive regimes. More positively, the evidence could be used to help us understand how oppression arises, that we might prevent it.*

Once you find your way around *the **DRREEEEEAAAMSS** system* you'll find some of the criteria to be more relevant, more often than others. *Extrapolation*, for example, is only really used for studies using non-humans. *Evidence*, meanwhile, is handy in most evaluation situations. The key strength of **DRREEEEEAAAMSS** is that when you've used it a few times, when you've memorised and familiarised yourself with these 14 criteria, you can highlight the strengths and weaknesses of any study, any theory, in any psychology assignment.

6 Monitoring – and accelerating – your own progress

What to look for in this section
- **Five reasons to actively monitor your own progress**
- How to **evaluate your own assignments**
- How to **make the most of tutor feedback**
- How to **set goals for future improvement**

Shouldn't my tutor monitor my progress?

Any tutor worth their salt works hard to monitor the progress of all their students. The problem is s/he has numerous students who all have progress that needs monitoring. You, on the other hand, only have one person to worry about – yourself. The aim of keeping a close eye on how well you're doing on your psychology course is to establish a clear vision of four key elements of your study; what you've achieved; what you need to achieve; what you're good at; and what you're not so good at. Once you know more about these four areas you're better placed to allocate your study time more efficiently. In part, this means devoting more effort to working on your weaknesses and less time practising skills that you're already pretty good at, in order to make you more of an all-round learner. This way, self-monitoring can play a part in accelerating your progress.

Five reasons to actively monitor your own progress

Self-monitoring is a bit like making a shopping list before planning to cook a meal. You spend a little time initially deciding what you want to buy, but in the long run this saves you an awful lot more time, effort and inconvenience once you get to the shops.

Box 3E

Why should I monitor my own progress?
Here are 5 good reasons

1 Because my tutor can't do all the work even if s/he wants to.
Whilst s/he'll have a record of my marks and a fairly clear sense of my rate of progress, my tutor has so many other students to keep an eye on that the amount of energy s/he'll invest in me is limited. If I really want to gain a clear idea of my strengths and weaknesses I should use my tutor's input as a resource, but try and work out for myself where I can improve.
KEY QUESTION **How can I turn my tutor's feedback into my own clear idea of where I'm succeeding and failing?**

2 Because it helps me compare present performance with past performance.
Careful self-monitoring at regular intervals helps me build a 'storyboard' to record changes in my performance throughout the course. Recording achievements, areas for improvement and plans of action each month or term, then comparing them with past performances, will tell me if I'm moving in the right direction. Without these regular snapshots it's more difficult to establish both how my performance is changing and where improvement is required
KEY QUESTION **Are my grades and tutor feedback better than they were last term?**

3 Because it helps me set goals for my future performance.
As well as keeping me abreast of how I'm doing compared with my past performance, self-monitoring helps me decide on my future direction. Once I have a clear idea about what I'm doing well at and which parts of my studying need improving I can set some realistic goals which will help me attain a desirable level in the weeks to come. I can also make concrete plans about how to achieve these goals
KEY QUESTION **Now I know what my main weakness is, what goals shall I set for this term?**

4 Because I want to be responsible for my own learning.
Making a decision to actively monitor my own progress is part of a wider decision to break away from 'tutor dependency' and become more independent as a learner. After all, this is my psychology course, no-one else's. I'm not doing this as a favour for anyone else. Self-monitoring is a natural consequence of this 'independent learner' status. If I'm failing in any particular aspect of the course it's up to me to discover this and sort it out.
KEY QUESTION **Now I'm in charge of my own learning, how can I use my tutor as an advisor?**

5 Because in itself it's a good way of learning, not 'yet another task to complete'.
Once I get used to the habit of monitoring myself it becomes clear that this isn't an additional task on top of learning. It's part of the learning process. By tracking my grades and comparing the strengths of past and present pieces of work, then setting goals for future work, I'm familiarising myself with what makes a good (and poor) assignment. Into the bargain I'm learning what gets me a good grade, how to be a more effective psychology student. It's not just something to do on top of learning, it's a part of it.
KEY QUESTION **How can I learn by self-monitoring?**

With a list there's no standing around in the supermarket asking yourself *Do I need cherry tomatoes for this meal? Do I already have any at home?* A self-monitoring strategy, like a shopping list, gives you an overview of what you've already got (skills-wise) and what you still need, which helps you spend your valuable time concentrating your efforts on trying to achieve what you need most – in other words, working on your weaknesses. For example, if your own progress report tells you that time after time you're losing marks on your evaluation skills, these are the skills you should practise.

The self-monitoring exercises included in this section should be seen as labour-saving devices. Using them to plot your progress through your psychology course will save you unnecessary work and improve your efficiency. **Box 3E** has five reasons to get more involved in self-monitoring for your own sake, not because your tutor might ask you to do so.

In practice, self-monitoring needn't be time consuming. **Boxes 3F**, **3G** and **3H** suggest three practical exercises that you can use to keep abreast of your progress during your psychology course. You needn't use all three. Rather, decide which ones suit your needs most. You can even adapt them for your own particular course or purposes. The important thing is to be doing something active, structured and regular to help you develop an overview of your strengths and weaknesses, of where you're going and where you've come from.

How to evaluate your own assignments

Use **Box 3F** in conjunction with the advice on writing assignments which appears earlier in this chapter. The idea is to rate your psychology assignments according to the criteria featured in the table **before you hand it in**. This way you can pick up on any weaknesses and tackle them before you finally submit. Hand in the completed table with your assignment so that your tutor knows how you feel about your own work.

How to make the most of tutor feedback

Use **Box 3G** to keep track of the feedback and grades your tutor gives you when s/he marks your assignments. Throughout your course this will help you compare your past and present performance. This exercise requires the co-operation of your tutor, but if you submit this tracking sheet with your assignments and ask for it to be filled in, s/he will, I'm sure, oblige. S/he may even ask to keep a copy of it herself. Better still, this table can be maintained electronically in a shared area so that you and your tutor have easy access. Notice how the feedback categories in **Box 3G** are separated into different skill areas. This helps you discover your own strengths and weaknesses and work a little harder on the latter.

How to set goals for future improvement

Use **Box 3H** to keep an overview of your progress on the course and to indicate the areas you need to focus on for future improvement. The idea here is to get a 'bird's-eye view' of your progress by keeping a record of which modules of the course you've already

Box 3F

Evaluate your own assignments

What to do: Submit a completed version of Box 3F with each assignment.

Am I happy with this assignment?

The figure in the right-hand column shows whether I strongly agree (1), agree (2) or disagree (3) with the statement on the left.

In this assignment I have . . .

. . . read and understood the **knowledge** and **instruction** words in the question.

. . . begun by defining the **knowledge** words.

. . . included material which is **relevant** and excluded that which is **irrelevant**.

. . . **planned** my assignment using a linear plan or mind-map.

. . . ended with a **summary/conclusion**.

. . . written for the appropriate **audience**: the intelligent, literate novice.

. . . used **paragraphs** with linkage throughout.

. . . included **DRREEEEEAAAMSS evaluations** whenever appropriate.

. . . understood and made use of appropriate **terminology**.

. . . used **arguments** with conclusions, supporting statements and evidence.

. . . **cited** secondary sources throughout and included **references** at the end.

Is my assignment self-evaluation TOTAL closer to 11 (dissatisfied) or 33 (satisfied)?

covered, how you did on them and what your main areas are for improvement. In short, it's a record of the past and a projection into the future. In the columns towards the right of the table you're asked to comment briefly on your strong and weak skill areas. These might include referencing, evaluating and so on. You're also asked to suggest how you're going to tackle you're weaker areas, by suggesting some practical strategies. Whilst these can be discussed with your tutor, remember that **Box 3H** is designed to be your own record of your progress, so there's no need to hand it in to anyone. To give a clearer idea of how to use this exercise I've filled in the top row as an example.

Box 3G

Tracking tutor feedback

What to do: Ask your tutor to fill in a section of Box 3G for each assignment.

(title, type, date)	Tutor feedback	grade
Assignment 1		
	Knowledge & academic content	☐
	Evaluation of research	☐
	Citing and referencing	☐
	Use of terminology	☐
Assignment 2		
	Knowledge & academic content	☐
	Evaluation of research	☐
	Citing and referencing	☐
	Use of terminology	☐
Assignment 3		
	Knowledge & academic content	☐
	Evaluation of research	☐
	Citing and referencing	☐
	Use of terminology	☐
Assignment 4		
	Knowledge & academic content	☐
	Evaluation of research	☐
	Citing and referencing	☐
	Use of terminology	☐
Assignment 5		
	Knowledge & academic content	☐
	Evaluation of research	☐
	Citing and referencing	☐
	Use of terminology	☐
Assignment 6		
	Knowledge & academic content	☐
	Evaluation of research	☐
	Citing and referencing	☐
	Use of terminology	☐

Projecting into the future

What to do: Track your own progress with Box 3H

Module	Assignment Grades				2 Strongest skill areas		2 Weakest skill areas		2 Strategies for improving performance	
	C	C	D	B	I have a good Understanding of main concepts e.g. obedience.	I have a good selection of studies are included in my essays.	My evaluations of research lack detail and scope.	I leave ethical issues out of my work, and fail to distinguish between these issues.	Keep a 'cribsheet' of DRREEEEAAAMSS evaluation issues and their meanings to use when writing assignments.	Learn the five different 'ethical issues' aspects of the umbrella term issues' (*deception, informed consent* etc.) and be sure to comment on these issues separately when appropriate.
Cognitive psychology										
Developmental psychology										
Physiological psychology										
Individual differences										
Social psychology										
Research methods										

● 7 Preparing for – and passing – psychology exams

> *What to look for in this section*
> ● Who likes exams?
> ● A 10-point plan for passing in psychology exams

Who likes exams?

It is often said that noone likes examinations. Arguably they turn assessment into a memory test, in which the ability to store knowledge is seen as more important than the ability to manipulate and apply it to the real world. There may be something in this view, though it's also true that some people thrive in timed assessments, which suggests that there are those who do like exams. Whatever your opinion, exams figure in virtually all psychology courses and ultimate success depends on being able to pass them and pass them well. Some exams are of the 'open-book' variety, though most require questions to be answered without notes, books, websites, mobile phones. . . . This presents a real challenge for most learners and it can be a nerve-wracking prospect for many. In this section I'll present a 10-point plan of action which is aimed at making psychology exams slightly less daunting – and passing them rather more likely. The advice contained here won't alter the fact that succeeding in exams requires a good dose of time and effort, though it should help you spend your time and effort more wisely, and yield greater rewards on the day of the exam. You don't have to be a genius to pass exams. Success really boils down to a decent knowledge of the subject, a positive attitude and clear planning – three qualities which anyone can learn.

A 10-point plan for passing in psychology exams

1   **Know your specification**: *summarise and colour code it*
   Box 3H helps you plot your progress through your psychology course by giving you an overview of the modules and how you performed on them. You can get a still more detailed overview by obtaining your course specification, which you can then use to help plan your exam preparation. It's a good idea to make a plan of your specification which fits on one page, showing all the topics you could possibly be tested on. It may also help to colour code this, showing topics which are to be tested in different exams in different colours. Stick your colour-coded specification on some easily visible wall space with the dates of your exams marked underneath. This document will provide an excellent starting point for your revision campaign.

2   **Know your exam**: *predict the future by looking into the past*
   Besides your specification, the other vital 'travel documents' which will ease your journey towards exam success are *past papers*. These are invaluable sources of inside knowledge. They reveal the kinds of questions you can expect to see when the big day finally comes. Having detailed knowledge of what's on the specification is quite a good preparation for the exam, but casting a close eye on past papers can help you to determine:

(a) Which *instruction words* (see **Box 3A**) tend to be used on particular papers.

(b) Whether questions on certain papers tend to be *all-in-ones* or *structured* questions (see p. 52) and how marks are allocated for separate parts of these questions.

(c) What the layout of the paper is likely to be.

These insights, along with a good overview of the specification, can really propel you towards exam success.

3   **Timing is everything**: *start early, revise regularly*
They say the secret of good comedy lies in the timing. This holds true for exam revision too. Specifically, there are two questions about revision timing which need to be considered. First, *how long before my exam should I begin my revision?* Second, *how much time per week should I spend revising?* Clearly these two questions are interlinked. If you begin revising only a few days before the exam you'll need to work round the clock even to gain a pass grade. If you begin in plenty of time you can put together a revision schedule that will enable you to have a life outside revision.

So how long before my exam should I begin revising?

There's no universal answer to this, though it should be measured in weeks and months, rather than minutes, hours or days. This is especially true if you're preparing for various timed assessments simultaneously. Approximately three months before your exam it's advisable to have a revision schedule drawn up and to have begun putting it into practice, gradually increasing the weekly doses of revision thereafter.

And how much time per week should I spend revising?

A well-organised revision schedule is characterised by regular, but not too lengthy, sessions of work, rather than infrequent, caffeine-induced marathons. 'Little but often' is the trick. In practice this means dividing revision time into two or three 45-minute sessions per day, increasing to four sessions as the day of the assessment gets closer. It's also important to have a 'revision Sabbath' – a weekly revision-free day. After all, all work and no play isn't very good – as the saying goes. To help you stick to your revision schedule it helps to physically draw one up, rather than simply having it as a notion. **Box 3I** gives you some idea of what such a document might look like. Obviously it may have to be modified to find room to revise other subjects. The timing of the sessions will also depend upon whether you're a morning, afternoon, or evening person. Once it is drawn, you can stick it up on your wall or website – next to your specification outline and your tracking sheet (**Box 3H**).

Box 3I

Revision schedule

My revision week for psychology looks like this . . .

	Mon.	Tue.	Wed.	Thu.	Fri.	Sat.
Session 1 (45 mins.)	Cognitive	Individual differences	Developmental	Social	Physiological	Cognitive
Session 2 (45 mins.)	Developmental	Social	Physiological	Cognitive	Individual differences	Developmental
Session 3 (45 mins.)	Physiological	Cognitive	Individual differences	Developmental	Social	Physiological

4   **Reinforce yourself**: *a behaviourist's method of exam preparation*

> *'You've done six whole days of
> revision. Now positively reinforce
> yourself. Take Sunday off.'*

Preparing for timed assessments isn't just about pain and suffering. True, it is hard work, but this work deserves to be rewarded, or as a behaviourist might say, reinforced. The ultimate reward comes in the form of a good grade in the exam, but realistically you deserve a few more treats along the way. Behaviourist proponents of operant conditioning, such as E. L. Thorndike (1874–1949) and B. F. Skinner (1904–90), wrote that the best way to increase the likelihood of a desirable behaviour (revision, in this case) is to reward it. Thorndike's (1898) *law of effect* states that

Any behaviour which produces a pleasant effect is likely to be repeated

Similarly, Skinner (1938) suggested that according to the law of *operant conditioning*, a desirable behaviour will be made more likely by the presentation of *positive reinforcement* (a reward), or by the removal of a threat or some other unpleasant stimulus (*negative reinforcement*). You might consider introducing these behaviourist principles into your own revision schedule. For example, when you've successfully adhered to your schedule for one week, some form of *positive reinforcement* might be in order. Give yourself a treat, such as a night out – or a night in, depending on your tastes. Alternatively you could use negative reinforcement to treat yourself by removing something unpleasant from your environment.

5   **Don't just sit there, do something**: *revision is an active process*
Sometimes you may tell yourself that you've been working hard for the last hour, only to find, on testing yourself, that very little of what you have been revising has stuck. Sitting, staring steadfastly at a book or a set of notes is seldom a successful strategy. Why? Because it's too passive. Effective revision is an active and varied process. You'll find your memory to be more engaged and capable of deeper processing if you perform activities while revising. Indeed, active revision helps you *recall* information at a later date, whereas passive revision is only likely to facilitate the *recognition* of information, which is really only useful in multiple choice assessments (and identity parades). Different activities suit different learners and different styles of learning, but **Box 3J** has some suggested revision activities.

Box 3J

Active revision

Colour-coded cue cards	Use your class and lecture notes as a starting point. Identify the key points (main ideas, findings, evaluations) of a topic and transfer them onto portable cue cards. Colour code them to distinguish between topics, between findings and evaluations, or between advantages and disadvantages etc. Actively making the cards is just as good a revision strategy as using them to revise with.
Grids and tables	Take a topic and transform your notes into a table or grid. Each cell in the grid has bullet-pointed details of a key theory or study, including evaluations. Once you've made a grid you can use it to test yourself by trying to reproduce it in all its detail without looking at the original. Done repeatedly this is an excellent way of committing material to memory.
Patterned plans	We've already looked at the advantages of using patterned plans for planning essays (see Box 3B). They can also be used for revision, largely in the same way as grids. Each spidery plan is constructed as a topic summary, and then can be used for self-testing.
Walkie-talkie	Doing revision actively sitting at your desk is one thing, but actually walking about whilst revising can get your frontal lobes working and your synaptic links sizzling into action. Once you feel you have a topic or a model answer set in your memory, go for a walk along the beach or through the woods and actually vocalise them out loud. This method of memorising is very popular with actors trying to learn their lines.
Practice questions	Of course there's no better way of revising actively than mocking up the exam itself and practising answering questions from past papers. Try with your notes at first, then without.

---

6   **Learning together**: *a social psychologist's method of exam preparation*

Ever since Norman Triplett (1898) demonstrated experimentally that, all other things being equal, cyclists riding in pairs worked harder than those riding alone, the potential role of *social facilitation* for improving performance has been well documented. The social facilitation effect predicts that the presence of others will influence performance on a variety of tasks. One example of social facilitation is known as *co-action*. In the co-action effect, performance on familiar tasks tends to improve when we work alongside others who are doing the same thing as us. There is also a suggestion that co-action may be even more effective with a dash of competition between the participants. Revising with fellow students in study groups can offer a nice blend of co-operation (helping each other revise) and competition (ultimately you'll all be in the exam together). As a supplement, not a replacement, for revising on your own, study groups can help in preparing for exams. They offer opportunities for discussion, for giving and receiving help with difficult topics and for sharing learning strategies. They also make a nice change from always working alone. Beware though. If not carefully organised, study groups can degenerate into 'groups that don't do very much studying at all'. **Box 3K** has some pointers as to how to revise effectively in groups.

Box 3K

Revising in groups can work

Study groups work most efficiently when . . .

. . . **it is decided beforehand exactly which topics are to be discussed**, so that everyone comes well-prepared and well-equipped. This additional structure is very helpful, as it cuts down on aimless, drifting sessions.

. . . **all participants have a clear role to play**, which is perhaps distinct from other peoples' roles. Individuals can take responsibility for certain studies or topics. This method cuts down on 'social loafing' (certain people not pulling their weight).

. . . **everyone is prepared to help those who are struggling**. Actually, explaining an idea to someone else is a really good way of learning it.

. . . **they're not too big or too long**. Four is a good number. Two hours is a good amount of time.

. . . **they're supplementary to, not a replacement for, revising alone**. Study groups make a good, interactive contrast to the more traditional revision, though this is because they can help to reinforce the hard work that's already gone on 'in the privacy of your bedroom'.

---

7   **Have a life**: *there's a whole world out there*

It's important that exams are taken seriously. But how seriously? There comes a point where this seriousness reaches a degree that is counterproductive. True, living in a tunnel-visioned state of perpetual dread in which the thought of failure turns you into an insomniac shows that you care about your studies. But does it increase your chances of success? Probably not. An optimum level of seriousness requires sustained, regular and productive revision, but it also requires you to have a life outside studying. A lively social life, a healthy diet and a good level of exercise will all increase your chances of success. And why not admit it – failing an exam is not the end of life. No-one is imprisoned or physically harmed as a consequence. A more likely result is an inconvenient re-sit and some more revision. So, during the revision period, try to maintain a sense of perspective. Prepare regularly and sensibly, but for your own sanity do other things as well.

8   **Stress-buster**: *a cognitive psychologist's method of exam stress reduction*
Negative thinking can cast a long shadow over the most carefully prepared revision schedule. Fears about *what if it all goes wrong?* or *what if everyone else is smarter than me?* or *what will happen if I fail?* are real cognitive obstacles to exam success, and it's best to try and address them head-on. One cognitive technique which is used to this effect is known as *cognitive restructuring.* It involves restructuring negative thinking into something more positive. Two stages of thought restructuring in order to improve performance have been identified, and these are summarised in **Box 3L**. If the stress of forthcoming exams does take hold, follow these steps to restore a sense of cognitive balance.

Box 3L

Defeating negative thinking with cognitive restructuring

STEP 1 Identify negative thinking	STEP 2 Accentuate the positive
What if I'm not smart enough?	Of course I'm smart enough. I was accepted on the course, and I've had several good grades along the way.
Oh no, I haven't done enough revision.	Alright I haven't been revising flat out but I should be fine as I have been following my revision schedule.
What will people say if I don't do well?	I've prepared properly so even if I don't get the top grade, fair minded people won't be too critical.
Revision reveals the gaps in my knowledge	The whole point of revision is to highlight the bits of the course I don't know so well, so that I can practise them. That's what I'll do.
What will happen to me if I fail?	In the unlikely event that things do go wrong, I can retake the exam. In any case it's only one exam and there's more to life than exams anyway.
Oh no, I'm stressed, which makes things worse	If I think through each of the issues that are stressing me, it seems they are all rather irrational.

Box 3M

Exam technique

Once inside the exam room you can maximise your performance by following these 6 guidelines.

1. **Take a deep breath before you start.**
   Remind yourself to think positive. The preparation is over now. It's time to make the most of what you've learned.

2. **Carefully read the words in each question you answer.**
   As we learned earlier in this chapter, exam questions feature 'psychology words' and 'instructions'. Before you begin each answer underline these words and ensure you know what you're being asked to do.

3 **Make plans.**
   Before embarking on any essays or longer answers, spend a few minutes making a legible plan. This will give structure to your answer and may even help you pick up extra marks since the examiner will see this evidence of your knowledge.

4 **Tailor your answers to the questions.**
   This may sound obvious but there are two mistakes that many well-prepared learners often make. First, they write everything they know about a certain topic, rather than what's relevant to the question. Secondly, they ignore the indication (given on the exam paper) of how many marks are available for each part of a question. If the first part of a question is worth 5 marks and the second part is worth 10, then clearly you need to allocate your time and space accordingly.

5 **Attempt all the questions you're supposed to attempt.**
   Most marks in most exam answers are earned in the first half of those answers. This has long been recognised by those who mark exam papers. Frustratingly then, when learners miss out questions – perhaps because they think they can't get a good grade – a disproportionately large number of marks are lost. The message here is that even if you feel you can only provide a partial answer to a question – do so, rather than missing it out and writing an extended answer to some other question you feel confident about.

6 **When time is running out . . .**
   How do you while away the final half-hour of an exam? Well, how you answer this question may well have a critical impact on your grade. Here are some popular strategies, in ascending order of effectiveness: (i) leaving, (ii) staring at the ceiling, (iii) checking through answers, spotting mistakes and trying to gain a few more marks, (iv) if running short of time on the final answer, abbreviating the last few points to note-form or bullets. These final two strategies are certainly the ones you can count on to inflate your grade.

---

9 **Play to your strengths**: *make the most of your learning style*
When preparing for your written assessment in psychology it's important to be aware of your own strengths and preferences as a learner. Some of us like to learn by using visual materials, others like to be actively making and doing things. These learning preferences can be utilised in your revision once you

know what your strengths are, although it's also important to brush up on your weaknesses. To find out more about tailoring your revision to your preferred style of learning go back to Chapter 2, which deals with this issue in some detail.

10   **On the day**: *what to do in the exam*

Once inside the exam room your success is not assured by your being well prepared. Putting preparation into practice is just as important. In fact, a well-prepared person can still mess up due to poor exam technique. Conversely, a half-prepared person can still get a decent grade with good technique. Ideally though, thorough preparation and excellent technique is the dream ticket, so take note of **Box 3M**, where you'll find some essentials of how to maximise your performance when the day finally arrives.

4 Conducting and Understanding Psychological Research

This chapter is a general introduction to all the main research methods in psychology. It is also a practical guide to doing research – a users' manual to planning, carrying out and reporting research. You'll find this useful because sooner or later your psychology tutor will invite you to do a study of your own. There's nothing like doing research to help you to appreciate how the studies you've read about turned out the way they did.

The decisions and compromises Milgram, Freud and others made whilst doing their studies will make more sense to you after you've been through the research process yourself. On the other hand, some of their decisions might seem even more baffling. Tough decisions have to be made about what to study, who to use as participants, which method to use, how to preserve the safety and dignity of everyone involved and how to encapsulate the study in the form of a Research Report. This chapter deals with each of these decisions.

Users Guide to Chapter 4

• 1 Deciding what to study

Step 1 Choosing a topic you're interested in
Step 2 Selecting a piece of evidence from your chosen topic
Step 3 Replication, modification, innovation?
Step 4 Selecting your research rationale

• 2 Research methods in psychology

Method 1 Controlled experiments
Method 2 Case studies
Method 3 Questionnaires
Method 4 Field studies
Method 5 Content analysis
Method 6 Correlational studies
Method 7 Cross-cultural studies
Method 8 Longitudinal studies
Method 9 Diary studies

3 Selecting participants for research

Method 1 Simple random sampling
Method 2 Stratified random sampling
Method 3 Systematic random sampling
Method 4 Quota sampling

4 Treating participants ethically

Eight steps to ethical research in psychology
How to produce a briefing document

5 Writing your research report

Abstract
Introduction
Method
Results
Discussion
References
Appendices

1 Deciding what to study

Deciding what to study is about selecting a **research rationale**. A **research rationale** is a **statement of the aims of your research**. It points an inquiring finger at that 'gap in our understanding' of a topic (or aspect of a topic) that your research proposes to help us fill. Deciding on a workable research rationale can be a bit of a 'gazing blankly into space' experience. To keep this difficult gazing period to a minimum try taking your decision in little steps, rather than in one big leap

Step 1   Choose a topic you're interested in

It's advisable to research a topic you've studied on your course. Going 'away from home' is a gamble that can lead to quite a bit of extra work. So if you're fascinated by the psychology of serial killers or animal husbandry and neither of them appear on your syllabus, try to compromise. But within the limits of your course, do choose something you're interested in. Choose a topic (or aspect of a topic) that grabbed you when you did it in class. Or maybe go for something you've been reading about. Researching something you're indifferent to, or something you've been told to research because you haven't come up with an idea yourself, can be a real ball and chain – especially when it comes to writing your *research report*.

I worked with a pair of students who nominated *the formation of relationships* as their research topic. I'll use their example to illustrate how to put together a *Research Rationale*.

Step 2   Select a piece of evidence from your chosen topic

You've made your task more manageable by focusing on a single topic. Now it's time to get even more specific. From your topic select a study or theory that you think is interesting and worthy of more investigation. When you have an idea in your sights, pause for a moment and ask yourself this question: *Has anything already been written about this study or theory?* If you can find some psychological evidence relating to the piece of research you've chosen, all well and good. You'll need to include relevant work from other authors when you write your *research report*. So check the course textbooks and make sure there's some material relating to the piece of evidence you've chosen before you do your study.

> *After reviewing work on* **the formation of relationships** *our exemplar students, Sid and Nancy (names fictitious), chose Markey and Kurtz's (2006) theory of complementary friendship development as their area for research. This states that as friendships progress, friendship pairs tend to exhibit increasingly pronounced opposite or complementary behaviour patterns, especially in terms of dominance and submissiveness. In other words, as they get to know each other, one becomes more dominant, the other more submissive.*

Step 3   Decide whether to replicate, modify, or innovate

You've settled on an interesting (to you), fairly well-documented piece of evidence. This will be the launch-pad for your own study. Now you face three choices:

- *Choice 1* is to **do the study in the same way the original authors did it**. Or, in the case of a theory, to test it in the same way someone else has already tested it. This is called **replicating** research. It's a good way to verify the original findings and to see if they're *replicable* (see **Chapter Three** for more on *replicability*).

- *Choice 2* is to **introduce a new element into the design of the original piece of research**. You do virtually the same study, with a new twist. You might, for instance, replace one variable with another. Let's say you find an original study about the influence of increased temperature levels on our ability to solve problems. Replace the word 'temperature' with 'noise' and you have a slightly different study. This is called **modifying** research. It's fine too. But there's a difference between *modifying* and *complicating*. By all means introduce a new element into the design of a study, but try not to make it any more complicated – especially when you're just starting out in research.

- *Choice 3* brings with it rather surprising news. You may not realise it but many psychology courses don't reward originality in research design. If you come up with an original, groundbreaking idea for researching your topic you probably won't gain any more marks than you would if you'd done a replication. Yet whilst **innovation (doing a study that isn't based on an**

original piece of research) may not improve your grade, you shouldn't be put off from going ahead with it if it's an idea you really want to try. So long as it isn't a complicated idea, and so long as you can find evidence by other authors that relates to it.

Remember Sid and Nancy were using Markey and Kurtz's (2006) theory of complementary friendship development as their starting point. Because they wanted to keep things simple, they decided to replicate a fairly straightforward way of testing this idea. They selected friendship pairs who had known each other either for around 2 weeks, or for around 16 weeks. They then gave these friendship pairs questionnaires which had been designed to rate their levels of dominance or submissiveness within these friendships. Markey and Kurtz would predict that the 16-week condition would display more pronounced levels of complementarity. In other words, the 16-week pairs would be more dissimilar in terms of dominance–submissiveness than would the 2-week pairs.

Step 4   And finally, select your research rationale

So now you've really narrowed things down. You've selected a topic and a piece of research from your chosen topic. You've decided whether you're going to replicate or modify the research you've selected. You may even be intent on doing an original study. Now, finally, you're in a position to set out your research rationale.

Remember, your research rationale is your answer to the question – *What is the aim of your study?* It should be a clear, precise statement of the gap in our understanding that the results of your research will help to fill. When you've decided how you're going to word it, pause for a moment and ask yourself *Is it really clear and precise?* A good way to check this is to show it to someone and see how they react. If they read it, look at you and say 'So what's the aim of your study then?' you probably need to clarify things a little.

Sid and Nancy's Research Rationale looks like this: **A study to find out if longer lasting friendships have more strongly opposed behaviour patterns in relation to dominance and submissiveness than do friendships that are only a few days old.**

When you've settled on the wording for your *Research Rationale* you shouldn't find it too hard to convert it into a **testable prediction** about what you think the outcome of your study will be. This **testable prediction** will be your **hypothesis** (see Chapter 1 for a full discussion of hypotheses).

Sid and Nancy's hypothesis is: **16 week old friendships will have more strongly opposed behaviour patterns in relation to dominance and submissiveness than will friendships that are only a few days old**.

Furnished with a clear *Research Rationale*, now it's time to settle on a **method**.

● 2 Research methods in psychology

A **method** is a **way of carrying out research.** Once you've got your *Research Rationale*, your next job is to decide which method you're going to use. You'll be spoilt for choice since there are plenty of alternatives. This section reviews the most popular methods in psychology. None of the methods featured here is superior to any of the others. They all have advantages and disadvantages. Some though are more popular amongst psychology tutors and students than others are. Also, some have more technical terminology attached to them than others do. In fact, **the controlled experiment** is the most popular method and it's the one that carries the most terminology. Because of this you'll find more space devoted to it than to any of the other methods in the section that follows.

Method 1   Controlled Experiments

Aren't they what chemists, physicists and biologists do?

Yes, and the ones they do have plenty in common with the ones psychologists do. For one thing, they do them in laboratories. So they're sometimes called **laboratory experiments**. For another thing, they follow the *Rule of One Variable*, which states that

> *If two substances are treated in identical fashion in all respects except one, any difference in the outcome of those substances must be due to that one variable.*

To illustrate this rule, let's say you've prepared two samples of the same chemical in two separate test tubes, *A* and *B*. You apply a flame to each test tube. You get no reaction from either of them. Next, you add a measure of another chemical, *Z*, to test tube *B* and apply the flame to each test tube a second time. This time *B* bursts into flames. You would probably conclude from this experiment that *B*'s bursting into flames was down to the introduction of *Z*. After all, *A* and *B* were treated in identical fashion *in all respects except this one.*

Controlled experiments in psychology work according to a similar principle. In a typical laboratory study you take two **groups** (or **conditions**, as psychologists call them) **of participants** and treat them identically in all respects except one. In other words, you try to ensure that your conditions are only treated differently according to one variable. This one variable is your **independent variable** (*IV*). It's **what separates *Condition A* from *Condition B*.** It's sometimes called the 'manipulated variable' because it's what you (the researcher) manipulate to ensure that it's present in one condition and absent in the other. We call the condition where the *IV* is absent the **control condition**, whilst the condition where the *IV* is present is called the **experimental condition**.

By the way, more adventurous researchers have three or more conditions in their experiments. Their *IV* would be absent in *Condition A*, present in *B*, present to a greater degree in *C* and so on. But most undergraduate experiments stick to two conditions, so these are the ones I'm going to concentrate on in this discussion.

> *Latane and Darley (1970) did a controlled experiment to investigate how people react in emergency situations. They created two conditions of participants, A and B. **One by one**, participants in Condition A were shown into a room and invited to sit down and fill in a questionnaire. Participants in Condition B were shown into a similar room and invited to sit down and fill in a similar question-naire **as a group**. In both conditions, after a few minutes, steam billowed into the room through a grille in the wall. The researchers recorded participants' reaction time (how long it took them to raise the alarm).*

Have you spotted the *IV* in Latane and Darley's study? What's present in Condition B (experimental condition), absent in *A* (control condition). It's *other people*. They wanted to find out whether their participants would react to the emergency in a differ-ent way in a group setting, compared with when they were alone.

Your independent variable (*IV*) is present in one condition, absent in the other. As an experimenter you're interested in the effect of the presence of your *IV* upon **some aspect of your participants' behaviour, which you'll observe and record during your experiment**. Latane and Darley were interested in the effect of their *IV* on their participants' reaction time. This aspect of behaviour – the one you observe and record in your experiment, the one that may be influenced by the presence or absence of the *IV* – is your **dependent variable** (*DV*). It's called this because its value may be dependent upon the presence or absence of your independent variable. To sum all this up, you could say that:

> **Controlled experiments investigate the influence of an *IV* (the difference between two conditions) on a *DV* (some aspect of partic-ipants' behaviour).**

What about those other types of variables, the ones that were featured in Chapter 1?

You mean **extraneous variables** (*EVs*). These are discussed in Chapter 1. There I said that a controlled experiment is a way of *studying the effects of a change in one variable (IV) on the value of another (DV), whilst attempting to control all extraneous variables.* You could say that **extraneous variables** are variables that break the *Rule of One Variable*. Any variable that's present in one condition of an experiment and absent in the other – *apart from the IV* – is regarded by experimenters as an *EV* that needs to be controlled, or, as we often put it, made constant across the two conditions.

> *Latane and Darley were looking at the effect of other people (IV) on their partic-ipants' response time (DV). Condition A were tested individually, Condition B were tested as a group. But what if Condition A had consisted entirely of males*

and B *had been all females? Here, gender would be an* extraneous variable. *The researchers would have to control it by making it constant across the conditions, by making sure they had equal numbers of males and females in* A *and* B. *Otherwise they would be unsure as to whether any differences in reaction time (between* A *and* B*) were due to gender or to the presence or absence of their* IV *(other people).*

As an experimenter you may feel like you need eyes in the back of your head to keep a check on all the *EVs* that need to be controlled. But, as Chapter 1 suggests, it's unrealistic to try to control every conceivable *extraneous variable* that might differ between the conditions of your experiment. Eye colour, intelligence, heart rate, fatigue . . . the list is endless. You can't control them all. But you can control the obvious ones. To help you decide which obvious ones to control, try dividing these *EVs* into two types: **extraneous *participant* variables** and **extraneous *situational* variables**.

> **Extraneous participant variables** (*EPVs*) are **characteristics of your participants that might vary between your conditions**. Gender and age are obvious examples. For instance, the average age of your *Condition A* might be ten years greater than in *Condition B*.

> **Extraneous situational variables** (*ESVs*) are **aspects of the *experimental setting* that might vary between your conditions**. These include temperature, time of day, background noise and season. For example, you might test *Condition A* in the morning and *B* in the afternoon.

As an experimenter it's your job to control the effects of these *EVs*. As you design your experiment think about how you can make them constant between your conditions; so that your *Rule of One Variable* remains intact; so that your *IV* is the only thing that distinguishes *Condition A* from *Condition B*.

> *In an experiment like Latane and Darley's, time of day is an example of an* ESV *that could be made constant across the conditions. A straightforward way of doing this would be to ensure that* Conditions A *and* B *are both tested in the morning. This way you could be confident in linking any change in the* DV *to the* IV, *rather than to the fact that* Condition B *was tested after a heavy lunch.*

Your most powerful tool for controlling troublesome *EVs* in your experiment is how you divide participants into conditions. There are three popular methods for doing this, or *experimental designs*, as psychologists call them.

- An **Independent design** has **no participant appearing in more than one condition** of the experiment. *Conditions A* and *B* have entirely different personnel, though they usually have equal numbers of participants.

Box 4A

All three experimental designs have advantages and problems

	An advantage of this design is . . .	A problem with this design is . . .
The Independent Design	. . . because participants only appear in one condition there are no **order effects**. . . . participants are less likely to display **demand characteristics**. As they're only tested once, they have less opportunity to 'work out' the aims of the experiment.	. . . **participant variables** (PVs). All participants have different characteristics and abilities. In Independent Designs some PVs will vary across conditions. Variables like intelligence, self-esteem (and many others) will be more in evidence in one condition than the other. The unequal distribution of these PVs between the conditions will ensure that the rule of one variable will always be bent a little. . . . you **need more participants** than you do in Repeated Measures designs, since each participant only produces one set of data.
The Repeated Measures Design	. . . **you need fewer participants** than you do in the other designs, since everyone is observed and tested twice. Effectively, you get two sets of data for the price of one participant. . . . you don't have the problem of participant variables (PVs). Participants are effectively being compared with themselves, so there are	. . . the **order effect**. These are a consequence of having participants that appear in both conditions. The order effect comes in two varieties. **First**, the **fatigue effect**. This is when your participants grow tired or bored. Their performance deteriorates the longer your study goes on. **Second**, the **practice effect**. Here, participants grow more comfortable, with their setting (or more competent at the tasks they're given). Their performance improves as the experiment goes on. Both these effects produce performances that vary between conditions for reasons other than the presence or absence

→

- A **Repeated Measures design** has **all participants appearing in both conditions**. So if you're a participant in an experiment with this kind of design you'll be observed twice – both in *Condition A and* in *Condition B*.

- In a **Matched Pairs design** the experimenter pre-tests participants in relation to the extraneous variable she's aiming to control. If she's trying to control the EV of age the she'll find out how old each participant is before

Box 4A (continued)

All three experimental designs have advantages and problems

	An advantage of this design is . . .	A problem with this design is . . .
The Repeated Measures Design (continued)	no characteristics or abilities that vary across the conditions.	of the IV. So the Rule of One Variable is broken. You can deal with the **order effect** by **counterbalancing** (there's an explanation of this coming up). . . . **demand characteristics** (DCs). This is when participants guess what the experimenter expects from the outcome of the study. They react in one of two ways. **Either** they try to make the study 'work out' the way the experimenter expects it to. **Or** they try to prevent the experimenter's expectations being fulfilled. As with the order effects, *DC*s produce behaviours that vary between your two conditions.
The Matched Pairs Design	. . . the reduced effect of participant variables. Pre-testing participants on one or more *PV* reduces the degree to which they vary between conditions. . . . order effects don't present a problem because your participants only appear in one condition.	. . . even though you've pre-tested your participants (on one or more *PV*) and divided them into conditions accordingly, the *PV* will still be a thorn in your side, for two reasons. **First** there will still be some variation between the two groups, even on the variables you've pre-tested. **Second**, there will still be a number of variables you haven't pre-tested for and these will vary between conditions. . . . compared with the other two designs, the pre-testing procedure makes this is a fairly time-consuming business.

dividing everyone up. If she's trying to control intelligence s/he'll give all the participants an IQ test before dividing them up. Armed with this data s/he'll then make sure that an equal number of old and young (or high and low IQ achievers) appear in each condition. A good way of doing this is by ranking the participants from eldest to youngest (or highest to lowest IQ), then putting the eldest in *Condition A*, the 2nd eldest in *Condition B*, the 3rd eldest in *A* and so on. Matched pairs designs are independent designs in that no-one appears in more than one condition of the experiment.

Latane and Darley could have used any of these designs for their experiment. An Independent design would have had Condition A *filling in their question-naires individually and* Condition B *filling theirs in as a group. In a Repeated Measures design', the same participants would have filled in the questionnaire twice – once alone, once as a group. A Matched Pairs design would have had all the participants being pre-tested on (for example) intelligence. Equal numbers of high and low achievers would then be put in two groups* A *and* B, *in an effort to make the* EPV *of intelligence constant across the two conditions. However, as* **Box 4A** *suggests, matching participants in this way doesn't yet eliminate* EPVs, *though it does help to reduce their effect.*

As **Box 4A** shows, none of these three designs is better than another. They all have advantages and problems.

Counterbalancing

What's counterbalancing?

Counterbalancing is **a way of dealing with 'the order effect' in experiments that have a Repeated Measures design**. Let's say you've set up an experiment in which all participants appear in *Conditions A* and *B*. And let's say they all appear in *A* first, then *B*. Chances are they'll become either fatigued or practised as the experiment wears on. This means they'll either do worse in *B* (fatigue) or better in *B* (practice), partly for reasons that have nothing to do with the absence or presence of the IV, but rather, because of the order in which they appeared in the two conditions.

If everyone in Latane and Darley's experiment appeared in Condition A *(alone) first, then in* Condition B *(group), they may have reacted faster in* B *because it was their second emergency of the day. They'd had practice. Their reaction time (DV) was dependent not only on the presence or absence of other people (IV), but also on the order in which they appeared in the two conditions (ESV).*

In situations like this *order* is an *extraneous situational variable*. It's your job as the experimenter to try and make *ESVs* like this constant between your two conditions. This is where counterbalancing comes in.

If your Repeated Measures experiment is susceptible to the order effect, divide your participants into two equal groups. Let the first group appear in *Condition A* first, then in *B*. Let the second group appear in *B* first, then *A*. This will neutralise the fatigue and practice effects. They'll still be present, but now they'll move in two directions, rather than just one. To put this another way – half your participants will be fatigued in *A*, half in *B*. Half will be practised in *A*, half in *B*.

Now you can be more confident in claiming that any differences in the behaviour of your two conditions are down to the presence or absence or your *IV*, rather than to the order in which they appeared in the two conditions. The precise name for this method of controlling the order effect is **ABBA Counterbalancing** (since half your participants appear in *A then B* and half in *B then A*). It's a handy device but it isn't perfect. It won't eliminate fatigue or practice from your experiment, though it will help you to control their effects.

> *If Latane and Darley's study were done as a Repeated Measures experiment, ABBA counterbalancing would be a handy device for controlling the order effect. If half the participants appeared in* A *then* B *and half in* B *then* A *the effect of 'practice' would be neutralised. It would affect performances in both conditions equally.*

You have to make compromises when you do controlled experiments in psychology. You're investigating the influence of one kind of variable (*IV*) on another kind of variable (*DV*), while trying to make a third class of variable (*EV*) constant across your conditions. Realistically you can't control every extraneous variable that threatens to bend or break the Rule of One Variable in your experiment. But don't lose hope. You're not entirely powerless. Controlled experiments got their name because they incorporate a number of handy tools to help you stay in charge of your research. Independent, Repeated Measures and Matched Pairs designs, as well as ABBA counterbalancing, can all help you deal with troublesome *EV*s. So that when you record a difference in the behaviour of your two conditions you can confidently trace it back to your *IV*, rather than to some other, extraneous feature of your experiment.

Your job as experimenter is to select the most appropriate tools for your research project. The ones I've featured in this section are all pretty handy, though they're not power-tools. They won't eliminate extraneous variables from your experiment, though they will help you to control their effects.

Controlled experiments are part of an overall approach to doing psychological research, called the **quantitative** approach. Psychologists who adopt this approach observe behaviour, then **express their observations in a *numerical* form**. In other words, they produce measurements of behaviour using graphs, tables, percentages. Doing research like this enables you to make comparisons between your participants' behaviour. Take Latane and Darley, for instance. Their results were expressed in seconds and minutes. They were measuring their participants' reaction time. The alternative to the quantitative approach in psychology is called the **qualitative**. The next section, on **case studies**, has more on this.

Like all methods controlled experiments have ADVANTAGES . . .

Doing research in laboratories gives you **control** over a lot of the variables that influence what happens in your study. In your laboratory (or in the classroom you're using as your laboratory) you can vary and manipulate variables you'd have no control over if you were working in a naturalistic setting. You select the lighting, the noise level, how many people are in the room. It's up to you if you want to make any of these variables constant across your conditions. Being in control is what draws people to this method.

Because of the amount of control they offer, laboratory experiments are highly **replicable** (see Chapter 3 for a discussion of **replicability**). It's an asset if your study can be repeated (replicated) by another researcher (or by you) at a later date, as it means that your original findings can be checked or verified. Because laboratory experimenters manipulate so many of their variables themselves, their studies are relatively easy to replicate – more so than studies that take place in naturalistic settings, where you'd have a difficult job reproducing the exact temperature, noise, and crowding levels of the original research.

Controlling your experimental variables means you can use a **standardised** procedure in your experiment. As far as you can, you need to make sure that all your participants are treated in the same way. This means giving the same instructions, with the same wording, the same amount of guidance, to everyone. Variation in how participants are treated will act as an *extraneous variable*, so it should be avoided. In a laboratory, where you can rehearse your procedure down to the last detail, you're less likely to fall into the trap of treating some people 'more equally than others'.

And DISADVANTAGES . . .

Like **ecological validity**. You should be getting used to this term now, so I won't labour the point again. Findings from laboratory experiments can't help us to under-stand how we behave in everyday settings because they're too artificial. They **lack ecological validity**. The laboratory setting is artificial, which leads participants to behave unnaturally. The tasks researchers ask participants to do in laboratory studies are also artificial, again leading to unnatural reactions. The upshot of this is that results gained from controlled experiments cannot confidently be used to inform us about behaviour in the outside world.

Watch out too for **demand characteristics**. These are particular problems in Repeated Measures experiments, where participants are being observed for a longer period of time, but they can crop up in all experiments. When participants know what the aim of your study is they may influence its outcome, consciously or otherwise. They may try to make the experiment 'work out' like (they think) the experimenter wants it to. Or else they'll try to sabotage its outcome to upset the experimenter's expectations. Influences like these will act as extraneous variables, so prevent them where you can. A good way of outlawing demand characteristics is to ensure your participants don't find out what the aim of your study is. Mind you, deceiving your participants like this could leave you open to cries of 'unethical'. There's more on these ethical dilemmas later in this chapter.

A related problem is **experimenter bias**. This can happen when the researcher knows the experiment's aims. Knowing what's expected to happen, s/he might – consciously or otherwise – influence its outcome to conform to these expectations. S/he may even communicate these expectations to the participants (consciously or otherwise), which would lead to demand characteristics. A good way of combating experimenter bias is to use competent researchers who are ignorant of the experimenter's aims and of what its outcome is expected to be. Experimenters who are kept naive in this way are usually referred to as **blind researchers**.

Controlled experiments are the most complicated of the methods, so if you've understood this part of the chapter you should be alright with the rest of it. Before you move on, pause for a moment and make sure you know what these terms mean:

The Rule of One Variable
Control and **experimental conditions**
Independent, **dependent** and **extraneous variables**
Independent, **Repeated Measures** and **Matched Pairs designs**
The order effect
Demand characteristics
ABBA counterbalancing
Standardised procedures
Experimenter bias
Blind researchers

Method 2 Case Studies

A Gordian knot is a type of knot that's hard to untie.

After studying the behaviour of Trobriand Islanders – in the Pacific Islands – in the 1920s, Bronislaw Malinowski came to the conclusion that 'although people feel or think or experience certain psychological states in association with the performance of customary acts, the majority of them surely are not able to put them into words' (1922). In other words, people aren't very good at 'speaking their minds'. This is rotten news for psychologists. How are we supposed to study what people think, feel and experience if we can't rely on what they tell us about their thoughts, feelings, experiences? Malinowski called this question 'the real Gordian knot of social psychology'.

Case studies are deeply entangled in Malinowski's knot because they involve psychologists asking people to talk about their feelings, thoughts, experiences. They also involve observing and recording people's behaviour. Doing case studies means making a combined record of what people say and do.

So how would you define a 'case study'?

It's **a detailed study of an individual or group**. Usually you're looking in detail at one person's life, past and present. Detail – the idea of looking at the small-print of someone's thoughts, feelings, experiences – is the essence of the case study. More so than with any method, case studies allow you to get 'close up' to the person you're studying. So you can arrive at an intimate portrait of them, their relationships, desires, weaknesses, strengths etc.

Case studies are part of an overall approach to doing psychological research called the **qualitative** approach. Psychologists who do qualitative research aren't satisfied with observing and recording people's behaviour, they want to know how people feel about their behaviour too. They want to know about the meanings people attach to what they do.

Let's say, for example, you notice that your next door neighbour has a habit of talking to himself. If you were taking a qualitative approach to researching this problem you wouldn't just record his behaviour, you'd go next door and ask him to tell you about what he was doing. As Malinowski put it, you'd try and grasp 'his vision of his world' (1922). In effect, you'd do a case study.

> In The Man Who Mistook His Wife for a Hat *(1985) Oliver Sacks reports his case study of Ray. From his conversations and observations Sacks tells the story of Ray's experience of Tourette's Syndrome – a neurological condition that leaves the individual with a number of uncontrollable tics, jerks and twitches. Sacks argues that in some ways Tourette's is the flipside of Parkinson's disease, since Touretters have an excess of the same excitor transmitter in the brain that Parkinsonians lack. Where the Parkinsonian is lethargic, the Touretter is frenetic. The case of 'Witty Ticcy Ray' is an intimate record of Ray's behaviour and of how he feels about his Tourettism.*

Different researchers do case studies for different reasons. Bilton et al. (1996) makes a distinction between **idiographic** and **indicative** case studies. Researchers who do **idiographic** studies are interested in a particular case because of its outstanding, unique qualities. '**Idiographic**' is a handy term to learn because it figures fairly often elsewhere in psychology. It means **referring to the unique qualities of an individual**. Authors of studies like these aren't so interested in shedding light on people's behaviour in general from what they've found out about their particular case. They're simply saying 'look, this case is unique and interesting'.

The aim of doing **indicative** case studies is to enlighten us about people generally. Here, the author feels that knowing more about their case – or an aspect of their case's life – will help us understand more about human behaviour in general. Another way of putting this is that the **insights gained from indicative case studies are generalisable to other cases and situations**.

> *Sacks's case of Ray tells us more about the inner world of the 'Touretter'. A quote from Ray himself illustrates this – 'You "normals", who have the right transmitters in the right places at the right times in your brains, have all feelings, all styles, available all the time – gravity, levity, whatever is appropriate. We Touretters don't.' Listening to Ray talk about his condition helps Sacks to understand how unpredictable the experience of Tourette's syndrome is. The case of Ray 'in particular' helps us to unravel Tourettes 'in general'. In this sense, Sacks takes an indicative approach.*

Doing case studies effectively involves negotiating a number of carefully laid traps. The trap you're most likely to stumble into when you do a case study is **the partiality**

trap. This relates to the subjective viewpoint of you, the researcher. When you're studying a participant 'close up' there's a danger that instead of reporting what s/he actually says and does, you'll report your interpretation of what s/he says and does. This can happen consciously or unconsciously. There's a greater danger of this when you have certain expectations about what s/he's doing or why s/he's doing it. It's all too easy to find yourself reporting behaviour the way you see it, rather than the way your participant intends it to be seen. You might, for instance, report a throwaway comment as a 'scathing aside'.

This kind of partiality is especially characteristic of the case study method. You could say it's the case study equivalent of 'experimenter bias'. Earlier in this chapter (in the section on controlled experiments) I suggested using 'blind' (uninformed) researchers as a technique for reducing experimenter bias. This isn't really appropriate in a case study setting. If you're making a detailed portrait of your participant's thoughts, feelings, experiences, it's a good thing if you and your participant are familiar with the aims of the research. But don't despair. There are ways of avoiding the partiality trap when you're doing a case study.

First of all, **be honest** about when you're being impartial and when you're not (Coolican, 1996). In your report, make it clear when you're offering your interpretation of what your participant said and did and when you're simply describing events *as they happened*. You might use phrases like 'it seemed to me that . . .' or 'you could say that . . .' where you're giving your own views.

Secondly, **quote your participant** (Coolican, 1996). If you include, as Sacks did in the case of Ray, some direct statements from the person you're studying, this adds credibility to your report. A direct, unadulterated transcription of something your participant actually said is less partial than your version of what they said.

Thirdly, '**touch base**' (Bilton, 1996). Good practice in qualitative research means involving your participant in the reporting process. There's no-one better to check the accuracy of what you're reporting than your participant. As you gather your notes, show them to your participant and ask if you're giving a fair representation of what they've been saying and doing.

When doing qualitative research it's impossible to banish your own interpretations from your report altogether. They're bound to creep in a bit. Being honest, quoting your participant and touching base won't eliminate partiality from your case study, though they will help you to reduce its effects.

Like all methods, case studies have ADVANTAGES . . .

Researchers are drawn to the case study method because of the level of **detail** it yields about a participant. You'll gather more data about a single participant by doing a case study than you would by using any other method. You'll be able to spend a good deal of time with your participant and so observe them in a variety of situations and speak to them about a variety of their thoughts, feelings and experiences.

Case studies allow you a good deal of **flexibility**. It may be that during your discussions with your participant you stumble upon something about them that you want to follow up. S/he may turn out to be a twin or a war veteran or an arachnophobic. With a case study you're free to follow up these new lines of inquiry because you don't set out with a rigid, clearly stated research rationale. The aims of case studies tend to be more open-ended.

And DISADVANTAGES . . .

Unlike controlled experiments, case studies are *not replicable*. Once you've done a case study you can't do the same study again, either with the same participant or with a different one. As a researcher doing a case study you have a lot of contact with your participant. You ask numerous questions, you make numerous observations. You enter into numerous complex interactions that can never be repeated.

Because they are unique, findings from case studies are **hard to generalise**. Although you might find out a lot about a particular participant, you'd be hard pressed to say with any confidence that your findings tell us much about the rest of the population. This is the downside of doing a study that only has one participant. S/he might, after all, be pretty unusual. No matter what you discover about him/her, it may tell us nothing about the rest of us. This is a real drawback if you're attempting to do an 'indicative' case study.

Method 3   Questionnaires

Most weekly magazines would seem incomplete without a questionnaire for readers to complete. They're good news for people with long train journeys ahead of them and they're good news for psychologists, who want to collect lots of data about a large sample of participants without spending very much time, effort or money. Whatever magazine takes your fancy you'll know that filling in questionnaires is straightforward enough. What you might not realise is that making them up is a bit of a puzzle. This section suggests some solutions.

How would you define a **questionnaire**?

As **a set of written questions to be answered by respondents**. In some studies the researchers are around while respondents fill in their answers – these are called *face-to-face* questionnaires. In others the researchers hand over the questionnaires, then leave the respondents to get on with it. These are called *self-completion* questionnaires. In a third category – *postal* or *e-questionnaires* – respondents never even meet the researchers. They receive the questionaires, fill them in and send the questionaires back by post or email.

> In 2003 Niens et al. carried out a questionnaire study in Northern Ireland, into
> prejudicial attitudes in Catholic and Protestant regions of Belfast. They wanted
> to find out whether increased inter-group contact was related to a downturn in
> hostile attitudes. Questionnaires asked participants (drawn from both religious
> groups) to comment on the amount of contact they had with 'outgroup'
> members, as well as on their levels of anxiety towards that group as a whole. In
> line with the so called 'contact hypothesis' (Allport, 1954), in this sample there

*was an inverse relationship between contact and anxiety. In other words, pres-
ence seemed to make the heart grow fonder.*

The questions on questionnaires are often called *items*. They come in two varieties:
closed and **open-ended** items.

Closed items are child's play for respondents. They come complete with suggested
responses. All they have to do is pick one. Typical suggested responses are 'yes', 'no'
and 'don't know'. A quantitative variation on this theme involves providing a numerical scale and asking respondents to say how much they agree with a statement, like,
for example, 'the earth is flat'. A response of 1 might mean 'I don't agree at all',
whereas 7 means 'I totally agree'. This kind of 1–7 method is called a Likert scale,
after its inventor, Rensis Likert (1903–81).

Are questionnaires quantitative or qualitative?

They can be either. **Open-ended** items are an example of *qualitative* research. Here,
items come minus suggested responses. Respondents have to make their own up,
which means they have more work to do. On the plus side, it also means you get
more detailed information about your respondents. Open-ended items are useful if
you're interested in your respondents' views and opinions about a certain issue.

Closed items allow you to gather data in numerical form. You can work out how
many people said 'yes', 'no' and 'don't know' to each item. If you're using a Likert
scale you can work out – numerically – how strongly your participants agree with a
statement. Collecting data numerically like this is an example of the quantitative
approach.

> *Niens et al. used a Likert scale in their questionnaire study. This involved
> presenting a series of statements and asking the participants to indicate how
> much they agreed with them, on a four-point scale. For example, one item read
> 'On a scale of 1 [unpleasant] to 4 [definitely pleasant], is contact with out-
> group members pleasant?' Data from such items enabled the researchers to
> apply a numerical measure to participant anxiety levels.*

Writing questionnaires effectively is a fine art. A well written questionnaire with
carefully crafted items can be the big difference between doing effective and ineffec-
tive research. As you sit down to write your questionnaire be on the look out for some
cunningly placed traps. Here are five of them, along with some strategies for side-
stepping them.

The 'throwing them in at the deep end' trap Anyone who's filled in a questionnaire knows that motivation amongst respondents is generally pretty low. As a rule,
respondents are a lethargic bunch who are easily distracted from their task.
Consequently they need to be wined and dined a little. With this in mind, the first item
on your questionnaire is critical. Don't throw your respondents in at the deep end.

Make item 1 nice and easy. It isn't there to yield data, it's there to welcome your respondents to your questionnaire and coax them towards item 2.

The 'irrelevance trap'   In the world of the questionnaire less is most definitely more. Effective questionnaires are short and sweet. Respondents lack stamina. Including items that don't relate to your research rationale – except for the first item – is a serious offence.

The 'terminology' trap   Think back to Chapter 3. Do you remember what 'psychology words' are? They're words that only make sense to people who've studied psychology. They're jargon, or technical terms that need explaining to non-psychologists. Including 'psychology words' in questionnaire items is like shooting yourself in the foot. Your respondents – who, remember, are in a state of low motivation in any case – will wander off and do something else as soon as they stumble across an item they don't understand. This problem is magnified if you're using *self-completion* questionnaires, where there's no one around to help out with any difficulties.

The 'leading questions' trap   Questionnaire respondents, like many of us, are easily led. Consequently you need to make sure you don't lead them towards making unnatural responses because of the way you phrase your items. Use neutral phrases like *Is the earth flat or spherical?* rather than leading phrases like *Do you agree that the earth is flat?* Also, if you're using closed items be sure to provide a healthy variety of possible responses. A choice of 'yes' or 'no' is often not enough. 'Don't know' is a popular answer to many questions. How many times have you used it today? Do you know?

The 'lies, fraud and mischief' trap   I'm not saying people who fill in questionnaires are liars. Mind you, they don't always give entirely honest responses. As a researcher there isn't a lot you can do about this. However, including a *lie detector* in your questionnaire might help. Put in two items that ask the same question using different wording. For example one item could say *Is the earth flat or spherical?* and another could say *Is the earth shaped more like a pancake or a beach ball?* It's a fair bet that anyone who gives conflicting responses to these items is either fraudulent or mischievous (not taking your questionnaire seriously). So you can discard their responses.

Like all methods, questionnaires have ADVANTAGES . . .

They're excellent for **reaching inaccessible respondents**. When doing research it's sometimes hard to find a time and a place to meet your participants to carry out your study. Questionnaires offer you a solution to this problem. You can distribute them in one meeting (or with no meetings at all, by post or electronic means) and while you're at it you can agree on a deadline for their return. When you're dealing with respondents who are either busy or a long way away this is a real lifeline for your research project.

When you do a questionnaire study you're more or less guaranteed of having a **standardised procedure**. In other words, it's easy for you to ensure that all your respondents are treated equally because your instructions and your items are incorporated onto the questionnaire itself. So there's little danger of some respondents being treated 'more equally than others'.

And DISADVANTAGES . . .

Asking someone to write down what they'd do in a certain situation is no substitute for observing what they do when they're actually out there, in that situation. Do you always do what you say you'll do? No, neither do I. The problem with questionnaires is that you're asking people to respond to **hypothetical items**. Even the most honest, diligent respondent is likely to say one thing and do another.

Response rates to questionnaires can be pretty low. Of the ones you do get back, some will be only half filled in or may have to be discarded because of the lie-detector. This is a particular problem with self-completion questionnaires.

Method 4   Field studies

Asking someone to write down what they'd do in a certain situation is no substitute for observing what they do actually in the situation (or *in the field*, as most researchers would put it). You may be one of those researchers who feel that so many people 'speak with forked tongues' about their thoughts, feelings and experiences that doing a questionnaire study isn't worth the bother. You'd rather observe what people actually do than read about what they intend to do. You may also be one of those researchers who see little point in observing and recording behaviour in laboratories, since all you get in the end are artificial responses to artificial requests.

If some of these views sound like yours there is a method that may suit you down to the ground.

How do you define a 'field study'?

As **a piece of research that takes place in a natural setting**. Its aim is to take your research to your participants, rather than bringing them into your laboratory to be studied. This means you can observe and record everyday behaviour in everyday settings. After all, psychology should help us to understand the ordinary things we do, not just the things we do in unusual, highly controlled situations. Another way of putting this is to say that doing field studies helps you improve the ecological validity of your research. Field studies come in two varieties.

Variety One: field experiments

These are controlled experiments, with one difference. As in laboratory experiments, you study **the effects of a change in one variable (*IV*) on the value of another (*DV*), whilst attempting to control all other extraneous variables**, but here you do it in a natural setting. You give up the warmth and predictability of your laboratory for the cold, wet, unpredictability of the outside world – the field. Popular venues for doing field experiments are restaurants, schools and public conveniences. You can do them wherever there are participants to be studied.

Most of what appears in the section, earlier in this chapter, on controlled experiments also applies to field experiments, so I won't dwell too long on them. But they do have a couple of distinguishing features.

First, because you're aiming to study everyday behaviour in everyday settings, you can't really tell your participants they're being studied. Would you act naturally if someone told you you were in a psychology experiment? No. So field experiments tend to be done **covertly – without the participants knowing they're being studied**. Other methods use covert methods too, but field experiments use them more often than most.

Secondly, because you've sacrificed the comfort of your laboratory for the cold, erratic outside world, you'll find **extraneous variables** harder to control. When you do a field experiment you're at the mercy of the elements far more than you are in your laboratory, where temperature, lighting and who's around are all down to you. The upshot of this is that some of these extraneous variables will vary between your conditions, thus bending your *Rule of One Variable* (see the section on controlled experiments for a full explanation of this rule).

> *Middlemist, Knowles and Matter did their business in a public toilet. Their field experiment – done in a gents' in 1976 – investigated the effect on physiological arousal of having someone standing next to you, which was measured by timing how long participants took to start urinating.* Condition A *had a confederate standing at the next urinal to the unsuspecting participant.* Condition B *had the confederate standing three urinals away. Another researcher hid in a cubicle with a home-made periscope and a stopwatch to record how long it took each participant to begin. The researchers found that having someone close by increased arousal, thus delaying urination. In this experiment the* IV *was the distance between the participant and the confederate, the* DV *was how long it took the participant to urinate.*

Are field experiments quantitative or qualitative?

Like laboratory experiments, they tend to err on the *quantitative* side. However, researchers who use this method often design their studies so they collect a mixture of the two types of data.

Variety Two: field observations

These involve **making a record of events and behaviour that take place in a natural setting**. Sometimes they're called 'non-experimental observations' to distinguish them from field experiments. There are no *IVs*, *DVs*, *EVs* or conditions in field observations. You could say they're a more straightforward way of recording everyday behaviour in everyday settings. You don't have to worry about controlling or manipulating variables when using this method

Field observations come in two types. The first – **participant observation** – isn't especially popular with students who've recently begun doing research in psychology as it requires a little more time and training than you may have access to at this early stage in your research career. Nonetheless, it's well worth knowing about.

Participant observation involves **gaining entry into and sharing the experiences of the group of participants you're studying, whilst at the same time gathering *qualitative* data.** The participant observer lives a kind of double life, participating in the life of the group as well as making descriptive observations, gathering field notes. Participant observation studies have famously been carried out in hospitals, on kibbutzim and even amongst street gangs. This method – often called *ethnography* – is much used by social anthropologists and can be carried out either overtly or covertly.

> In 1973 a team of researchers led by Rosenhan bluffed their way into a number of psychiatric wards by simulating minor schizophrenic symptoms. Once inside they carried out covert participant observations into the daily interactions between patients and medical staff. The resulting paper, 'On being sane in insane places', startled the psychiatric profession on two counts. First, it highlighted how easy it was to get committed into a psychiatric ward. All you had to do was say you were 'hearing voices'. Second, it highlighted how difficult it was to persuade medical staff that the researchers were sane enough to get out. In some cases it took weeks for the researchers to extricate themselves.

A more popular choice for psychology undergraduates is the second type of field observation – **non-participant observation**. Whilst *participant observation* involves studying a group from the inside, **non-participant observation** is about being on the outside looking in. It involves **making a record of events and behaviour that take place in a natural setting, *without becoming part of the group you're studying*.**

Non-participant observation can be done overtly (where participants know they're being studied) or covertly (where they don't). There are positive and negative sides to each of these. Studying participants overtly can produce demand characteristics (the section on controlled experiments earlier in this chapter has an explanation of these), whilst covert research raises ethical issues (see the section on ethics later in this chapter for more on these).

Are field observations qualitative or quantitative?

They can be either. Doing them quantitatively involves observing participants' behaviour and recording it in a numerical form. Researchers who do quantitative observations use a technique called *systematic observation*, which is explained below. Doing qualitative observation involves recording behaviour in a descriptive way. This method is favoured by researchers who prefer to use a participant observation method.

*Tronick and Morelli (1992) observed parenting styles amongst the Efe commu-
nity of the Democratic Republic of Congo (formerly Zaire). This covert observation began with a period of familiarisation with local customs and beliefs. The
observation itself was systematic (see below), meaning that certain prescribed
behaviours were pre-selected, then recorded when they occurred. These behaviours were deemed to indicate levels of sociability in development. They
included playing alone, or interacting with father, mother, sibling etc. Noting
down prescribed behaviours in this way allowed the researchers to generate
quantitative results and to give structure to their observations.*

Wait. Aren't there a lot of different varieties of field studies?

It may seem so, though actually, no. But if it's bothering you, pause for a moment and
take a look at **Box 4B**, which should clear things up a little.

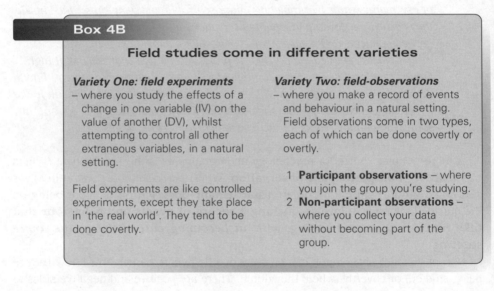

Box 4B

Field studies come in different varieties

Variety One: field experiments
– where you study the effects of a
change in one variable (IV) on the
value of another (DV), whilst
attempting to control all other
extraneous variables, in a natural
setting.

Field experiments are like controlled
experiments, except they take place
in 'the real world'. They tend to be
done covertly.

Variety Two: field-observations
– where you make a record of events
and behaviour in a natural setting.
Field observations come in two types,
each of which can be done covertly or
overtly.

1 **Participant observations** – where
  you join the group you're studying.
2 **Non-participant observations** –
  where you collect your data
  without becoming part of the
  group.

As I said a few paragraphs ago, field experiments are really a version of controlled
experiments, so for tips on how to do them go back to the section that deals with that
method earlier in this chapter. As I also said a few paragraphs ago, doing participant
observations tends to be beyond the scope of undergraduate psychology students, but
here are some tips on how to deal with the non-participant variety.

Doing non-participant observations effectively involves treading carefully to avoid
a number of smartly positioned traps. Here are some especially notorious ones, along
with some tips for bypassing them.

The 'no system' trap You can't record everything about your participants'
behaviour. Some things will escape your notice. Neither is it a good idea to record

as much as you can of what your participants do. This will leave too much open to interpretation. An alternative approach is to devise a *system for observation*. Decide on certain prescribed behaviour/s to focus on and record these and these only. Be sure that the prescribed behaviours you focus on are easy to recognise and define. This will make them easier to record. For example, 'finger-pointing' is easier to spot than, say, 'flirting'. So let's say you do decide to record 'finger-pointing' in a cafeteria. There are a number of ways you could do this. You could count the number of 'finger-points' in an hour; you could compare males with females on 'finger-pointing'; you could measure the average duration of a 'finger-point'. Any of these would be fine, since you'd be observing a prescribed behaviour that's easy to recognise, easy to define and therefore easy to record. This strategy of **focusing on a prescribed behaviour, then recording it numerically** is called **systematic observation**.

The 'no recording' trap   Recording what happens during your observation is a useful back-up when you're analysing your data. During your study you're likely to miss or misunderstand some of the things your participants say and do. If you record what happened on video or audio equipment you can go back and clarify a few ambiguities. A word of warning though, recording participants' behaviour should only be done with their consent, so this is a luxury that's restricted to overt research.

The 'lone-observer' trap   Doing an observation alone means backing yourself to be competent enough to make an accurate record of what your participants say and do. This is a big responsibility. You can relieve some of it by having two or more observers working independently (so as not to influence each other during the observation session). You'll probably find that even though they'll be dealing with prescribed behaviours (so they'll know what they're looking out for) your observers will still produce slightly differing accounts of what went on. This is inevitable. Everyone has their own interpretation of events. But if your observers produce extravagantly differing records it might be worth checking a few aspects of the design of your study. Are your observers really clear about their roles? Are they really focusing on prescribed behaviours that are easy to define?

The 'blowing cover' trap   If you're doing *covert* research, try not to look and behave like someone who is doing psychological research. Avoid appearing shifty, standing around with notepads, discussing the ins and outs of your study within earshot of your participants. If you draw attention to yourself, participants may not realise you're doing psychological research but they may well think something's not quite right. This may lead them to behave unnaturally, which is precisely what you don't want. So keep a low profile.

If you're doing overt research it's still worth keeping a low profile. Although your participants know they're being studied, this won't be uppermost in their minds throughout the entire session. After a few minutes of uncertainty they'll probably forget about you and get on with whatever they're doing. So once the observation is underway try to blend into the background. Keep quiet, avoid rustling, scribbling and fiddling with cameras and stopwatches.

Like all methods, field studies have ADVANTAGES . . .

It takes something fairly special to drag psychologists out of their laboratories to do their research in the field. The main incentive for going out into the field can be summed up in three words: **good ecological validity**. Field studies enable researchers to study everyday behaviour in everyday settings, and to generalise their results to the wider world. They're the ideal response to anyone who says psychologists draw their findings from giving people artificial tasks to do in artificial settings.

Because so many field studies are done covertly, you tend to get **no demand characteristics** (the section on controlled experiments has more on these). Participants who don't know they're in a study won't try to 'make it work out' the way the researcher wants it to. Nor will they try spoiling things for the researcher. Reducing the effects of demand characteristics is really another consequence of allowing participants to behave naturally, the way they usually behave when no-one is watching them.

And DISADVANTAGES . . .

Some who favour a qualitative approach to doing research object to the use of systematic observation techniques in field studies. They say that if you focus in on prescribed behaviours and record these and these alone, you miss the full richness and variety of your participants' behaviour. This is an example of **reductionism** (see Chapter 3 for more on this). You're also unable to take account of any unexpected behaviour that arises, if it falls outside the limits of your prescribed behaviour. In other words, systematic observation makes researchers too limited, too inflexible in what they observe.

The problem with working in the field is that **extraneous variables** are hard to control. Temperature, noise and many other variables are less predictable once you're outside the laboratory. With field *experiments* (as opposed to field observations) this lack of predictability is a particular drawback, since with this method you're trying to control any extraneous variables that might vary between your conditions. But the truth is that whatever variety of field study you're doing, you're only ever a moment away from complete disruption. Blizzards, dogs and marching bands can confound even the most carefully designed study. Could this be why most research is done under controlled conditions?

Method 5 **Content analysis**

A good private detective can find out a lot about someone simply by snooping around their living room, even when the subject of their investigations is dead, missing or on the other side of town. Once inside the living room, your private eye may well focus on two sources of information. First, she'll look at the books and DVDs that are lying around. Second, she'll look out for any scribbled notes, diaries, drawings or letters that carry the subject's signature. In short, she'll sift through the media messages the subject is exposed to (you could call these 'incoming messages') and the messages the subject has produced ('outgoing messages'). Messages like these will help the intrepid investigator build up a useful profile of the subject's tastes, motivations, desires, hang-ups, heartaches...

Content analysis resembles this sort of detective work. It's a way of studying people *indirectly*, by analysing messages they expose themselves to and messages they produce. The TV and films they watch, the books and newspapers they read, their letters, diaries, drawings and graffiti. Researchers who use this method reckon that *analysing* the *content* of messages helps us understand more about people's behaviour. For example, analysing what's in the cartoons we watch could tell us something about how violent we are in the playground, at work, and at home. Or analysing the content of our newspapers might tell us something about how we voted in the last election.

How do you define content analysis?

As **a technique for assessing the content of messages**.

Is content analysis quantitative or qualitative?

You can do it either way. But for students who are just beginning their careers as researchers the quantitative method tends to be favourite, so you'll find more space devoted to that approach in this section. Nevertheless, here are some details about the qualitative approach.

Qualitative content analysis is usually done by trained coders or 'content analysts'. This is sometimes called *semiology*, and involves interpreting what's contained within a message in the light of what's known about its sender and its recipient. In other words, you're looking at the context that the sender and recipient of a message are working in. This means taking notice of who's talking, as well as what's being said. Qualitative content analysis might, for example, involve studying the use of persuasive communication between two people conversing outside a bar. Or it might involve scouring TV news coverage for examples of political bias.

When you use this *interpretive* approach to content analysis you see the messages you're studying as being constructed as part of an interaction. They're not just messages studied in a vacuum. They're part of a conversation or discourse. And of course, because this method is so interpretive, different researchers are likely to analyse the content of the same messages in different ways.

> In 1980 Bruner and Kelso published a study of 30 years of graffiti in public toilets. The content of these scrawlings was analysed qualitatively, for example in terms of gender differences. Female graffitists were reported as adopting a more interpersonal style, posing questions about relationships. Males took a more egocentric, confrontational approach to their art.

Meanwhile **quantitative content analysis** places the emphasis on studying *the message itself*. Rather than studying the people who produce and receive messages, the focus is on what's in the messages on their TVs, in their diaries, their newspapers, in their books, websites, emails . . .

In fact, when you do **quantitative content analysis** your first job is to select your **source material**. That's **what you're going to analyse the content of**. You can select more or less anything, so long as it's some form of material that contains messages. This gives you a pretty big choice. So big, in fact, that I'd be a fool to try and give you a definitive list of possible sources. Instead, here's a continuation of the list that appears in the previous paragraph...radio news, magazines, graffiti, movies, advertisements, children's drawings and stories, CCTV footage . . .

Once you've chosen your source material it's time to select a **target message**. In other words, **what you're going to focus on in your source material**. You can't analyse the entire content of your source material any more than you can observe everything your participants do in a field observation. So you need to focus in on a specific message from your source material. Your choice of possible target messages is roughly as wide as the Grand Canyon, so again I'll avoid attempting to offer you a definitive list. Here's one idea, borrowed from some undergraduate students I worked with.

> *Gilbert and George (names fictitious) chose a series of Postman Pat story books as their source material. For their target message they focused on how many characters were shown driving vehicles in the stories. They wanted to see if there were more male or more female drivers in Greendale (the village Pat calls home). The aim of their study was to find out whether children's books portray males and females in stereotypical gender roles.*

Doing quantitative content analyses effectively involves stepping between a series of smartly concealed traps and potholes. Here are a few of them, plus some suggested routes between them.

The 'no system' trap   Yes, this is the same trap that appears on the road to doing non-participant field observations, so you can backtrack to the section on field studies for more on this. The key point here is to focus on a target message that's easy to recognise, easy to define and therefore easy to record numerically.

The 'lone analyst' trap   Again, a throwback to the section on non-participant field observations. Remember, using more than one researcher means you can be more confident about the reliability of your data.

The 'Itchy and Scratchy' trap   Imagine you want to find out how much violence there is in an episode of *The Simpsons*, yet you restrict your content analysis to the bit with Itchy and Scratchy in it. (For non-Simpsons-literate readers, the violence level in the 'Itchy and Scratchy' bit of *The Simpsons* is unrepresentative of the violence level in the show as a whole.) What's the problem with your study? You've selected a section of source material that's unrepresentative of the whole thing. Avoid this trap by analysing a healthy slab of material, whatever it is. Rather than using a few pages of a children's story, use a series of stories, like Gilbert and George did.

The 'no comparison' trap If Gilbert and George had just counted how many male drivers were careering around Greendale this study would have lacked something. Instead, they compared the number of male and female drivers. Analysing two elements from your target message means you can make comparisons between them. Analysing only one element often produces research that has an empty feel about it.

Like all methods, content analysis has ADVANTAGES . . .

Doing content analysis allows you a high degree of **control** over your research. Because you're analysing messages that people produce (outgoing) or expose themselves to (incoming), rather than actual behaviour of participants at the time that it occurs, you're spared the unpredictability of the live research situation. Once you've got hold of your source material you can analyse it when and where you want.

When you do content analyses your **choice of source material** is, to put it mildly, extensive. Researchers are drawn to this method because it enables them to study more or less any kind of message they choose. In the case of incoming messages – media output – the amount of material that's available for study is huge. And it's getting bigger.

And DISADVANTAGES . . .

Coolican (1996) describes quantitative content analysis as a method for reducing qualitative data to a numerical form. Researchers who take a qualitative approach to research say that if you focus on a specific target message in your source material, then just count how often it appears, you're bound to miss a lot of what's going on in the material. They say you're being **reductionist**, that you're reducing a complex set of messages to an oversimplified form. Researchers who take this view prefer to carry out qualitative content analyses.

Doing content analysis is about studying messages, rather than the people who receive or produce them. So you could say it's a rather **indirect** form of research. Arguably, psychological research should focus on the person, not the message. We should study how people respond to incoming messages, like the books they read. We should try to find out how people produce outgoing messages, like pictures or stories. In short, we should be more direct.

Method 6   Correlational studies

Every summer when the men down our street ditch their long trousers and start wearing shorts, ice-cream sales go sky high. Also, the rise in average annual temperature around here has been accompanied by an escalation in violent crime. In fact, our town is full of relationships like these – relationships between *pairs of variables* that appear to vary together, or **correlate**. Researchers use this term when they discuss variables that occur in 'real life'. Sometimes these are called **naturally occurring** variables, since they are **neither manipulated nor controlled by researchers**, in contrast to the controlled variables that are manipulated in laboratory experiments.

To say that a pair of variables **correlates** means they **alter their value at the same time as each other**. This can happen in two different ways. First, as one goes up (or down), so does the other one. They follow each other. Like a window cleaner and his shadow. Correlations like these, where **an increase (or decrease) in the value of one variable is accompanied by an increase (or decrease) in the value of the other**, are called **positive correlations**.

Another kind of correlation is called **negative correlation**. Here, **an increase (or decrease) in the value of one variable is accompanied by a decrease (or increase) in the value of the other**. Like the two ends of a seesaw. Sometimes this is called *inverse* correlation. For example, the fewer men in long trousers, the more people buying ice creams.

So how would you define a 'correlational study'?

It's **where researchers select a pair of variables and measure the degree to which they vary together**. Your first job when you're planning to do a correlational study is to choose a pair of variables. Remember, you're looking for naturally occurring, 'real-life' variables. What you're investigating is the kind of relationship that exists between two variables that would be at large in the world (and going up and down) anyway, whether or not you were studying them. Examples of naturally occurring variables are climatic changes, crime figures, library attendances, college enrolments, ice cream sales, dog immigration figures etc. Naturally occurring variables that are not manipulated by researchers can also include characteristics of people, such as extroversion scores or the incidence of emotional states. They are measured, but not manipulated, as the following study illustrates.

> *Izard et al. (1993) looked at a proposed correlation between participants' experiencing two emotions – guilt and shame. Questionnaire responses from participants indicated how frequently – on a scale of 1–9 – they experienced a range of emotions, including guilt and shame. A positive correlation between these two was uncovered, suggesting that they do tend to co-exist.*

Are correlational studies quantitative or qualitative?

Quantitative. Another look at our definition of correlational studies shows why. The word *measure* gives it away. Correlating a pair of variables involves assigning a quantitative value (a number) to the relationship between a pair of variables. So instead of saying that the rise of the multiplex cinema positively correlates with an increase in joyriding *'a lot'*, a correlational study allows you to say that these variables have a correlation of a particular numerical value. It's this numerical precision that draws many researchers to this method. The numerical value assigned to a pair of variables in a correlational study is called a **correlation co-efficient**. This is **a number measuring the degree to which pairs of variables are correlated**. It's always a number between 1 and +1. The closer it is to −1, the more negatively correlated a pair of variables is. The closer it is to +1, the more positively correlated they are. A co-efficient of around zero shows little or 'no correlation'. **Box 4C** summarises some of this information, and more.

> *Izard et al.'s research yielded a correlation co-efficient of +0.61 for guilt and shame. This suggests a positive correlation which exceeds that which would be expected if the relationship were purely down to chance.*

Box 4C

A correlation co-efficient is a number between −1 and +1

	A	B			C	D	E			F	G
Correlation co-efficients:	−1	−0.8	−0.6	−0.4	−0.2	0	0.2	0.4	0.6	0.8	+1

The scale shows correlation co-efficients of varying strengths. Co-efficient **G** indicates **perfect positive correlation**, where two values move up and down together like a window cleaner and his shadow. Co-efficient **A** shows **perfect negative correlation**, where two values move in opposite directions, like the ends of a seesaw. Perfect correlations such as these are rare in real life. **F** and **B** show strongly positive (**F**) and negative (**B**) correlations respectively. **C** and **E** show weak correlations. Co-efficient **D** shows a relationship of **no correlation**, where **variables in a pair alter their values independently of one another**, as in the relationship between egg consumption and the popularity of lepidopterology (moth collecting).

So how do you work out the correlation co-efficient for a pair of variables?

Having established which pair of variables you're going to use, calculating a correlation co-efficient involves using a set of fairly straightforward statistical procedures. The section on **inferential statistics** in Chapter 5 has a guide to *calculating correlation co-efficients*.

Doing correlational studies effectively involves treading lightly around and between a few notable trapdoors. Here are some of the more dangerous ones, with suggestions on how to steer clear of them.

The 'un-operational variable' trap Psychologists have pilfered the idea of correlation from mathematicians. Doing correlational studies boils down to assigning a mathematical value to the relationship between a pair of variables. Given its quantitative nature, you shouldn't be too shocked to discover that the key to doing effective correlational research is selecting quantifiable variables. This means ensuring the pair of variables you're correlating are **variables that can be observed and measured**. Sometimes these are called **operational variables**. Good examples of *naturally* occurring, operational variables are temperature, unemployment, ice cream sales. Bad examples are morale and happiness, unless of course you know of any effective ways of measuring these elusive qualities.

The 'correlation and cause are two different things' trap Although 'men wearing shorts' and 'ice cream sales' are positively correlated, it would be foolish to assume that one *causes* the other. Both these variables owe their fluctuations to a third variable – summer. It is a mistake to assign cause-and-effect relationships to variables that are correlated. Correlation and cause are two different things. Even where cause-and-effect relationships do exist, it's beyond the scope of correlational studies to uncover them. This is because this method doesn't involve the strict controls that are necessary to even contemplate the establishment of cause-and-effect links. Correlation shows an association or coincidence between pairs of variables, that's all. Chapter 1 has a lengthy discussion of the uses and misuses of the word 'cause' in psychology.

The 'no means no' trap It's silly I know, but people who aren't fully concentrating on what they're doing sometimes get 'no correlation' mixed up with 'negative correlation', probably because of their negative connotations. Just to be sure this never happens to you, look again at the definitions of the two. They're pretty different, I think you'll agree.

Like all methods, correlational studies have ADVANTAGES . . .

Correlational studies involve neither the manipulation nor control of environmental variables. This is advantageous on two counts. One is that because you're using naturally occurring variables, your study will have a high degree of **ecological validity**. The other advantage of not manipulating the environment is that your study is likely to **ethically sound**. Specifically, issues relating to participants' safety, their right to withdraw and debriefing don't arise at all in correlational research.

What draws many researchers to this method is the mathematical tool of correlation itself. Using co-efficients to measure relationships between pairs of variables means you can claim a high degree of **empiricism**. This means you can point to observable, measurable associations between variables to support your theories, rather than simply supporting them with unsubstantiated observations, ideas and anecdotes.

And DISADVANTAGES . . .

The criticism on everybody's lips when it comes to correlational research is its **inability to establish cause and-effect links**. Researchers who favour more controlled methods, such as laboratory experiments, claim they can establish causal links, though even this is open to dispute (the section on 'causing' in Chapter 1 covers this debate). Still, it's widely accepted that correlational research hasn't a hope of establishing causal links – only coincidences – between pairs of variables.

Findings from correlational studies measure how groups of people behave, yet **they tell us little about any given individual's behaviour**. It might be beneficial to know that as a male you're likely to behave in a certain way as the temperature rises in the summer, because you're part of the male population. But findings like these tell us nothing about the individual motivations of particular male participants. You could say correlational studies treat people 'in herds'.

Method 7   **Cross-cultural studies**

As the name suggests, cross-cultural research is largely driven by the concept of **culture** itself. We can distinguish culture from a number of related notions such as 'nation', 'ethnicity' and 'race'. A nation is a political entity with defined, yet malleable geographical boundaries. Ethnicity is a psychological concept referring to a person's sense of belonging to a distinct social group. Race is a physical category referring to how groups with distinct ancestries differ from each other, often in terms of appearance. Rather than being to do with politics (nation), biology (race) or identity (ethnicity), culture is a sociological concept which refers to the norms and beliefs held by certain groups of people. A useful working definition of culture is **a sociological concept referring to how social groups are distinctive in terms of attitudes, norms and behaviours**. According to this understanding, 'my culture' is something which is open to change by assimilation, should I be integrated into another culture. Another interesting aspect of culture is that it is not necessarily assumed that groups of people with different cultures live in separate nations, or locations (though often they do). So it is perfectly conceivable for cross-cultural research to compare the behaviours of two cultural groups who reside in one nation.

So how would you define a 'cross-cultural study'?

As **a study which seeks to identify how human behaviour and experience manifests itself differently in different cultures**. In practice this means taking an aspect of behaviour (intelligence, aggression, visual perception) and comparing how it looks under the differing lights that are cast by various cultures. In essence then, a cross-cultural study involves a selected behaviour being observed in more than one cultural group, while a number of extraneous variables are held constant by the researcher. To all intents and purposes, culture acts as the independent variable in studies like these, since it is the difference between the conditions. A specific behaviour (say, *obedience to authority* or *perceiving pictures in three dimensions*) acts as the dependent variable. The researcher strives to set up equivalent testing conditions in two or more cultural settings. In this way established theories are tested in various locations. Such research is also known as *culture comparative* or *replication research*, since it involves original research being replicated in different cultures.

Peng and Nisbett (1999) compared cognitive styles in two groups of participants from the US and China respectively (part of the Chinese sample resided in the US). They wanted to find out whether participants from the two groups employed different kinds of arguments when trying to solve disputes. Specifically, it was hypothesised that North Americans would be more likely to apply 'differentiating' decision-making, whereby in any dispute one side of the argument is favoured over the other. Meanwhile the Chinese 'dialectical' tradition would predict that the Chinese condition would be happier to tolerate contradiction in disputes and therefore pick out the appealing parts of two apparently conflicting arguments. Such a predicted cultural difference in cognitive styles was revealed in the samples tested.

Are cross-cultural studies quantitative or qualitative?

They often combine elements of both, although some form of quantifiable data is generally favoured by those who work cross-culturally. Indeed, a qualitative approach to researching culture and behaviour fits in more closely with using the *ethnographic observation* method (see p. 115). This is because a more detailed observation of one cultural group is more compatible with qualitative research techniques. Typically then, a cross-cultural researcher will observe a specific aspect of behaviour (dependent variable) in respondents from two or more cultures, and allot a quantifiable value to that behaviour. This allows the influence of culture on at least one aspect of behaviour to be observed in a quantifiable form.

Peng and Nisbett presented participants with stories and proverbs with either differentiated or dialectical elements. Participants were then asked to indicate, on a seven-point scale, which ones they agreed with or liked best. This seven-point Likert scale gave researchers a quantifiable measure of culture's influence on cognitive style.

Doing cross-cultural research effectively involves being aware of the possible perils of using culture as an independent variable. Here are some examples of these perils, plus some techniques which can be used to avoid them.

The 'like-for-like' trap   Essentially the typical cross-cultural scenario sees the replication of original research in different cultural locations to see if similar results occur. The researcher takes several steps to ensure a high level of standardisation and control in each testing situation. In other words, she needs to ensure that, as far as possible, like is being compared with like. For example, whilst it is important that participants are from different cultural backgrounds, it should be ensured insofar as this is possible that they are of similar age, and educational level, or from a similar demographic group. It would, after all, be misleading to compare data gathered from doctors in Indonesia with those obtained from a sample of athletes in Canada.

The 'uncontrolled researcher' trap   Cross-cultural replications often involve conducting similar testing situations in different locations, often many miles apart. The practicalities of this mean that very often, different trials are conducted by different personnel, based at different universities in different countries. This additional link in the chain of communication may present a problem if all team members do not apply a standardised level of experimental control and ethical good practice. It is paramount that all the researchers apply the experimental controls of the testing scenario to the same extent.

The 'lost in translation' trap   In any controlled study it is important that all participants receive similar instructions. Typically, researchers either read out or distribute pre-prepared instruction sheets so that everyone is equally well (or badly) informed. In cross-cultural research these instructions often have to be translated into different languages. It is in the nature of language that some terms don't translate with perfect equivalence across languages. For example, the requirement to 'say the first thing that comes into your head' has varying connotations across different languages. It is sometimes conventional in this type of research to translate instructions twice, in an effort to reduce misunderstanding. First, text is translated from the original language to that of participants; secondly, it is translated back into the original by another translator to see if the original meaning is preserved. This is the *back translation* method. Besides translating researchers' instructions, the translation of what participants say during research is a task that faces just as many equivalence issues.

The 'sampling error' trap   Comparing results gathered from samples in two or more cultural settings helps cross-cultural psychologists draw conclusions about the cultural universality (or relativity) of certain behaviours. They might, for example, suggest that strategies for coping with stress differ between Scots and Rwandans. Yet conclusions like these barely conceal a serious **sampling error**. Samples used in cross-cultural research cannot reliably be treated as representative of their culture as a whole. Indeed, the realities of research often dictate that participants are drawn from the most accessible sectors of society. These may be students, since these are the people most available to psychological researchers based in universities.

The 'cultural stalemate' trap   Even the most meticulous translation and standardisation measures cannot mask the fact that there are some concepts which simply do not have equivalent meaning in different cultures. Certain concepts that are studied in original research become meaningless once they're taken into other cultural settings. Take 'stress', for example. Arguably the meaning of stress is 'situated' in western, industrialised cultures. In other words, it gains its meaning from the cultural context in which it is observed most. Thus it is very difficult to design a study in which stress levels are tested across cultures if the idea of stress is not fully recognised in some of the testing sites. This creates a kind of 'cultural stalemate'. It is better to conduct cross-cultural research using a dependent variable which is meaningful in all of the places where the study is being carried out.

Like all methods cross-cultural studies have ADVANTAGES . . .

The culture-comparison approach lends a global dimension to mainstream psychology. Too often, theories emerge from research which comes from a restricted geographical region. Cross-cultural psychology bucks this trend. A key benefit from testing theories globally is that it justifies researchers' claims that their findings can be applied to an international population. Ultimately this should help to **reduce ethnocentrism** in psychology.

Culture-comparative researchers aim to set up equivalent testing conditions in different cultural settings. This means that as much as possible, standardised procedures are used with all samples. For example, though instructions to participants are translated into various languages, attempts are made to convey equivalent meanings to all participants. This enables the cross-cultural researcher to claim that the main difference between the samples in their studies is cultural background. This high level of *empiricism* allows us to make inferences about the influence of culture on behaviour.

And DISADVANTAGES . . .

Critics of cross-cultural research sometimes refer to it as the 'transport and test' method of investigating the relationship between culture and behaviour. By this they are referring to a tendency for researchers to transport theories, often from the US or Europe, into the developing world, where they proceed to conduct research to see whether these theories are valid or not. This approach clearly has strains of **ethnocentrism**. It ignores the reality that psychology is now a global discipline and that psychologists from the developing world generate many theories of their own. Arguably, cross-cultural psychology might learn more about the concept of culture by researching 'home grown' ideas in collaboration with indigenous psychologists.

Culture-comparison studies characteristically face **the paradox of difference and equivalence**. The samples used in these studies need to satisfy rather contradictory requirements. First, they need to be *different* in relation to the independent variable, which is generally some aspect of culture. Yet they also need to be *equivalent*, or comparable, in relation to various other aspects of culture. They should be drawn from equivalent (comparable) social groups in their populations, or be matched for affluence, age and so on. This paradox arises from the researcher's desire to perform the difficult manoeuvre of isolating one aspect of culture in order to observe its effect on behaviour. The difficulty lies in the fact that a complex idea like culture is not easily dissected into its discrete, constituent parts (diet, schooling, sexuality etc.) The upshot of this paradox is that comparison groups are often used which differ not only on the *IV*, but also on a series of other, extraneous cultural variables.

Method 8 Longitudinal studies

As the name suggests, this type of study sees the research team in for the long haul. Longitudinal research involves tracking a single group of participants at regular intervals over a long period in order to assess the influence of time itself on their development, personality or behaviour. Since the same group (or *cohort*) is studied repeatedly during longitudinal research, you could say that this method is a kind of extended *Repeated Measures* study (see **Box 4A**), in which time itself is the independent variable.

> *Caspi et al. (2000) have been following up a cohort of 1000 or so participants who were born in Dunedin, New Zealand, in the early 1970s. The cohort has been regularly assessed (for example at the ages of 3, 18 and 21) and several measures of personality and behaviour have been taken. The researchers looked at alcohol dependency, and at incidents of violence and aggression, as well as taking measures of personality by questionnaire and non-participant observation. An interesting finding showed that those who were classified as 'uncontrolled' at 3 years were more likely to offend at 21.*

As this study from New Zealand illustrates, longitudinal research is useful for plotting developmental aspects of personality, and for helping researchers to establish links between incidents in early development and later behavioural manifestations.

So how would you define a 'longitudinal study'?

It's **a study in which a researcher assesses the responses of the same individual or individuals on two or more occasions during their lifetime**. Longitudinal designs can be incorporated into other research methods, such as case studies or questionnaires, whilst some studies can be regarded as explicitly and primarily longitudinal in nature. Typical longitudinal research involves the selection of a **birth cohort**, which is **a sample of participants who were born during a given time period, such as a year**. This cohort is then visited several times during their lifespan, as in the popular British TV documentary *7-UP*, in which a cohort of 22 males have been visited and interviewed every 7 years since 1964.

Are longitudinal studies qualitative or quantitative?

It varies. At each visit the cohort members may be interviewed or subjected to a series of psychometric tests relating to the variables selected for study. These variables may include cognitive, behavioural or stress-related behaviours. The rationale is that since all the participants are the same age and are likely to have similar cultural backgrounds, behavioural differences on subsequent trials might reasonably be put down to the passage of time, or to cultural changes. Links between early experience and behaviour later in life can also be established.

Doing longitudinal research effectively requires a great deal of care and attention to detail over a long period, during which several traps can halt the progress of the research. Here are a few of the most common traps, along with some tips on how to forestall them.

The 'attrition' trap   The danger of *participant attrition* – losing touch with participants during the study – is of course more real than ever in a longitudinal context. Migration, mortality and motivation (the lack of it) can all intervene and account for the loss of participants along the way. But there are steps that can be taken to reduce attrition's effects. To begin with, it is important to ensure that a fairly large sample of participants is used in the first place – enough to absorb a certain amount of natural wastage. Secondly, attrition is less likely if researchers keep regular contact with participants throughout, and give clear instructions about what is required of each participant.

The 'uncommon threads' trap   Since longitudinal research can span decades, research teams will vary in their personnel during the study. This means that extra care is taken so that as the years pass, the focus of the study remains constant. For instance, if the study began as an interview-based investigation into drug use, care should be taken that this rationale is only altered with very good reason. Ideally, to fully appreciate the effects of cultural change and the passing of time, the questions being asked by researchers should remain standard throughout, allowing common threads of data to emerge.

Like all methods longitudinal studies have ADVANTAGES . . .

The rationale of longitudinal research is to assess the effects of the passage of time and cultural change on the development of a set of individuals. This makes it an ideal method for highlighting **age-related changes** in personality and behaviour. Since the research involves detailed quantitative and qualitative data collection over a long period, it is arguably the most effective method for investigating the way age influences behaviour and personality in a given cultural setting.

Longitudinal designs are arguably a **reliable** method for investigating the effects of early experience on behaviour later in life. Compared with, say, case studies, and retrospective, historical designs, in which present behaviour and personality are seen in comparison with events in the past, the longitudinal design does not rely on memory or the recovery of historical social documents.

And DISADVANTAGES . . .

Longitudinal studies rely on data which is drawn from particular birth cohorts. In its own way this constitutes a restricted sample, which means **results cannot be generalised** to participants born in other years.

The practicalities of longitudinal research demand that time, expense and the effort of maintaining the interest and motivation of participants are all resources which are heavily drained. In other words, for all its rich data, this is an **expensive and labour-intensive** research method.

Method 9   Diary studies

Leafing through someone's diary is every psychologist's fantasy. If you want to know what someone's been up to, could there be a more reliable source than their own personal record – straight from the horse's mouth?

A diary can be an honest, intimate account of what's going on in someone's life. True, you can find out plenty about a person by observing their behaviour or reading their responses to a questionnaire, but neither of these methods produces first-hand tales, told in the participants' own words.

Most people have a go at keeping a diary. The popular technique is to compile a general, 'Captain's log' style résumé of the important events of the day. Who decides which events are important? The diarist does, and here lies a key difference between traditional diaries and the diaries psychological researchers use. In research, it's *the researcher* who decides which topics are covered in that day's entries, not the diarist.

At the beginning of a diary study the diarist – or participant – is given what's called a **target variable**. This is **the aspect of the participant's life the researcher is interested in**. From then on the diarist is expected to keep a 'one-track minded' record of their behaviour relating to that variable.

> *In a study by de Castro and de Castro (1989) participants were asked to record all their food-related behaviour for a week. Food-related behaviour was the target variable. They wrote down descriptions of their meals, where they ate, who they ate with and so on. The researchers observed a strong relationship between 'meal size' and the number of people who were present while it was being eaten.*

There's another striking difference between traditional diaries and the ones used in research. They look very different. Rather than slim, personalised little volumes, a research diary usually takes the form of a standardised set of response sheets (often completed electronically or online, blog-like) with spaces for participants to fill in each day, hour, afternoon, or whatever 'time interval' is being used. As well as having 'open-ended' spaces, these sheets often have standard questions to be answered each time the dairy is filled in.

So how would you define a **diary study**?

Often called a 'self-report', it's **a study where you ask participants to keep a personal record of their behaviour relating to a variable over a specified time period**.

Are diary studies qualitative or quantitative?

They tend to combine both. Typical diary studies have participants making descriptive entries in their diaries. They would write in detail about their behaviour relating to the target variable. This descriptive element makes it a qualitative study. Yet quantitative elements also play a part. For example, you might ask participants to record the number of times a particular behaviour occurs, or to record (say on a scale of 1 to 7, a so-called Likert scale) how strongly they feel about an event or behaviour.

What happens to the diaries once they're complete?

When the diaries have been compiled and returned to you, you can set about analysing their content.

Analysing their content? That sounds familiar.

So it should. At this point a diary study really becomes an exercise in *content analysis* (see earlier in this chapter for a full description of this). The researcher now summarises, interprets or collates the participants' diary entries. How this is done depends on the target variable.

When conducting a diary study one way of analysing data is to pick out the most common categories of behaviour, thoughts or feelings that feature in the diaries. For instance, if you were studying eating habits you might want to pick out what your participants have recorded as the most important features of a desirable eating environment. This would be a descriptive, qualitative exercise. You may also want to take quantitative measures. For instance, you might be interested in the average number of people present at each meal or how long the average meal takes to eat.

Doing diary studies effectively involves side-stepping several treacherous traps. Here are some of the most treacherous, plus some ideas on how to steer clear of them.

The 'no system' trap   This one's common to *diary studies*, *content analysis* and *field studies*. Backtrack to the section on field studies for a full explanation. The key here is to limit your research to a target variable that's easy to define, easy to measure and therefore easy to record numerically.

The 'censorship' trap   Doing effective diary research means striking a balance between freedom of expression and censorship. Allowing participants freedom to write what they want about a target variable may yield a stack of (albeit interesting) diaries that are difficult to content analyse because they're written in a multitude of individual styles. On the other hand, if diarists are prevented from expressing themselves they'll be well and truly censored. Their diaries will be nothing more than standardised (questionnaire-style) response sheets that prevent them from telling first-hand tales in their own words. So strike a balance. Design response sheets that incorporate some room for standardised responses on the target variable and some room for 'open-ended' reflections. Remember, one aim of diary research is to let participants tell their tales in their own words. So take care to preserve your diarists' own wording when recording qualitative data in your research report.

The 'great expectations' trap   However generous they are, your diarists won't care about your research as much as you do. Yes, most of them will be happy to fill out their diaries each day but don't expect them to, say, give up all their afternoons.

Ask yourself how long your response sheets take to complete. Then ask yourself how much time you can realistically ask of your participants. Half an hour a day is a lot to ask. Ten minutes is nearer the mark. It's a good idea to include, on your response sheets, clear recommendations about how much to write each day.

The 'disappearing diarists' trap   Diary research can come to a sorry end when researchers lose touch with diarists in mid-study. Response sheets are duly delivered to participants with clear instructions about what's expected of them – and that's the last you see of either of them. Disappearing diarists (or *participant attrition*) is bound to happen occasionally. But there are steps you can take to minimise it. Above all, make sure diarists have clear written instructions about what to write about, when and how to return the diaries when the deed is done, how to contact you with any queries, and so on. Also, it's a good idea for you to contact each diarist once the study is underway, just to remind them that you're interested in what they're up to.

Like all methods, diary studies have ADVANTAGES . . .

Diary studies **raise the participants' profile** in psychological research. So many methods reduce participants to the level of 'objects to be studied' (controlled experiments, field studies), whose own voices are rarely heard in the research. In diary studies participants' voices come through loud and clear. They retain some control over what is reported and the style of reporting that's used. After all, in self-report research, participants are reporting on themselves, rather than being reported on by others.

Self-report diaries give you access to **relatively private behaviours that are unobservable in the field or in the laboratory**. They give you a backstage pass into the lives of your participants. This means you can develop an interest in aspects of behaviour that are normally kept fairly private – such as diet, health, hygiene and sexual behaviour. Using a self-report method has the added advantage of allowing you to study your participants in a fairly detailed way without resorting to deception.

And DISADVANTAGES . . .

Since self-report research relies on the participants taking control of data collection, it's bound to yield **unverifiable data**. Checking how truthful or accurate diarists have been with their entries is, of course, out of the question. No second opinion is available. Perhaps this explains why diary studies remain outside the mainstream of psychological research.

Once the diaries are returned to the researcher, a process of interpreting, summarising and making sense of text can all too easily descend into **reductionism**. In other words, you may find yourself reducing the complexities of the diary entries to soundbites.

Before leaving this section let's eavesdrop on a group of psychology students to find out what they have to say in response to the question – *Why do you think these methods are so popular and practical for doing research on undergraduate psychology courses?* **Box 4D** has their answers.

Box 4D

Why do you think these methods are so popular and practical?

A popular, practical method is . . .	'I think it's popular and practical because . . .
Controlled experiment	. . . it enables you to do your study "all in one go". Once you've found yourself a room to use as a laboratory and gathered together your participants, the whole study can be done in an afternoon.'
Case study	. . . you only need one or two participants. So although you're gathering detailed data, you don't need to spend time finding lots of participants.'
Questionnaire	. . . once you've constructed your questionnaire it's a fairly straightforward task to collate your results. Also, using questionnaires means you can combine the quantitative and qualitative approaches.'
Field study	. . . it enables you to do your study in the real world, like in a shopping mall or in the street. This means that as long as you don't inconvenience anyone, you can do your study "undercover".'
Content analysis	. . . you find out a lot about TV programmes, magazines or whatever it is you're studying. You can look "behind the headlines" and "inbetween the lines" of what journalists and programme makers are really saying.'
Correlational study	. . . you can draw links between variables that move up and down together and you can measure the size of the link. Plus, you don't actually have to assemble any participants. You can use crime figures and such like.'
Diary studies	. . . you get to hear how participants describe what they're doing and how they feel about it. You can hear they're way of putting it. It's more personal, somehow.'

Now you have some idea about *how* you're going to do your study, it's time you turned your thoughts to *who* you're going to study.

● 3 Selecting participants for research

Unless you're doing a content analysis (in which case you won't need any participants) or a case study (where you'll need precious few) your next job is to find a sample of participants to study. Whether you're planning a controlled experiment, a questionnaire or a field study, you'll need to consider who your participants are going to be and how you're going to get hold of them.

One thing's for sure. You can't study everyone. It would take too long. Instead, you need to find yourself a select group of participants to take part in your research. This select group will be your **sample**. The art of selecting them is called **sampling**.

How about going out and picking the first twenty people I bump into?

You could do that. But it's risky. The first twenty people you bump into will probably include quite a few representatives from some groups in society and hardly any representatives from others. You might bump into fifteen men and only five women. Or twenty people without disabilities. Or a marching band. So you might end up with **a group of participants that over-represents some groups in the population and under-represents others**. This is what we call an **unrepresentative sample**. It's your job to find a way of stopping yourself from selecting this kind of sample.

In this section I'm going to suggest four ways of avoiding unrepresentative samples. First though, there are three groups of people I really must introduce you to. No doubt you yourself are a member of at least one of these groups.

Samples, sampling populations and populations

Introducing *Group A*, **the sample**. These are **the participants you'll study in your research**.

Introducing *Group B*, **the sampling population**. These are the people who are *in danger* of being selected as participants for your research. This is **the group who you'll draw your sample from**. If you're doing your study at a university, you're drawing your sample from a sampling population of the students from a particular university. If you're doing your study at a leisure centre, your sampling population is the users of a particular leisure centre.

Introducing *Group C*, **the population**. These are **the group to whom the results of your study will apply**. If you're doing a study about problem-solving amongst university students, you'll no doubt want to apply your results to a population of 'all normal problem- solving adults'. If you're doing a study about courtship and flirting behaviour amongst leisure centre users, you'll probably go on to apply your results to a population of 'normal adults'.

Psychology's best kept secret

Now stop. Look again at *Groups B* and *C*. They're not quite the same are they? *Group B* is smaller than group *C*. Psychology's best kept secret is that researchers regularly draw their samples from a particular, restricted sampling population. Namely, university undergraduates. Then they go on to apply their results to a population of 'all normal adults'. You could say they're shooting themselves in the foot by doing this, since they're bound to end up doing research on unrepresentative samples of participants. So why do they do it? They do it because psychological research takes place in universities and universities are teeming with undergraduates. They're widely available. For this reason some critics of psychology have mischievously altered its name from *the study of human behaviour and experience* to *the study of undergraduate behaviour and experience.*

Four ways to select a representative sample

Having exposed psychology's best kept secret, let's get back to the business of selecting a sample of participants that neither under-represents, nor over-represents, any particular social group. Here are four popular sampling methods

Method 1 Simple random sampling

When you use this method **everyone in your sampling population has an equal chance of being selected** as a participant. Note that this isn't the same as saying that everyone in the population has an equal chance of being selected. Populations are bigger than sampling populations, remember? However, the bigger your sampling population is, the more representative of the population as a whole your sample will be. Here are some techniques of doing random sampling:

> The *'college roll' technique* is useful if you're using your college as your sampling population. It's a bit restricted, but very convenient. Simply give everyone on the roll a number, then select a random sample of numbers. Most spreadsheet or statistics software packages incorporate a *random number generator*. You'll find a *random number table* in **Appendix 2**. Alternatively, do it manually. Have all the names from the roll on bits of paper and pick a sample of them out of a hat. Or a box, if you're working in a big college. This technique works well for controlled experiments.

> The *'electoral roll' technique* is useful if you're looking for a sampling population that covers your community, rather than just your college. Virtually every adult is on the electoral roll (this isn't true of, say, your local phone book, which omits non-phone-owners and subscribers who have chosen to be 'ex-directory'). Once you've got hold of a copy of the electoral roll for your area, use any of the methods I suggested in the previous paragraph for selecting your random sample (although this method's a bit beyond the scope of the 'names out of a hat' method). This technique works well for questionnaire studies.

Method 2 Stratified random sampling

This method is similar to simple random sampling, with an additional, preliminary phase. Before selecting your sample you do a little detective work on your sampling population. You find out its proportions, according to certain variables that you think are relevant to your study. For example, if you're doing a gender-related study you might take the trouble to find out that 50% of your sampling population are male, 50% female. Or if you're doing a health-related study you might take the trouble to find out that 30% of your sampling population are smokers, 70% non-smokers.

Following this preliminary, detective stage, you go on to select your participants, taking care to **reproduce, in your sample, the proportions that exist in your sampling population**. So let's say you want a sample of 50 participants. In the case of the gender-related study you separate your sampling population into males and females, then randomly choose 25 of each (using any if the methods I suggested in the simple random sampling section). For the health-related study you'd randomly select 35 participants from the non-smoking contingent and 15 from the smoking contingent.

Stratified random sampling works well with any method so long as you're able to find out the proportions that make up your sampling population. True, it requires some extra detective work, but this helps you to make sure that certain groups that are relevant to your study are fairly represented in your sample.

Method 3   Systematic random sampling

Again this method is simple random sampling with a difference. Instead of selecting your sample from your sampling population by using some form of *random number generation*, you do it by nominating a *system* by which you select every 5th, 10th, or whatever number you prefer-th, member of your sample population until you have enough participants for your study. For instance, you might select every 10th name on your college roll, every 17th person who walks down a corridor. You might even call at every third house in your street. This method works well with research that takes place in the field, though it's a fair method for using with questionnaires and controlled experiments, too.

Method 4   Quota sampling

If you don't have any details about the proportions that make up your sampling population (for example, if you haven't had time to do the necessary detective work), **quota sampling** could be for you. As with stratified random sampling, the aim here is to **reproduce, in your sample, the proportions that exist in your sampling population**. But unlike stratified random sampling, you do it **without knowing the proportions that exist in your sampling population**.

Hang on. How can you reproduce the proportions of something you don't know the proportions of?

Easy. Guesswork. Make an informed guess. Again, let's say you're looking for a sample of 50 participants. In the case of gender you can make an informed guess that 50% of your sampling population are female, 50% male. Then, when you've done your guessing, you go ahead and find yourself 25 males and 25 females to do your research on. These are your quotas. Or in the case of smoking you can make an informed guess that 30% of your sampling population smoke, 70% don't. Then you go ahead and select quotas of 35 non-smokers and 15 smokers.

So quota sampling is based on 'informed guesswork' rather than detective work, right?

Right. It's different from stratified random sampling in another way, too. Once you've decided (guessed) how many representatives you want from each group, instead of selecting them randomly you go out and pick the first, say, 25 males you come across, or the first 25 females. You could say that, once you've decided on the size of your quotas, all you're doing is choosing the first 25 people you bump into.

Now let's do some more eavesdropping. This time on a group of first-year under-graduate psychology students who are discussing the merits and demerits of different sampling methods. See **Box 4E**.

Box 4E

What are the merits and demerits of the different sampling methods?

	'One of its merits is . . .	'One of its demerits is . . .
Simple random sampling	. . . its 'randomness'. Everyone in your sampling population has an equal chance of being picked'.	. . . you can get an unrepresentative sample because you don't take into account the proportions in the sampling population'.
Stratified random sampling	. . . that in relation to a variable like gender you can make the proportions in your sample the same as those in your sampling population'.	. . . that you can only use it if you know all about the make-up of your sampling population'.
Systematic random sampling	. . . it stops you choosing people who you like the look of and avoiding people who you don't like the look of. You have to follow your system'.	. . . it could produce unrepresentative samples. Like if you chose every 10th house on a street and they were all even numbers. They might all be on the posh side of the street'.
Quota sampling	. . . you don't need to know the make-up of your sampling population and you still get a pretty representative sample'.	. . . it's a bit unreliable because you have to guess the proportions of your sampling population. You might guess wrong'.

Now you've chosen your sample, it's time think about how to treat them *ethically* during your research.

● 4 Treating participants ethically

Post-traumatic stress disorder (PTSD) affects people who've been exposed to distress-ing incidents. Fires and floods are typical examples. People who experience PTSD find it hard to expel the incident from their thoughts. They have bad dreams and flash-backs. In a word, they're traumatised. In 1980 American psychiatrists included PTSD in their directory of psychiatric disorders'- the *Diagnostic and Statistical Manual (DSM)* – for the first time. Inclusion in the *DSM* made PTSD a properly recognised mental illness. People had always suffered from it, but now it was official.

PTSD isn't like other psychiatric disorders. It has a different legal status from all the other 550 or so conditions in the *DSM*. Unlike depression, schizophrenia and the rest, legally speaking you can trace the onset of PTSD back to a specific incident. This means you can blame its onset on whoever was responsible for exposing you to the incident, then try and claim compensation. Employees regularly sue employers on these grounds. Some day someone will blame their bad dreams or flashbacks on an incident they were exposed to not by an employer, but by a psychological researcher whilst participating in one of their studies.

Eight steps to ethical research in psychology

To make sure your research doesn't end this way, observe the **eight guidelines for treating human participants ethically** outlined in this section as you do your study.

Guideline One   When writing your research report avoid mentioning participants' names. They'll be happier to take part in your research (and for you to write
   about what they did) if you guarantee, before your study starts, that you'll respect their **ANONYMITY**. Tell your participants **'Rest assured, your names won't be used when we write our research report'**.

Guideline Two   If you're doing overt research (where participants know they're being studied) inform your participants what the study involves and about any incon-venience they're likely to suffer. Do this before the study starts. If they know what they're letting themselves in for they can give you their **INFORMED CONSENT**. However, there may be some things you don't want to divulge, since doing so might lead participants to behave unnaturally. In cases like this, let your participants know they're not being told everything. This gives them the option to withdraw. If the partic-ipants are children, consent has to be obtained from whoever's responsible for them. Tell your participants **'Since the aims of our study require you to behave natu-rally, we're keeping some of its procedures secret. But rest assured, you're in no danger. However, if you're concerned about not being fully informed, feel free to withdraw at any stage'**.

Guideline Three   Most psychological researchers conceal some details about their research from their participants. Some degree of **DECEPTION** is commonplace, espe-cially where it's reasonable to assume that complete openness might lead to unnatu-ral behaviour. But how far should you go? How do you decide how much deception to employ? To help answer these questions there are two groups of people you can consult before your study begins. First, people of a similar age and background to your participants. Secondly, your own fellow researchers. Ask people from both groups if *they* think you're deceiving your participants in a way that could cause them anxiety if they were to find out about it at a future date. If they say you're overstepping the mark, alter your design. Say to your colleagues *'Here's an outline of what we intend to do in our research. If you were a participant in this study, would you be anxious about the level of deception involved?'*

Guideline Four   Leave participants as you found them by giving them a thorough **DEBRIEFING** after the study is done. Try to ensure that anyone who takes part in your study feels as comfortable with themselves (and with psychological research) as they did beforehand. All experiences affect us in some way, so they won't feel exactly the same as they did before taking part. But by explaining the true aims of your study and thanking them for their co-operation you can ensure that your participants don't walk away with bad memories, muttering to themselves about how they'll never take part in psychological research again. Tell your participants *'Thanks for your time and co-operation. If you'd like to know more about the true aims of our study I'll be happy to go over them with you. If you'd like a copy of our research report, remember to leave us your e-mail address before you leave. Do take a biscuit on your way out'*.

   Guideline Five   The politeness of some participants is such that even if they're experiencing pain and distress during your study, they won't say anything, not wanting to rock the boat. Suffering in silence like this is clearly of benefit to no-one. You can't prevent it altogether, but you can make it less likely. Before your study begins, explain clearly to your participants that they have the **RIGHT TO WITH-DRAW** *at any stage*. And if, at any stage, you feel that your participants are experiencing pain and distress, close it down. Don't just grit your teeth and hang on until the end. Err on the side of caution. Tell your participants *'As it says in our briefing document, if you begin to feel uneasy about anything that happens during our study you can withdraw at any stage. And if, after the study is finished, you'd prefer us not use the data relating to your behaviour, we'll be happy to withdraw and destroy them there and then '*.

Guideline Six   Be sure to inform your participants that anything you find out about them during your study will be treated with **CONFIDENTIALITY**. Assurances like these are especially important when you're dealing with responses to questionnaires about sensitive subjects (religion, sex, food etc.). Tell your participants *'As it says in our briefing document, you can rest assured that any information you provide during our study will be treated in confidence'*. If, however, one of your participants commits a misdemeanour or felony (theft, violence, damage etc.) during your study, you're within your rights to break this confidence.

Guideline Seven   A recent change in psychological terminology has seen researchers adopt the term 'participant', rather than 'subject', to refer to the members of their sample. This signals a change in attitude, too. Researchers are keener to see those who take part in their studies as having feelings and rights. The old 'it's alright to *subject* people and animals to physical and psychological discomfort, so long as it's in the interests of science' attitude is thankfully on the wane. ***PROTECTION OF PARTICIPANTS*** is de rigueur ('required behaviour', i.e. essential). So it's up to you to protect your participants from any discomfort during your study. One of way of showing your concern is to find out, before your study begins, if anyone taking part in your study has a medical condition that might put them at risk. Tell your participants *'Rest assured, during our study you won't experience any more physical or mental stress than you would if you weren't taking part. Remember, you can raise the alarm if you do experience any discomfort at any stage. We'll be on hand if you need us. Also, if anyone has any of the medical conditions listed on our briefing document, please let us know before we start'.*

Guideline Eight   Doing research involving **COVERT PARTICIPATION** means dealing with a peculiar set of circumstances. You can't obtain consent from your participants. Deception is inevitable. The right to withdraw is inapplicable. Debriefing is impractical. So how can you do a covert field study ethically? As a rule of thumb you should ensure that you don't study participants in situations where they aren't on public view *in any case*. Since most of these studies take place in public places like malls or cafes, you shouldn't have any problems there. If your study involves intervening in what your participant is doing (as in many field experiments) rather than just observing them (as in field observations) make sure you don't have them doing anything they wouldn't be likely to do in the normal course of events. Asking someone the time, or for assistance in crossing a road, is fine. Stealing their shopping isn't.

How to produce a briefing document

Treating participants with courtesy, gratitude and consideration makes sense twice over. First, they'll be more likely to behave naturally. Secondly, they'll be more likely to volunteer to take part in psychological research again. The last thing you want is a sample of seething, short-tempered participants, desperate for clear instructions about what they're meant to be doing and how long they're expected to hang around. Remember, these people don't have to take part in your study. So in the interests of keeping them well-informed it's a good idea to present them with a **briefing document** before your study begins.

*What's a **briefing document**?*

The aim here is to answer some of the questions participants typically ask about something which is, after all, an unusual situation for them. The scope of the document will vary according to the kind of study you're doing, but generally it will include:

- Advice about medical conditions that might put them at risk if they take part.

- Assurances about anonymity, confidentiality and their right to withdraw.
- Information about the level of deception in your study.
- Information about the aims of your study.
- Instructions about what they're expected to do during the study.
- Your email address, in case participants want a copy of your research report.
- Your gratitude for their time and effort.

Apart from making everyone feel more at ease, your briefing document saves you the headache of having to remember to make a series of announcements at the beginning of the study. Much easier to have it all pre-prepared. Plus, it gives you an air of professionalism that ought to make your participants take you and your research seriously.

If you treat your participants ethically the chances of them walking away from your study with bad memories of what you put them through will be slim. By treating people right you can uphold the reputation of psychological researchers as a communicative, considerate, competent bunch who don't mean any harm. As a representative of a bunch with a reputation like that, you ought to find willing participants for future studies easier to come by.

What about the ethics of doing research on animals?

Psychological research using non-humans has its own set of ethical guidelines. Since I'm writing for students on undergraduate courses which – (I assume) – only use human participants, I'm skipping these guidelines here. If you want to know more about the ethics of doing research with non-humans *or* human participants, publications by the British Psychological Society – 'Guidelines for the use of animals in research' and *Ethical Principles for Conducting Research with Human Participants* – should tell you all you need to know.

Let's conclude this section by eavesdropping on a group of psychology students who are discussing ethical issues relating to three familiar studies. See **Box 4F**.

You've done your ethical research. Now it's time to encapsulate it in your *Research Report*.

● 5 Writing your research report

However skilfully you design and execute your study, you'll gain most of your marks for the way you write it up. Writing research reports isn't like writing essays. True, there are similarities. You need a similar level of detail. The word limit is similar (around 2000 words on most undergraduate courses, though it varies). The big difference is, research reports follow a recommended format. There's a set of conventions for dividing them into predetermined sections. Although following the format isn't compulsory, it's conventional on most courses, so I'm going to stick to it here.

Box 4F

Did these researchers treat their participants ethically?

Latane and Darley's laboratory experiment (1968)	'Not really. For one thing they deceived them by not initially revealing the true aims of the study. Though if they had they might not have acted naturally. For another thing, the smoke coming out of the wall might have been traumatic. Especially if there were any pyrophobics in the sample.' (See p. 100 for an outline of this study.)
Niens et al.'s questionnaire study (2003)	'Frankly, yes. Although the participants weren't fully aware that the study was about Allport's "contact theory", they did know it was about religious tensions. Also they weren't likely to be harmed and the questionnaire scripts were filled in anonymously.' (See p. 110 for an outline of this study.)
Middlemist et al.'s field experiment (1976)	'Definitely not. Being a typical field experiment, no consent was obtained. Although these toilets were public, it isn't really the kind of place you expect to be observed. It's in that public–private "neither-world". What's more, it can be traumatic to crowd someone whilst the are trying to "go". Also, I bet there was no debriefing. Would you want to debrief someone after a study like that?' (p. 114 has an outline of this study).

Before guiding you through the format though, let me introduce you to the kind of pearl of wisdom that might easily fall out of a cracker at the British Psychological Society Annual Party

> *Effective Research Reports should be written clearly enough for the reader to replicate the research without asking for any further clarifications.*

If you say these words to yourself before you start writing your report, then again at regular intervals whilst you're writing it, your work will be better for it. The recommended format for a *2000-word* report goes like this

Your *TITLE* shouldn't just tell your readers what your research is about. It should tell them which variables you're studying. So *The relationship between gender and the criteria we use for making moral decisions* is a more informative title than, say, *An investigation into moral dilemmas.*

Abstract

Your *Abstract* summarises your report. When you pick up a book in a shop you base your decision about whether or not to buy it on the blurb on the back. Abstracts have a similar function. They provide a summary, in around *150 words*, of the aim of your study, its method, the make-up of your sample, and your findings (including, where appropriate, the outcome of any inferential statistical tests you've done). After reading your Abstract your reader should be able to make an informed decision about whether to bother reading your entire report. Although the Abstract appears at the beginning of your report, some students prefer to write it last, since by then they're able to take a step back and summarise what they've done.

Introduction

Your *Introduction* is the first long section in your report, at around *500 words*. An effective Introduction does three jobs. It explains the background to your study, its aims, and your expectations about its findings.

Explain the background to your study by giving your reader a round-up of the relevant psychological research into the area you're studying. It's the convention to move from the general to the particular. In other words, set the scene first, then get to the specifics. Start by introducing the general psychological concepts you're dealing with (and describe some theories or studies that relate to them), then introduce the specific concepts your research addresses (and again, describe some related studies and theories). An example of a general psychological concept is 'prejudice'. A specific concept would be 'prejudice towards particular racial groups.'

To explain the *aims* of your study set out your research rationale and relate it to the research you described in the first part of your Introduction. Show how research by other psychologists leaves a gap in our understanding that still needs to be filled. Your study is an attempt to fill this gap.

To explain your *expectations* about the outcome of your study, spell out your *hypothesis* (see the section on *proving* in Chapter 1 for a full discussion of hypotheses). This is the culmination of your Introduction. You've written generally about the background to your study, now finish with a specific prediction about what you expect to find. An effective hypothesis is **operational**. This means it should **clearly state the variables that appear in your research**. An hypothesis like *There will be less inter-group tension between participants who know each other better* is too vague. A clearer, more operational hypothesis would be *Participants will show more positive inter-group attitudes when they have more contact with out-group members.*

If your reader is still in the dark about what your research is about and what you expect to find after reading your Introduction, something has gone badly wrong.

Method

Your *Method* should be written *clearly enough for the reader to replicate your research without asking for any further clarifications*. Here's where that pearl of wisdom comes into its own. This is the instruction manual section of your report. It's where your readers find out how they can do your research for themselves. The Method should be around **250 words** long. It's conventional to break it up into four sections:

1   **The design**   Here, set out the structure of your study. Describe what *method* you used, how many *conditions* you had and how you divided your participants into conditions. Did you use the *Independent, Repeated Measures* or *Matched Pairs* design? Say also what your *independent* and *dependent variables* were. You should also explain what measures you used to control any *extraneous variables*. Did you, for example, use *counterbalancing*? (See the section on *controlled experiments* earlier in this chapter for a fuller discussion of all these design concepts.)

2   **The sample**   Explain *which* sampling population you drew your participants from, *how many* of them were in each condition and *how* you selected them. Explain which *sampling method* you used. (See earlier in this chapter for a round-up of these *sampling methods.*)

3   **The materials**   What equipment or props would a would-be researcher need, to replicate your study? Set this out either as a list or as a short description, so long as it includes all the necessary items. The usual suspects are things like *briefing documents* (see the section on *ethics*, earlier in this chapter, for more on these), stopwatches, questionnaires, word lists, white-boards, calculators . . .

4   **The procedure**   This is a concise, step-by-step account of how you did your study. As always, employ a written style that's explicit, unambiguous and uncluttered. Don't complicate your *procedure* with your feelings about how you think it went. Just say what you did. Include word-for-word transcriptions of any instructions you gave to your participants. If you used a *questionnaire* don't forget to outline how you wrote it.

Results

Your **Results** section sets out, in around **300 words**, what you found from your research. This word limit doesn't include tables or graphs. As for raw data and statistical calculations, save them for your Appendix. It's conventional to divide this section into two parts. If you're doing quantitative research your report will only be complete if it has *parts 1* and *2*. If you're doing qualitative research, include *part 1* only.

1   **Describing the results**   Present your findings in a way that's easy to understand and easy on the eye. Start by outlining your main findings *in words*. Either use point form or write clearly laid out paragraphs, whichever you're most   comfortable with.

     If you're doing *qualitative* research, illustrate your description with key observations or quotes from your participants. If you're doing *quantitative* research, use key numerical findings to illustrate your description – for example, measures of **central tendency** (showing average scores) and

dispersion (showing how well spread your scores are). Also, support your descriptions of *quantitative* findings with other **descriptive statistics** (*Chapter 5* has a full discussion of these). This means using one or two charts, graphs or tables where you feel they add to the clarity of your descriptions. Present them attractively and label them so clearly that someone with a poor attention span, hardly any patience and no interest in psychology can make sense of them.

2   ***Analysing the results***   Here, deal with any **inferential statistical test** you use to support your findings. Chapter 5 has a detailed guide to using these. The aim of this part of your report is to answer three burning questions for your reader. First, which **inferential test** did you use? Second, why did you select this **inferential test** ahead of all the others? Third, did the outcome of this **inferential test** give statistical support for your findings? The conventions involved in answering these and other burning questions about **inferential tests** are dealt with in Chapter 5, so I won't dwell on them here.

Discussion

Your ***Discussion*** is the second long section in your report, at around **500 words**. Your first long section, the Introduction, moved from generally familiarising your reader with your research area to dealing with the particulars of your study. Your Discussion does the reverse. Here you're going to re-state what your particular study found, then relate it to the general research area. So your research report should have a kind of 'zoom in–zoom out' feel to it.

Start by *re-stating your findings*. Say whether your hypothesis is supported or not (remember, hypotheses aren't proved or disproved, they're supported or rejected – see Chapter 1 for a detailed discussion of this).

Next, *relate what you've found to other researchers' findings*. Do your results support or challenge what other psychologists have found? Your aim here is to place your own research back into the context you plucked it from in your Introduction. You've zoomed in, now you're zooming out. For instance, Middlemist et al. (see the section on *ethics* in this chapter for more on this study) might include the following statement in this part of their discussion – *The findings from our work in public conveniences are supported by a number of other studies that have looked at the effects of stress. An example of such a study is . . .*

Next, *evaluate your study and suggest how, if you did it again, you might alter its design.* As a guide to evaluating your research use *the DRREEEEEAAAMS system*. You'll find a detailed explanation of this Chapter 3. Although *DRREEEEEAAAMS* is designed to help you pick out positive and negative features of research, when applying it to your own study, err on the critical side. Identify weaknesses in your research, then suggest some possible modifications to the design. Middlemist et al. might, for instance, say something like – *Although we did our observations in a 'public' toilet, you could say it was unethical because you don't normally expect to be observed in such a setting. If we repeat this study it might be better to observe the effect of stress on a truly public activity, such as giving directions or reading a newspaper.*

Finally, *suggest some uses for your research findings and some ideas for future studies into your chosen topic.* Your aim here is to convince your reader that your research contributes to psychology's grand project of promoting human welfare. Middlemist et al. might argue that *Research of this kind has implications for education. Educationalists could benefit from understanding how putting people in stressful situations can adversely affect their performance. It could explain why some 'bright' students perform poorly in examinations.*

References

Your **Reference** section should include all the books and articles you've referred to in your report. Chapter 3 has a guide to the conventions of referencing.

Appendices

Your **Appendix** section is a repository for all the bits and pieces you want your tutor, lecturer, examiner to see, though you feel they're too rough and ready for the main

---

Box 4G

What are the most common mistakes in each section of a research report?

Title	'Being vague. In other words, not stating the variables that the research is dealing with.'
Abstract	'Forgetting to put the results in. An abstract is meant to include the results, plus the outcome of any statistical tests. Plenty of students miss this out.'
Introduction	'Missing the hypothesis off the end. This is a common error and it's such a shame because the hypothesis is meant to be what the introduction is leading up to. Would you tell a joke with no punch line?'
Method	'Omitting important details from the procedure, so that anyone wanting to do a replication wouldn't have a clue.'
Results	'Badly labelled graphs and tables. In other words, descriptive statistics which are only decipherable to the person that wrote the report.'
Discussion	'Overly hurried work. Since this is the last big section, students tend to fluff it by doing it in a hurry. They can see the end in sight, I suppose.'
References	'Leaving it out altogether – which is peculiar, since it's simple to do and it does gain a couple of marks.'
Appendices	'Unlabelled data and questionnaires that aren't referred to in the main report.'

body of your report. Include raw data, examples of questionnaires, transcriptions of broadcasts or interviews, instructions to researchers or participants, briefing documents (see the section on *ethics* in this chapter for a guide to these), stimulus materials, calculations from statistical tests, photographs – whatever you feel is necessary to supplement your report. Most importantly, be sure to label whatever you include and refer to it in your main report.

Let's end this section with a final bit of eavesdropping. This time, on an email discussion between a group of psychology tutors. They're considering some common mistakes made by students when writing research reports. See **Box 4G**.

Now you've selected your *research rationale*, settled on a *method*, picked your *participants*, studied them *ethically* and all but written your *research report*, your study is just about done – unless you need help with your **descriptive** and **inferential statistics**. In which case you'll be needing Chapter 5.

5 Using Statistics in Psychology

To newcomers in psychology it isn't entirely obvious why there's any need to develop statistical skills in a social science that's meant to be about human behaviour. In fact, many psychologists who prefer to do qualitative research have very little to do with statistics. But as you'll have realised from reading Chapter 4, it's very common for psychologists to measure human behaviour quantitatively, and whenever behaviour is measured thus, skills for using statistics are high on the agenda.

This chapter is a guide to how and why statistics are useful for studying psychology. It provides you with as many statistical skills as you'll need, to prosper at undergraduate level. A calculator will be handy now and again. Expertise in mathematics will be surplus to requirements.

Users Guide to Chapter 5

● 1 Two kinds of statistics

Not all psychologists use statistics. If you're doing qualitative research you might prefer to describe your findings in words – without graphs, tables or numbers. But wherever there's a quantitative aspect to your research you'll find some of the skills in this chapter useful.

Imagine a pair of psychology undergraduates doing their research. Call them Terry and Geri. They've chosen their *research rationale*, settled on a *method*, picked their *participants*, studied them *ethically* and all but written their *research reports*. Their research is nearly done. All that remains is for them to dabble in two kinds of statistics so they can complete their study and put the finishing touches to their research reports. These two kinds of statistics have different uses. They look different on paper. They have different names. One is called **descriptive statistics**, the other **inferential statistics**. This chapter is a guide to their use.

First, let's take a look at Terry and Geri's research.

> *Terry and Geri did a modified version of Latane and Darley's controlled experiment, which looked at participants' reactions to an emergency situation. As you may recall, half of Latane and Darley's participants were asked to fill in a questionnaire individually, whilst the other half completed theirs in a group situation. So the Independent Variable (IV) was 'other people'. Latane and Darley pumped steam (mimicking smoke) through a grille in a wall of the experimental room and recorded how long it took participants to raise the alarm. So the Dependent Variable (DV) was 'response time'.*
>
> *Terry and Geri modified Latane and Darley's study by replacing the IV of 'other people' with an IV of 'gender'. Condition A consisted of 25 males, Condition B 25 females. All the participants completed their questionnaires individually, alone in a room. They introduced another modification too, for practical reasons. Instead of using Latane and Darley's 'smoking grille effect', Terry and Geri created their emergency by sounding their college fire alarm. Their research rationale was **A study to find out if there's a difference between the average response times of males and females in an emergency situation**. This converted into an experimental hypothesis that predicted: **There will be a difference between the average response times of male and female participants in an emergency situation**. What they found is shown in **Box 5A**.*

Box 5A shows Terry and Geri's **raw scores**. This term is used by psychologists to refer to **research results that are yet to have descriptive or inferential statistics applied to them**. When you see raw scores from a psychology study you usually see every single participant's score, presented in the form of lists. You'll notice that the scores have been set out in order, from lowest to highest. Otherwise, these raw scores are 'unsummarised'. They're yet to be subjected to the rigours of our **two kinds of statistics**.

Box 5A

Response times for Terry and Geri's participants, measured in seconds

Condition A (male)
4, 5, 5, 6, 8, 8, 8, 8, 9, 9, 10, 10, 10, 10, 11, 11, 11, 11, 11, 11, 12, 12, 13, 14, 14

Condition B (female)
1, 1, 3, 3, 4, 4, 5, 5, 6, 6, 6, 6, 7, 7, 7, 7, 8, 8, 8, 8, 10, 11, 12, 18, 21

Introducing descriptive and inferential statistics

Isn't it high time to explain what these 'two kinds of statistics' are?

Descriptive statistics are used by researchers to make raw scores easier to digest. They're used to **encapsulate the most important findings from a study** in manageable, bite-size chunks, as an alternative to presenting readers with long lists of raw data. Descriptive statistics are good news for anyone who reads research reports, since they reduce large amounts of data to much smaller helpings. They also make data more presentable, easier on the eye. In short, they summarise. A common use of descriptive statistics is to show the *average score* of a group of participants, rather than showing every individual score. So in their *research report* Terry and Geri might include the *average response times* for males and females, rather than simply listing all fifty raw scores and letting you work it out for yourself.

   Inferential statistics are used for reasons associated less with presentation and more with confidence. When researchers come up with an experimental hypothesis they make a prediction about how a sample of participants will behave in a certain situation. If the research findings support the prediction, they'll conclude – with a high degree of confidence – that everyone in their population would behave in a similar way in a similar situation. In other words, they'll generalise their findings from their sample to their population.

   Researchers make predictions about the effect of independent variables (*IVs*) on dependent variables (*DVs*). Typically they predict that a change in the value of their *DV* will be attributable to a change in the value of their *IV*, whilst extraneous variables (*EVs*) are held constant (the section on *laboratory experiments* in Chapter 4 has a detailed explanation of these variables).

> *Terry and Geri are researching the effect of gender (IV) and response time (DV). If their findings support their hypothesis they'll conclude that any differences in the response times of their two conditions are attributable to gender. Furthermore, they'll conclude that these differences exist in the population as well as in their sample.*

But wait. Isn't there a problem with making conclusions like these?

Yes, there is. What if the difference in the response times of Terry and Geri's conditions isn't due to gender at all? What if it's due to something else? Chance, for instance. What if, just by chance, their female condition reacts more quickly than their male condition? After all, even if they'd used two male groups (instead of a male group and a female group) there'd almost certainly be some difference between the reaction times of the two groups – owing to chance, random variation.

So how can Terry and Geri defend themselves against the claim that the difference in the value of their *DV* between the two conditions isn't attributable to their *IV*, but to chance, random variation? The answer is, by using **inferential statistics**.

Researchers use **inferential statistics** to **demonstrate that a change in the value of a dependent variable can be confidently attributed to a change in the value of an independent variable, rather than to chance, random variation**. Inferential statistics enable researchers to be more confident about generalising their findings from a sample to a population.

Sounds like a useful safety net. So how do inferential statistics work?

The second section of this chapter is a guide to skills for using inferential statistics in psychological research. First though, a guide to the other kind of statistics.

● **2 Using descriptive statistics in psychology**

Descriptive statistics reduce large amounts of data to smaller, more manageable helpings. A common way of doing this is to work out the average, middle or most typical score for a group of participants in a study. This enables you to condense a long list of raw scores to a single value. These **average, middle or most typical scores for a set** are called **measures of central tendency**.

Three measures of central tendency

The mean is the **average score for a set**. To calculate the mean for a set of scores,

---

Box 5B

Working out the mean for *Condition A* in Terry and Geri's study

Step 1 *Add up all the scores in the set.*

4 + 5 + 5 + 6 + 8 + 8 + 8 + 8 + 9 + 9 + 10 + 10 + 10 + 10 + 11 + 11 + 11 + 11 + 11 + 11 + 12 + 12 + 13 + 14 + 14 = 241

Step 2 *Divide the total by the number of scores in the set.*

241 ÷ 25 = 9.64

The mean response time for males in Terry and Geri's study is 9.64 seconds.

add up all the scores in the set, then divide your total by the number of scores in the set. **Box 5B** shows how to work out the mean for Terry and Geri's male condition.

The Median is the **middle score in a set**. To work out the median, set out all the scores in a set in sequence, from lowest to highest. The median value is the number that lies half way along the sequence. So if there are five scores in a set, the median is the *third* number in the sequence. **Box 5C** shows you how to calculate the median for Terry and Geri's males.

Box 5C

Working out the median for *Condition A* in Terry and Geri's study

Step 1   Set out all the scores in the set in order, from lowest to highest.

4, 5, 5, 6, 8, 8, 8, 8, 9, 9, 10, 10, 10, 10, 11, 11, 11, 11, 11, 11, 12, 12, 13, 14, 14

Step 2   Find the number that lies at the midpoint in the set.

4, 5, 5, 6, 8, 8, 8 ,8, 9, 9, 10, 10, *10*, 10, 11,11, 11, 11, 11, 11, 12, 12, 13, 14, 14

The median response time for males in this study is 10 seconds.

Wait a minute. What happens if you have a set that has an even number of scores in it? How do you find the middle value in a set of, say, six scores?

Good question. In cases like these the median value is halfway between the *middle two numbers*. So in a set of six scores like 3, 4, 6, 7, 8, 9 the median is halfway between 6 and 7. So it's 6.5.

The mode is the **most typical score for a set**. To spot the mode in a set, simply see which value occurs most frequently. **Box 5D** shows the mode for Terry and Geri's males.

Box 5D

Working out the mode for Condition A in Terry and Geri's study

Simply find the most commonly occurring score in the set.

4, 5, 5, 6, 8, 8, 8, 8, 9, 9, 10, 10, 10, 10, **11, 11, 11, 11, 11, 11**, 12, 12, 13, 14, 14

The mode response time for males in Terry and Geri's experiment is 11 seconds.

Wait. What if you have a set of scores that has two most frequently occurring values; for example: 3, 6, 6, 6, 7, 8, 8, 8? How do you select the mode then?

Unusual cases like these are called **bi-modal sets**; **a set of scores that has two modal scores**. Another unusual case is where you have a set of scores with **no mode**. For example, in a set like *4, 5, 6, 7, 8, 9*. Here you'd have to say there's *no modal score*.

Mean, median and mode complement each other

If you've had your eyes peeled you'll have noticed that these three measures of central tendency give three different values for the scores in Terry and Geri's male condition. Since the mean, median and mode are all worked out differently, this shouldn't be too much of a surprise. In fact, although mean, median and mode are all measures of central tendency, they don't all do the same thing. They each reveal something different about the set. The mean reveals the average score. The median reveals the middle score. The mode reveals the most typical score. And since each one tells us something that the other two don't, you could say the mean, median and mode complement each other.

Mean is a popular measure of central tendency, but median and mode are useful too

Occasionally the mean, median and mode are all the same. This happens when a set of scores approximates to **normal distribution**. This 'special case' comes up for discussion later in this section, so I won't dwell on it here. For now it's sufficient to say that when your research throws up a set of scores you have a choice of three measures for working out its central tendency. You might choose to use one of them, two of them, or all three. The choice you make will depend on what you want to know about your scores. Researchers usually find the average score to be the most useful measure of central tendency, so they plump for the mean. No doubt the mean is a very popular measure of central tendency, but median and mode are pretty useful too. Indeed, on many occasions a mixture of more than one measure of central tendency is effective. Here are some examples:

> ### Example 1   *When the median is a useful complement to the mean*
> *What if Terry and Geri's male condition had an extra participant who dozed off and consequently took five minutes to react to the emergency? His extreme, 'outlying' score dramatically alters the mean value for the set. Now the mean is 20.8 seconds, instead of 9.64 seconds. Whilst this mean value still gives the true average score for the set, as a measure of central tendency it's rather misleading. In this kind of situation, where a set has an extreme, untypical 'outlying' score, the median is a useful complement to the mean. The median score for the set, including the dozing participant, is 11. It's unaffected by the extreme 'outlier'.*

Example 2 *When the mode is a useful complement to the mean*
Look again at Terry and Geri's male condition. It has a mean of 9.64. Let's round it up to 10 for the moment. In this set, four males scored 10. But what if two of these had scored 9, not 10? And what if another two had scored 11, not 10? Now we have a situation where the mean remains 10, yet nobody actually scored 10. So although the mean gives true average value, it doesn't tell us what most people have scored. Indeed, it doesn't tell us what anyone scored. It may well be that Terry and Geri are interested in what the most popular, most typical score was. If so, the mode would be a useful complement to the mean.

Example 3 *The mean is not even an option*
If a set of scores is presented at the **ordinal** *or* **nominal levels of measurement**, *it's impossible to calculate their mean, so the median or mode are used as measures of central tendency. Only scores at the* **interval level** *can be used to calculate a mean value (***interval, ordinal** *and* **nominal levels of measurement** *are dealt with in some detail in the second half of this chapter).*

Measures of central tendency are usually presented alongside **measures of how well spread a set of scores is**. These measures of spread are called **measures of dispersion**. They show whether the scores in a set are all clustered around a central point, or whether they're spread out. The combination of central tendency and dispersion gives a well-rounded picture of how the scores in a set are distributed. Presenting one without the other is frowned upon by most psychology tutors.

Three measures of dispersion
The range is the most straightforward way to work out the spread of a set of scores. It's **the difference between the highest and lowest scores**. Work out the range by subtracting the lowest score from the highest. **Box 5E** shows you how to calculate the range for Terry and Geri's male condition.

Box 5E

Working out the range for Condition A in Terry and Geri's study

Step 1 *Set out all the scores in the set in sequence, from lowest to highest.*

4, 5, 5, 6, 8, 8, 8, 8, 9, 9, 10, 10, 10, 10, 11, 11, 11, 11, 11, 11, 12, 12, 13, 14, **14**

Step 2 *Subtract the lowest score from the highest score.*

14 − 4 = 10

The range of response times for males in Terry and Geri's study is 10 seconds.

The mean deviation shows **the mean of the deviations from the mean.** In other words, it states the average amount by which all scores in a set differ (deviate) from the average. To work out mean deviation, first find the mean for a set of scores. Then work out by how much each individual score deviates from the mean. Finally, calculate the mean of all these deviations. **Box 5F** shows the mean deviation calculation for Terry and Geri's males. Take note though – mean deviation is seldom used. Mathematicians regard ignoring all the negative and positive signs when totalling the deviations for individual scores as a rather clumsy manoeuvre that's best avoided. Consequently, **standard deviation** is a more respectable measure of dispersion.

Box 5F

Working out the mean deviation for Condition A in Terry and Geri's study

Step 1 *Find the mean for the set: 9.64*

Step 2 *Work out how much each individual score deviates from the mean. Do this by subtracting the mean from each score. In the list below, the figures in brackets are the deviations for each score.*

   4(–5.64), 5(–4.64), 5(–4.64), 6(–3.64), 8(–1.64), 8(–1.64), 8(–1.64), 8(–1.64),
   9(–0.64), 9(0.64), 10(+0.36), 10(+0.36), 10(+0.36), 10(+0.36), 11(+1.36),
   11(+1.36), 11(+1.36), 11(+1.36), 11(+1.36), 11(+1.36), 12(+2.36), 12(+2.36),
   13(+3.36), 14(+4.36), 14(+4.36)

Step 3 *Work out the mean of all the deviations. Do this by adding all the deviations together, **ignoring all the positive and negative signs**, then dividing the total by the number of deviations.*

   5.64 + 4.64 + 4.64 + 3.64 + 1.64 + 1.64 + 1.64 + 1.64 + 0.64 + 0.64 + 0.36
   + 0.36 + 0.36 + 0.36 + 1.36 +1.36 + 1.36 + 1.36 + 1.36 + 1.36 + 2.36 + 2.36
   + 3.36 + 4.36 + 4.36 = 52.8

   52.8 ÷ 25 = 2.1

The mean deviation for Terry and Geri's male participants is 2.1 seconds.

The standard deviation (*SD*) is **a way of working out dispersion in a more mathematically sophisticated way than by using mean deviation**. Using *SD* enables you to avoid the rather clumsy manoeuvre of *ignoring all the positive and negative signs* when totalling the deviations for the individual scores. *SD* can be calculated in seven steps, as follows:

Step 1: Find the mean for the set of scores. *Step 2*: Work out how much each score deviates from the mean by subtracting the mean from each score. *Step 3*: Square each of the deviation values from *step 2*. *Step 4*: Add up all the squared values from *step 3* to give you *the sum of the squares*. *Step 5*: Subtract 1 from the number of scores in the set to give you *N – 1*. **Step 6**: Divide *the sum of the squares* by *N – 1*. This gives you the **variance** of the set of scores. **Step 7**: Find the square root of the **variance** to give you the *SD* for the set.

Standard deviation throws up a couple of questions

Before applying this procedure to Terry and Geri's scores you may feel that SD throws up a couple of questions that need answering. First, what's **variance**? Well, it's the term used to refer to **the square of standard deviation**. Variance is sometimes used as a measure of dispersion in its own right, though here we're using it as a step on the way to calculating *SD*. Second question: when calculating *SD* why do we divide

---

Box 5G

Working out the SD for Condition A in Terry and Geri's study

Step 1 Find the mean for the set of scores: 9.64.

Step 2 Work out how much each score deviates from the mean by subtracting the mean from each score. The figures in brackets are the deviations for each score.

4(–5.64), 5(–4.64), 5(–4.64), 6(–3.64), 8(–1.64), 8(–1.64), 8(–1.64), 8(–1.64), 9(–0.64), 9(–0.64), 10(+0.36), 10(+0.36), 10(+0.36), 10(+0.36), 11(+1.36), 11(+1.36), 11(+1.36), 11(+1.36), 11(+1.36), 11(+1.36), 12(+2.36), 12(+2.36), 13(+3.36), 14(+4.36), 14(+4.36)

Step 3 Square each of the deviation values from **step 2**. In the list below, the figures in brackets are the squared deviations for each score.

4(31.8), 5(21.5), 5(21.5), 6(13.2), 8(2.7), 8(2.7), 8(2.7), 8(2.7), 9(0.4), 9(0.4), 10(0.1), 10(0.1), 10(0.1), 10(0.1), 11(1.8), 11(1.8), 11(1.8), 11(1.8), 11(1.8), 12(5.6), 12(5.6), 13(11.3), 14(19.0), 14(19.0)

Step 4 Add up all the squared values from **step 3** to give the sum of the squares.

31.8 + 21.5 + 21.5 + 13.2 + 2.7 + 2.7 + 2.7 + 2.7 + 0.4 + 0.4 + 0.1 + 0.1 + 0.1 + 0.1 + 1.8 + 1.8 + 1.8 + 1.8 + 1.8 + 1.8 + 5.6 + 5.6 + 11.3 + 19.0 + 19.0 = 171.3

Step 5 Subtract 1 from the number of scores in the set to give N – 1: 25 – 1 = 24

Step 6 Divide the sum of the squares by N – 1 to give the variance of the set.

171.3 ÷ 24 = 7.1

Step 7 Find the square root of the variance to give the SD for the set.

$\sqrt{7.1}$ = 2.7

The standard deviation for Terry and Geri's male participants is 2.7

the sum of the squares by $N - 1$ and not by N (the number of deviations)? Well, dividing by $N - 1$ rather than N raises the value of the variance and SD for a set. It produces a measure of dispersion that's a little on the generous side. The reason for this is that we're calculating the standard deviation for a *sample* of scores, rather than for an entire *population* (see **Chapter 4** for an explanation of samples and populations). Since the scores for a sample are unlikely to be perfectly representative of the scores for a population, we tend to slightly inflate our estimate of variance and SD to allow for this discrepancy (or **sampling error**, as it's often called). This means we can be more confident about generalising our measure of dispersion to the entire population.

Not all measures of dispersion are equally useful

It was suggested a few paragraphs ago that mean deviation is seldom used. You'd be right to conclude from this that not all measures of dispersion are equally useful. However, the *range* and SD both have their uses, depending on what you want to know about your scores. If you want a quick, easy way to work out how widely spread a set is, the range is ideal. If you want a measure of dispersion that's sensitive to every value in your set, SD is the popular choice. But since these two measures tell you different things about how a set is dispersed, you may want to use them both. Like mean, median and mode, they complement each other.

Now you're skilled in working out measures of central tendency and dispersion, you may want to 'please the eye' of whoever is reading your research report with some graphical summaries of your participants' scores. Graphs for summarising sets of scores can be used alongside measures of central tendency and dispersion. This combination of 'pictures and numbers' neatly encapsulates your data in a way that's both informative and nice to look at. There are several ways of summarising scores using graphs.

Three ways of summarising scores graphically

The first two are **histograms** and **bar charts**. I'll introduce these together, since they have plenty in common.

Histograms are graphs that show how frequently scores appear in a set. Each individual score can be represented by an interval along the horizontal axis. The frequency of each score's appearance in the set is shown by a tower extending up the vertical axis. Where you have a large number of individual scores you can create **grouped scores along the horizontal axis**. These grouped scores are called **class intervals**. This way, each group of scores (class interval) is represented by a separate tower. **Box 5H** as two examples of histograms – one for each of Terry and Geri's conditions. **5H(a)** uses individual scores on the horizontal axis, **5H(b)** uses class intervals.

Bar charts have a lot in common with histograms. Like histograms, they **show the frequency of a particular variable**. In other words, they can tell the reader how often a particular event occurs in a study. Also like histograms they use vertical towers (bars) to indicate frequency. For example, the bar chart in **Box 5J** shows how frequently males and females in Terry and Geri's study responded to the emergency in under ten minutes. As well as showing the frequency of a variable, bar charts can be used to compare mean scores, percentage scores, proportions and so forth.

So what's the difference between a histogram and a bar chart?

It concerns the kinds of variables that appear along their horizontal axes. Along the horizontal axes of histograms you'll find continuous, numerical variables. Typical examples of these are time and temperature. Variables like these are measured at what's called the **interval level of measurement** (the second half of this chapter has an explanation of **levels of measurement**). Since histograms have *continuous variables* along their horizontal axes, their towers are shown side by side, with no gaps between them. Along the horizontal axes of bar charts you'll find discrete, discontinuous variables. For example, gender. Gender has just two values (male or female) rather than a sequence of values along a continuum. Variables like these are measured at the **nominal level of measurement** (see the second half of this chapter). Other examples of discrete, discontinuous variables are eye colour and nationality. As bar charts show discontinuous variables along their horizontal axes, their towers are separated. They have gaps between them. Look out for the horizontal axis on the bar chart in **Box 5I**.

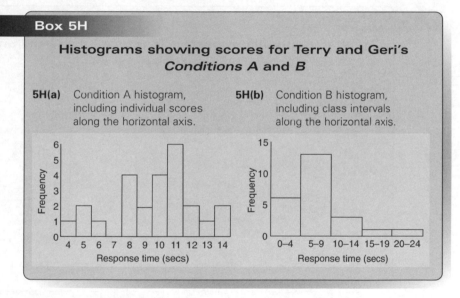

Box 5H

Histograms showing scores for Terry and Geri's *Conditions A and B*

5H(a) Condition A histogram, including individual scores along the horizontal axis.

5H(b) Condition B histogram, including class intervals along the horizontal axis.

Pie Charts are a third way of summarising scores graphically. They're useful when you want to **show how a particular variable divides up proportionally between a number of groups**. In effect, they show how big a piece of a pie each particular group has. The pie charts in **Box 5J** show the results of an exit questionnaire Terry and Geri gave to their participants. They were asked to indicate whether they had felt *very scared*, *a little scared* or *not at all scared* during the emergency situation.

Box 5I

Bar chart showing how frequently Terry and Geri's males and females responded in under 10 seconds

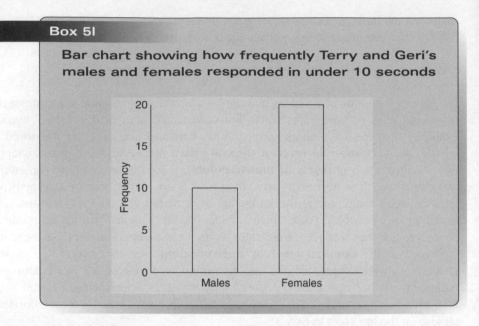

Box 5J

Pie charts showing reported fear levels for Terry and Geri's participants

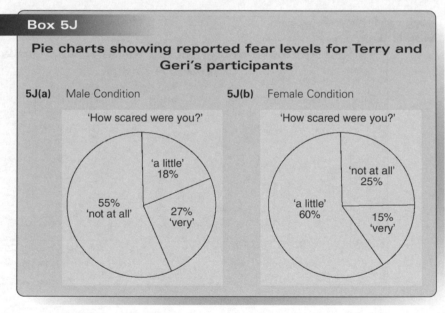

5J(a)   Male Condition   5J(b)   Female Condition

'How scared were you?'   'How scared were you?'

Measures of central tendency and dispersion, as well as the graphical summaries covered here, are all useful ways of describing research data. Thanks to these descriptive statistics your research report will be more concise and easier on the eye. Before crossing the border from descriptive statistics to inferential statistics there's one more idea to explore. It's another handy tool for describing data, but it also provides a key to unlock some of the puzzles that lIE in wait in the second half of this chapter.

The normal distribution and z-scores

Let's say Terry and Geri repeat their experiment on a larger scale. Rather than having 50 participants, let's say their follow-up study has 100 participants; 50 males, 50 females. Let's say the histogram in **Box 5K** *shows the reaction times for the male and female participants in this second, larger experiment.*

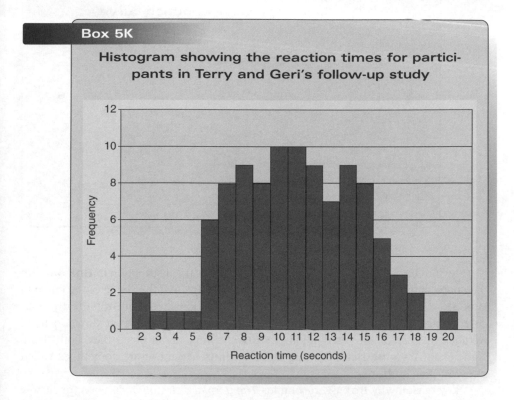

Box 5K

Histogram showing the reaction times for participants in Terry and Geri's follow-up study

Terry and Geri's follow-up study shows a distribution in which a lot of scores are clustered around a central score of 10 to 12 seconds, whilst a few scores are spread out towards the extremities (or tails). You could say this distribution goes 'up in the middle and down at the sides'. Distributions like this are approximations of a theoretical, mathematical model called **the normal distribution**. It's a kind of ideal distribution of scores against which other distributions can be compared. Whilst the distribution in **Box 5K** approximates to **the normal distribution**, it falls short of replicating it perfectly. In fact, real-life distributions never perfectly replicate the **normal distribution**. It is, after all, a theoretical, ideal distribution.

So what are the characteristics of this theoretical, ideal distribution?

The **normal distribution** has four distinguishing characteristics. *First*, it is **shaped like a bell**. *Secondly* it is **symmetrical**. *Thirdly*, the **mean, median and mode for the set are the same**. *Fourthly*, its **extremities (tails) don't touch the horizon-**

tal axis, but carry on out towards infinity. **Box 5L** shows the shape of this theoretical, ideal distribution. It has a shape that's often known as *the normal distribution curve*.

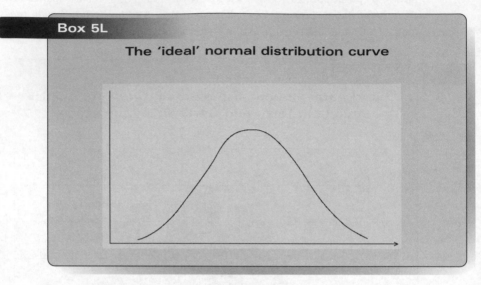

Box 5L

The 'ideal' normal distribution curve

Now turn back a page or so. Compare the shape of the distribution in **Box 5K** with the shape of the distributions in **Box 5H**. Now look again at the shape of the curve in **Box 5L**. You'll notice that whilst none of the distributions in **5H** or **5K** perfectly replicate normal distribution, the one in **5K** provides the closest approximation to it. Actually, neither of the distributions in **5H** is symmetrical, since they both 'lean' somewhat. **Asymmetrical**, **leaning distributions** like these are sometimes called **skewed distributions**.

A key reason why **Box 5K** resembles *The normal distribution curve* more closely than **Box 5H** does is that **5K** describes a set that has more scores in it than **5H** has. After all, the histogram in **Box 5K** includes scores from 100 participants, whereas those in **5H** show scores from only 25. In fact, for many of the variables psychologists are interested in (like reaction time, problem-solving ability, memory performance) as well as lots of other variables relating to human characteristics (such as height, weight, shoe size), it is generally true to say that *the more scores there are in a set, the greater the probability that it's shape will closely resemble the normal distribution curve*.

Properties of the area under the normal distribution curve

As well as the characteristics outlined above, there are a number of other assumptions you can make about a set of scores that closely approximates (remember, absolute 'normality' is a theoretical idea) to a normal distribution. These assumptions relate to the area beneath the normal curve.

Assumption 1   *50% of the scores in the set fall above the mean, 50% below it.*

This one's fairly obvious when you consider that the normal distribution curve is symmetrical. However, coming up are some other, less obvious assumptions that can be made about sets that closely approximate to normal distribution. First though, a short but necessary digression about the link between two closely related concepts.

Standard deviation and z-scores

As you know, standard deviation (*SD*) is a measure of dispersion. For the scores in Terry and Geri's follow-up study, the mean reaction time is 11 seconds, the *SD* (calculated using the formula featured earlier in this chapter) is 3.6 seconds. From this we can say that a score of 14.6 (11 plus 3.6) lies *1 SD above the mean*, a score of 7.4 (11 − 3.6) lies *1 SD below the mean*, 18.2 lies *2SDs above the mean*, 3.8 lies *2SDs below the mean* and so on.

Now, a **z-score** is **a measure of how many *SDs* a score lies above or below the mean**. In our example, a score of 14.6 *has a z-score of* +1, 7.4 *has a z-score of* −1, 18.2 *has a z-score of* +2 and so on.

So, back to those assumptions about sets of scores that closely approximate to normal distribution.

Assumption 2   *68.26% of scores always fall between the mean and 1 SD above and below the mean.*
Assumption 3   *31.74% of scores always fall beyond 1 SD above and below the mean.*

Box 5M

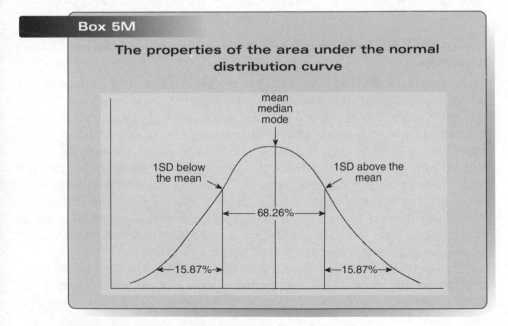

The properties of the area under the normal distribution curve

These assumptions are often referred to as *the properties of the area under the normal distribution curve*. They apply to all sets of scores that have normal distribution. Treat them as statistical 'facts of life'. **Box 5M** summarises them.

About these z-scores. Are they useful?

For working out the position of a particular score in relation to the other scores in a set that closely approximates normal distribution, they're really useful. They enable you to calculate *what proportion of scores (in a normally distributed set) lies between a given score and the mean*. They also enable you to calculate *what proportion of scores (in a normally distributed set) is higher or lower than a given score*.

z-score calculation   For example, imagine you're a participant in Terry and Geri's follow-up study and your reaction time is 9 seconds. So your score deviates from the mean (11) by 2 seconds. Another way of putting this is to say that you have a *deviation score* of –2 (which has a negative sign because it lies below the mean). Now, to work out your z-score, simply use the following calculation

> *z-score = the individual's deviation score ÷ SD for the set*

So in this example,

> *z-score = –2 ÷ 3.6*

So you have a z-score of –0.56. This means your score lies 0.6 *SDs below the mean*. Now, assuming the set closely approximates to normal distribution, you can find out what proportion of scores lies between your score and the mean, or what proportion of scores is higher or lower than yours, by using the table in **Appendix 3**.

How to decide whether a set of scores closely approximates to normal distribution

You already know that normal distribution is an ideal that never properly models real life scores. You already know that some real-life sets approximate to normal distribution more closely than others do. However, you may not yet know how to decide whether or not a set of scores closely approximates to normal distribution. This is worth knowing, whether you're working with *descriptive* statistics or in the neighbouring territory of *inferential* statistics. After all, the z-score manipulations featured above can only be performed on 'normally distributed' sets – sets that are close approximations to normal distribution. And as you'll discover in the second section of this chapter, there are some inferential manipulations that only apply to sets that closely approximate to normal distribution. So how *do* you decide whether a set *closely approximates* to normal distribution? Here are two methods.

First, use an **eye-ball test**. To 'eye-ball' a set of scores, first draw a histogram, then **look at the shape of the distribution** to see if it closely approximates to the normal distribution curve. Does it go up in the middle and down at the sides? Is it approximately symmetrical? Is it approximately shaped like a bell? Are the mean, median and mode approximately the same? If the answers to these questions are yes, yes, yes and yes respectively, you can safely say your set closely approximates to normal distribution. For most psychology tutors, 'eye-balling' is an accurate enough test of close approximation.

Alternatively, use a **goodness of fit test**. This is **a statistical test for establishing how closely a given set of scores conforms to the ideal, normally distributed set**. You'll find an example of a goodness of fit test in **Appendix 4**. These are best used where an eye-ball test leaves you undecided about close approximation. They're very much for the perfectionist.

Before crossing the border into the other half of this chapter, the half where statistics are used for making *inferences* about data rather than for *describing* it, make sure you've grasped each of the key terms in **Box 5N**.

Box 5N

Using descriptive statistics: B-Z of terms to remember

Bar charts are graphs that show the frequency of a particular variable. Along the horizontal axes of bar charts you'll find discrete, discontinuous variables.

Bi-modal sets are scores that have two modal values.

Correlation co-efficients are numbers for measuring the strength of the correlation between two variables.

Descriptive statistics encapsulate the most important findings from a study.

Dispersion measures how well spread a set of scores is.

Histograms are graphs that show how frequently scores appear in a set. Along the horizontal axes of histograms you'll find continuous, numerical variables.

Mean is the average score in a set.

Mean deviation is the mean of the deviations from the mean in a set.

Measures of central tendency are average, middle, or most typical scores for a set.

Median is the middle score in a set.

Mode is the most typical score in a set.

Normal distribution is a theoretical, mathematical model in which a lot of scores are clustered around a central point and a few scores are spread out toward the extremities.

Pie charts show how a variable divides up proportionally between a number of groups.

Range is the difference between the highest and lowest scores in a set.

Raw data are research results that haven't had descriptive or inferential statistics applied to them.

Sampling errors happen when a sample's scores are unrepresentative of a population's scores.

Skewed distributions are asymmetrical, leaning distributions.

Standard deviation is a way of working out dispersion in a more mathematically sophisticated way than by using mean deviation.

Variance is the square of standard deviation.

Z-scores measure by how many *SD*s a score lies above or below the mean for a set.

● 3 Using inferential statistics in psychology

The opening pages of this chapter outline the aims of inferential statistics. After reading this outline you'd be right to regard statistics of inference as a kind of 'researchers' defence' against anyone who might attribute the findings from a study to chance, random variation, rather than to the influence of an independent variable (*IV*) on a dependent variable (*DV*).

Sounds like a useful safety net. So how do inferential statistics work?

To answer this question let's stick with the case of Terry and Geri's study on *male and female responses to an emergency situation* (the first half of this chapter has a full account of this study).

> *Terry and Geri's hypothesis predicts that* **there will be a difference between the average response times of male and female participants in an emergency situation.** *Their results show there is a difference. The mean response time for* Condition A *is 9.64 seconds. For* Condition B *it's 7.28 seconds (***Box 5A***). Females, on average, responded more quickly than males.*

Having observed a difference between the response times of their samples, Terry and Geri would like to generalise these findings to the populations from which their samples are drawn. But they'll only be justified in doing so if the difference between their two sample means is big enough – or, as researchers prefer to put it, *significant enough* – for them to do so.

Who decides if the difference between their two sample means is significant enough?

Researchers decide for themselves, by applying **inferential tests** to their data. More will be revealed about **inferential tests** shortly. First though, here's a short but necessary digression on the subject of *hypotheses*. Did you know they come in different varieties?

Varieties of hypotheses

A testable prediction about the outcome of a study is called a *research hypothesis* or *experimental hypothesis*. But this isn't the only variety of prediction in the researchers' repertoire. Another is the **null hypothesis**. Null hypotheses predict the opposite of research hypotheses. If a research hypothesis predicts a difference between two samples of scores on a particular variable, the **null hypothesis** predicts that there will be *no difference*. In fact, the **null hypothesis** is sometimes called the **prediction of no difference**. When you have research findings that *support* a research hypothesis it's customary – according to statistical convention – to say that you *reject the null hypothesis*. This simply means that the prediction of no difference has been thrown out.

One tail or two?

Two other types of prediction are **one-tailed** and **two-tailed hypotheses**. The first of these is very specific, the second isn't. **One-tailed hypotheses specify the *direction* in which an *IV* will influence a *DV***. For instance, they specify that a change in an *IV* will *either* increase *or* decrease the value of a *DV*. **Two-tailed hypotheses predict that an *IV* will influence a *DV*, but they don't specify the direction**. In other words, they predict that a change in the *IV* will influence the *DV*, but the direction of change isn't specified.

Researchers who use one-tailed hypotheses are generally pretty confident about the direction of influence of their *IV* over their *DV*. A word of warning, though; your choice of a one-tailed or two-tailed hypothesis influences the kind of **inferential test** you'll apply to your data, so be sure you know which is which and which one you're using for your research.

> *In Terry and Geri's study the null hypothesis predicts that **there will be no difference between the response times of the two conditions**. A closer look at the research hypothesis for this study reveals it to be **two-tailed**. It predicts that response time (DV) will be influenced by gender (IV) but it doesn't specify whether male or female response times will be higher. A one-tailed hypothesis for this study would be **females will respond more quickly to the emergency situation than males will**.*

So what are these 'inferential tests'?

I'll come to them presently. First, a word about *errors*.

Two types of error

As in most fields, human error flourishes in the field of inferential statistics. So you need to have your wits about you. But researchers who use inferential statistics are prone to two types of errors in particular. First, there's the **Type One error**. This error results from being overly optimistic. Researchers who claim their results are *significant* – that they are attributable to the effect of an *IV* on a *DV* – when in fact they're simply the result of chance, random variation – are committing a **Type One error**. In short, they're **rejecting a null hypothesis that should be accepted**. Then there's the **Type Two error**. This is the opposite of the Type One. Researchers who claim their results have come about because of chance, random variation when they're attributable to the influence of their *IV* on their *DV* are making a **Type Two error**. They're **accepting a null hypothesis that should be rejected**. You could say this error comes from being overly pessimistic.

> *If Terry and Geri attribute the difference in response times between their male and female conditions to gender (IV) when in fact it came about by chance, random variation, they'd be making a **Type One error**.*

What about these inferential tests?

All in good time. First, a word about something called **the 5% level of significance**.

The 5% sinificance level: Researchers who reject null hypotheses are only 95% sure of what they're saying

Imagine you've done a piece of research and obtained sets of scores for two conditions. Your *two-tailed* research hypothesis predicts a difference between the two sets. Your null hypothesis predicts no difference. Let's say there is a difference, but you're not sure it's big enough to make your results significant. To find out whether it is big enough you do an **inferential test** on your data. Basing your design on the outcome of this test, you go ahead and *reject your null hypothesis*. Now pause for a moment and ask yourself a question. *What is the probability that you've rejected a null hypothesis you should have accepted?* In other words, what's the probability that you've made a Type One Error? Generally researchers set this level of probability at 5%. This means there's one chance in twenty of wrongly rejecting the null hypothesis. This is **the 5% level of significance**. It's **a** *set* **'level of doubt' that researchers conventionally operate at when rejecting null hypotheses**. When you do an **inferential test** on your data you'll arrive at a statistical value which may show your results to be significant at the 5% level. If they are significant at this level, you'll reject your null hypothesis. But you'll do so with a 5% 'level of doubt', a one-in-twenty chance that you've made a Type One error. An interesting consequence of this '5% convention' is that psychologists who reject null hypotheses are only 95% sure of what they're saying. By implication, the use of a 1% significance level means that this confidence level rises to 99%. The use of a 10% significance level is associated with a confidence level of 90%.

> *Terry and Geri have observed a difference between the mean scores of their two conditions. To find out whether the difference is significant they'll select an* **inferential test***. This will throw up a statistical value which they'll check against the 5% level of significance. If they find there to be a less then one-in-twenty chance that they've made a Type One error, they'll reject their null hypothesis and conclude that in the population at large, female responses to emergencies are significantly faster than male responses.*

Isn't it high time you explained these inferential tests?

Almost. First though, some thoughts about something called **levels of measurement**.

Three levels of measurement

A sprinter's success can be quantified in different ways. What's her fastest time? What's her world ranking? Is she in the Olympic team? Similarly, psychological research data can be quantified in different ways. Three main ways in fact, called **levels of measurement**. The reason for these different levels is that different research situations call for behaviour to be quantified in different ways. And the level at which behaviour is quantified in a study will determine how its data are presented. That is, what form they're presented in. In short, **levels of measurement** are **different ways of quantifying behaviour and presenting research data**. The level of measurement used by a researcher has a bearing on the kind of **inferential test** that will be applied to it.

Level 1   **the nominal level** (pass or fail)
Here, **data is presented in separate, discrete groups**. If you participate in a study that measures behaviour at this level your performance leads to your being put into one of a number of separate, discrete groups, in that each participant is placed in one group or another, not at some point in-between. For example, after a spelling test you might be put into a 'pass' group or a 'fail' group. In studies like these the researcher wants to know the number (*frequency*) of participants in each separate, discrete group. In the 'spelling' example, participants are divided into two groups. This is very common, though some (more complex) studies use more than two.

Level 2   **the ordinal level** (rank order)
Here, **data is presented in rank order**. As a participant in a study using the ordinal level you're given a *rank position* (like *2nd* or *5th* or *50th*) to show how you faired on whatever variable was measured. An ordinal score shows your position relative to the other participants in the group, as opposed to which group you belong to, which is what a nominal score shows.

Level 3   **the interval level** (actual scores)
Here, **data is presented as scores on a scale with equal units**. As a participant in a study with interval data you find out how much better or worse than the other participants you did, rather than just being given a rank position. So instead of finding out that she was the *5th* fastest in her race, the sprinter finds out her *actual score* or *time*. From this she can work out how much faster she was than the 6th fastest runner. Some examples of interval scales are seconds, metres, kilos. A key feature of interval level is that it uses scales that have equal units. This means that *each interval on the scale has the same value*. So on a scale that measures time in seconds the difference between *8* and *9* seconds *is equal to* the difference between *12* and *13* seconds or *17* and *18* seconds. This feature of the interval level of measurement has, from time to time, caused confusion. The next paragraph explains why.

Some scales appear to present data at the interval level when they don't

Imagine you're a participant in a study involving a spelling test. You spell sixteen out of a possible twenty words correctly. A fellow participant, Kim, spells fifteen correctly. Two other participants, Tim and Sim, score eight and seven respectively. *Is the difference in spelling performance between yourself and Kim equal to the difference in performance between Tim and Jim?* Arguably not. Why? Because the scale you're being measured on is man-made and doesn't have *equal units* like a proper interval scale does (e.g. seconds). After all, it would be inaccurate to say that the difference in 'spelling performance' between someone who scores sixteen and someone who scores eight *is equal to* the ability difference between someone who scores eight and someone who scores zero. Only scales that have *equal* units are regarded as proper interval scales. So beware. Some man-made scales appear to present data at the interval level when they don't. Famous and notorious examples are intelligence and personality scales, generically known as *psychometric* scales. They're perfectly legitimate in psychological research, though they're not regarded as proper interval scales. For the purposes of doing **inferential tests** it's conventional to 'downgrade' data from scales that appear – falsely – to present data at the interval level to the next lowest level of measurement. This means downgrading them to the ordinal level by giving each score a rank position. **Appendix 5** has a guide to *ranking scores.*

> *Terry and Geri's experiment measured response time (DV) in seconds. This is a widely used scale with equal units, so it's fine to regard it as an interval scale. Yet it might have been so different. Rather than recording each participant's time in seconds they might have given them all a rank position. The first to react would have been ranked 1, the last, ranked 50. This would have been an ordinal scale. Then again, they might have divided their participants into two separate, discrete groups. One group that responded in 'under 10 seconds', one that didn't. Then they'd have been using a nominal scale.*

Isn't it high time you explained these inferential tests?

Inferential tests

Tests of inference **enable you to *infer*, from the data you've collected in your study, whether or not your results are significant at the 5% level**. In other words, they tell you whether or not to *reject your null hypothesis.*

Most of the inferential tests featured in this section are for working out if the difference between the scores in your conditions is big enough to be regarded as statistically significant. Tests that do this are sometimes called *tests of difference.* Two bonus tests are also featured in this section. These are especially designed tests for working out the significance of data from correlational studies. In other words, they're *tests for calculating correlation co-efficien*ts (Chapter 4 has a guide to the correlational – and other – methods).

The tests covered here should cater for all your inferential statistical needs, especially if you're still in the early stages of your research career.

Hang on. With all these tests to choose from, how do you decide which one to select?

Good question. Your choice of test will depend on the nature of your study and on the kind of data it produced. **Box 5Q** offers you *a detailed guide to selecting the appropriate inferential test for your data.* **Box 5P** offers *a quick guide to the same.* Be warned, selecting an inappropriate test may lead to your arriving at inappropriate conclusions about the significance of your data, which is frowned upon by tutors, lecturers and examiners alike. So make sure you know which test is which and which one's best for your data.

Box 5P

A quick guide to selecting the appropriate inferential test for your data

	Tests of difference		Tests for calculating correlation co-efficients
	INDEPENDENT design	**REPEATED MEASURES or MATCHED PAIRS**	
NOMINAL level	Chi-square (*see* **Box 5S**)	Sign (*see* **Box 5R**)	
ORDINAL level	Mann–Whitney U (*see* **Box 5U**)	Wilcoxon (*see* **Box 5T**)	Spearman's rho (*see* **Box 5Z**)
INTERVAL Level	Unrelated t (*see* **Box 5W**)	Related t (*see* **Box 5V**)	Pearson's product moment calculation (*see* **Box 5Y**)

The *t-tests* on the bottom row of **Box 5P** are regarded as the most 'statistically powerful' of all the inferential tests included here. Sometimes these 'extra powerful' tests are called *parametric* tests. Predictably, the others are known as *non-parametric* tests. Once you've selected the appropriate test for your research, go ahead and apply it to your data. The rest of this chapter guides you through the calculations for the tests shown in **Boxes 5P** and **5Q**.

Box 5Q

A detailed guide to selecting the appropriate inferential test for your data

The most popular inferential 'tests of difference' are the **Sign test**, **Chi-square test**, **Wilcoxon test**, **Mann–Whitney U-test**, the **Unrelated t-test** and **Related t-test**. Also, there are the two 'bonus' tests, designed for working out the significance of data from correlational studies – the **Pearson product-moment calculation** and **Spearman's rho**. To ensure you make the appropriate selection, ask yourself some questions about your study and about the data it's produced.

Question 1   What kind of method have I used?
If you've conducted a **correlational study**, skip to **Box 5X**. Otherwise, go to *Question 2*.

Question 2   What kind of DESIGN does my study have?
If it has a **Repeated Measures** or **Matched Pairs** design select from **Sign test**, **Wilcoxon test** or **Related t-test**. If it has an **Independent** design select from **Chi-square test**, **Mann–Whitney U- test** or **Unrelated t-test**. Now go to *Question 3*.

Question 3   What LEVEL OF MEASUREMENT does my study use?
If it uses the **Nominal** level, select the **Chi-square test** (for Independent designs) or the **Sign test** (for Repeated Measures or Matched Pairs designs). If it uses the **Ordinal** level, select the **Mann–Whitney U-test** (for Independent designs) or the Wilcoxon test (for Repeated Measures or Matched Pairs designs). If your study uses the **Interval** level you may be able to select what's called a **parametric** test. The **Unrelated t test** and the **Related t-test** are examples of these. In order to 'gain access' to them you need to subject your data to the further rigours of *Questions 4* and *5*.

Question 4   Do the sets of scores from both my conditions approximate to NORMAL DISTRIBUTION?
If the sets of scores from both your conditions approximate **Normal Distribution** you're on course to select a parametric test. To make a decision on this use an 'eye-ball test' or a 'test of goodness of fit' (**Appendix 4**). If your answer to *Question 4* is 'no', convert your data to the *Ordinal* level by putting them into rank order (**Appendix 5** has a guide to ranking scores). Then select one of the inferential tests recommended in *Question 3*, for *Ordinal* scores. If your answer to *Question 4* is 'yes', go to *Question 5*.

Question 5   Are the sets of scores from both your conditions SIMILARLY DISPERSED?
In other words, are they 'spread out' to a similar extent (the first half of this chapter has a discussion of *Dispersion*)? If your sets are similarly dispersed you're on course for selecting a parametric test. There are two methods for making a decision on 'similarity of dispersion'. First, you can plot your sets on histograms and judge – using an 'eye-ball method' – whether they look like they're similarly spread. This method is usually precise enough. If you're looking for extra precision there's a statistical test specifically designed for measuring 'similarity of dispersion'. It's called the **F-test**. You'll find it in **Appendix 6**.

If you have *Interval* scores and you've answered 'yes' and 'yes' to *Questions 4* and *5* respectively, select the **unrelated t-test** for *Independent* designs or the **related t-test** for *Repeated Measures* or *Matched Pairs* designs.

Box 5R

The sign test

Select this when you have **nominal** data and a **Repeated Measures** or **Matched Pairs** design. For example, Terry and Geri contacted ten of their male participants six months after their original study and asked them to rate how scared they were during the original emergency. These second responses were compared with the ones they originally made six months earlier. Terry and Geri used a Sign test to find out if there was a significant difference between the two sets of responses.

Step 1 *Arrange the pairs of scores in two columns.*

participant	original response	second response	signs
1	very scared	very scared	
2	not at all	very	–
3	very	not at all	+
4	not at all	a little	–
5	very	a little	+
6	a little	not at all	+
7	a little	not at all	+
8	very	very	
9	a little	a little	
10	not at all	very	–

Step 2 Subtract the value in the second column from its pair in the first and enter the sign of the outcome in a third column. For example, if the value in the second column is smaller than the value in the first, enter a '+' sign in the third column.

Step 3 Count the number of times the least frequent sign occurs in the third column to find 'S'.
The least frequent sign is '–', which occurs 3 times. So $S = 3$.

Step 4 Total the number of '+' and '–' signs to find N.
There are four '+' signs and three '–' signs. So $N = 7$.

Step 5 Look in the table in **Appendix 7** to find out whether the result is significant at the 5% level.

Box 5S

The Chi-square test

Select this when you have **nominal** data and an **Independent** design. For example, let's say Terry and Geri divided their participants into separate, discrete groups: those that responded in 'under 10 seconds' and those that didn't. Here's how Terry and Geri would use a Chi-square test to find out if there was a significant difference between the number of males and females in their original study who responded to the emergency in under 10 seconds.

Step 1   Arrange the data in a 2 × 2 table. Call the number in each cell the 'observed' frequency (if your data is more complex and requires, say, a 2 × 3 table, you'll need to use a different form of the Chi-square test – called the Complex Chi-square test).

	Column 1 (males)	Column 2 (females)	Column 3 (totals)
row 1 reacted in under 10 secs	*cell A* 10	*cell B* 20	30
row 2 reacted in ten secs or more	*cell C* 15	*cell D* 5	20
row 3 totals	25	25	50

Step 2   Calculate the 'expected' frequency for each cell. Do this by multiplying the row total by the column total for each cell, then by dividing the outcome by the overall total. Note that an 'expected' frequency of less than 5 for any cell is regarded as so small as to invalidate the Chi square test. In such cases, abandon the test and accept your null hypothesis.

cell A $(30 \times 25) \div 50 = 15$ expected frequency = 15
cell B $(25 \times 30) \div 50 = 15$ expected frequency = 15
cell C $(20 \times 25) \div 50 = 10$ expected frequency = 10
cell D $(20 \times 25) \div 50 = 10$ expected frequency = 10

Step 3   For each cell find the difference between the OBSERVED and EXPECTED frequencies. Do   this by subtracting the smaller value from the larger.

cell A   15 (expected) – 10 (observed) = 5
cell B   20 (observed) – 15 (expected) = 5
cell C   15 (observed) – 10 (expected) = 5
cell D   10 (expected) – 5   (observed) = 5

Step 4   Square each of the values from step 3, then divide the outcome by the expected frequency for that cell.

cell A $5^2 (15 = 1.7$
cell B $5^2 (15 = 1.7$
cell C $5^2 (10 = 2.5$
cell D $5^2 (10 = 2.5$

Step 5   Total the values from *Step 4* to find X^2: 1.7 + 1.7 + 2.5 + 2.5 = 8.4, so $X^2 = 8.4$

Step 6   Look in the table in **Appendix 8** to find out if the result is significant at the 5% level. In our example, X^2 exceeds 3.841 for a two-tailed hypothesis, so our result is significant at the 5% level.

Box 5T

The Wilcoxon test

Select this when you have **ordinal** data and a **Repeated Measures** or **Matched Pairs** design. For example, Terry and Geri contacted ten of their male participants six months after their original study and tested their reactions to a similar emergency. They wanted to compare the reaction times in this second trial with those from the original research. To see if there was a significant difference between the two sets of scores they opted for a non-parametric test. The Wilcoxon test was the appropriate choice.

Step 1   Arrange the pairs of scores in two columns.

participant	Column 1 1st reaction time (in seconds)	Column 2 2nd reaction time (in seconds)	Column 3 difference	Column 4 ranked difference
1	3	3	0	
2	5	1	4	4.5
3	8	2	6	6
4	8	15	–7	7.5
5	8	1	7	7.5
6	11	9	2	3
7	11	7	4	4.5
8	11	10	1	1.5
9	14	14	0	
10	21	22	–1	1.5

Step 2   Work out the value for 'difference between each pair' (see column 3 above). Do this by subtracting each value from its pair. For each pair be sure to subtract in the same direction. For example, in the above table the second pair value is always subtracted from the first.

Step 3   Rank the 'differences between each pair' values from *Step 2*. Give the smallest difference the rank of 1 (see column 4 above). While ranking the scores, **ignore all positive and negative signs** and **ignore all scores of zero**. The latter are excluded from this test. **Appendix 5** has a guide to ranking scores.

Step 4   Add up the ranks for all the 'differences between each pair' that are positive, then add up the ranks for all the 'differences between each pair' that are negative. Let the smaller of these two totals be '*T*'. In our example there are only two negative 'differences between each pair'. Their ranks are 1.5 and 7.5, so *T* = 9.

Step 5   Look in the table in **Appendix 9** to find out if the result is significant at the 5% level. As you do so, be sure to exclude any zero 'differences between each pair' values from *N*. So in our example, since there are two such zero values, *N* = 8. In our example, *T* exceeds 4 for a two-tailed hypothesis, so the result is not significant at the 5% level.

Box 5U

The Mann–Whitney U test

Select this when you have **ordinal** data and an **independent** design. For example, say Terry and Geri did their original study with twenty participants in each condition and their data fell short of the criteria for selecting a parametric test, so they opted for a non-parametric test. The Mann–Whitney would be the appropriate choice.

Step 1 Arrange the scores in columns. If one set has fewer scores, make this 'Set *A*'. Here are the columns for the example described above. The values in brackets are the rank scores (see *Step 5*).

Set A *male condition*	Set B *female condition*
4 (5)	1 (1.5)
5 (7)	1 (1.5)
6 (9.5)	3 (3.5)
8 (12.5)	3 (3.5)
9 (14)	5 (7)
10 (15)	5 (7)
11 (16.5)	6 (9.5)
11 (16.5)	7 (11)
14 (18.5)	8 (12.5)
14 (18.5)	18 (20)

Step 2 Count how many scores are in each set to find NA and $\underline{NB}$. Multiply NA by NB to find $NANB$.
In our example $NA = 10$, $NB = 10$. So $NANB = 100$

Step 3 Add 1 to NA.
$NA + 1 = 11$.

Step 4 Multiply $NA+1$ by NA, then divide the outcome by 2.
$(11 \times 10) \div 2 = 55$.

Step 5 Rank all the scores from both sets, **taken as one set**. **Appendix** 5 has a guide to ranking scores. Give the smallest score rank 1. In the table in *Step 1*, ranks are shown in brackets.

Step 6 Add up the ranks from the scores in Set *A*.
$5 + 7 + 9.5 + 12.5 + 14 + 15 + 16.5 + 16.5 + 18.5 + 18.5 = 133$

Step 7 Add $NANB$ to the outcome of *Step 4*, then subtract the outcome of *Step 6*.
$100 + 55 - 133 = 22$

Step 8 Subtract the outcome of Step 7 from NANB.
$100 - 22 = 78$

Step 9 Call the outcomes of *Steps 7* and *8* 'U' and 'U''. Whichever is smallest is U.
$U = 22$, $U' = 78$

Step 10 Look in the table in **Appendix 10** to see if the result is significant at the 5% level. In our example, U does not exceed 23 for a two-tailed hypothesis, so the result is significant at the 5% level.

Box 5V

The Related t-test

Select this when you have **interval scores**, when sets **approximate to normal distribution** and are **similarly dispersed** and when you have a **Repeated Measures** or **Matched Pairs** design. For example, Terry and Geri contacted twenty of the participants from their follow-up study (see the section on normal distribution for details of this) at a later date and tested their reaction time in a similar emergency. They measured reaction time at the *interval* level of measurement. Both their sets approximate to normal distribution and were similarly dispersed. So the *Related* t was the appropriate test of significance.

Step 1   Arrange the scores in two columns

participant	Set A (reaction time 1)	Set B (reaction time 2)	A–B (Step 7)	(A–B)² (Step 8)
1	2	1	1	1
2	2	7	–5	25
3	3	2	1	1
4	5	3	2	4
5	6	3	3	9
6	7	4	3	9
7	8	4	4	16
8	8	7	1	1
9	9	7	2	4
10	9	6	3	9
11	10	6	4	16
12	10	6	4	16
13	10	8	2	4
14	11	5	6	36
15	11	8	3	9
16	12	10	2	4
17	12	11	1	1
18	13	9	4	16
19	15	5	10	100
20	16	13	3	9
			Total 54	**Total 290**

Step 2   Count up the pairs to find N: $N = 20$

Step 3   Calculate $N - 1$ to find df: $20 - 1 = 19$, $df = 19$

Step 4   Multiply the N by df: $20 \times 19 = 380$

Step 5   Find the mean for each set.
   Set A: $2 + 2 + 3 + 5 + 6 + 7 + 8 + 8 + 9 + 9 + 10 + 10 + 10 + 11 + 11 + 12 + 12 + 13 + 15 + 16 = 179$
   $179 \div 20 = 9$ Set *A* mean = 9
   Set B: $1 + 2 + 3 + 3 + 4 + 4 + 5 + 5 + 6 + 6 + 6 + 7 + 7 + 7 + 8 + 8 + 9 + 10 + 11 + 13 = 125$
   $125 \div 20 = 6.3$ Set *A* mean = 6.3

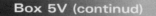

Box 5V (continud)

Step 6   Find the 'difference between the means' by subtracting the smaller one from the larger:
9 – 6.3 = 2.7

Step 7   Subtract each score in Set *B* from its pair in Set *A*. See the table in *Step 1* for the outcomes of these calculations.

Step 8   Square the outcome of *Step 7* for each pair, then add up the squared values. See the table in *Step 1*.
Total of the squared values = 290.

Step 9   Add the differences between each pair from *Step 7*, **taking negative signs into account**. See the table in *Step 1*.
Total of the differences between each pair = 54.

Step 10   Square the outcome of *Step 9*, then divide by N: $54^2 \div 20 = 145.8$

Step 11   Subtract the outcome of *Step 10* from the outcome of *Step 8*, then divide by the outcome of *Step 4*.
(290 – 145.8) ÷ 380 = 0.38

Step 12   Find the square root of the outcome of *Step 11*: √ 0.38 = 0.62

Step 13   Divide the outcome of *Step 6* by the outcome of *Step 12* to find *t*:
2.7 ÷ 0.62 = 4.35, so *t* = 4.35

Step 14   Look in the table in **Appendix 11** to see if the result is significant at the 5% level. In our example, *t* exceeds 2.093 for a two-tailed hypothesis, so the result is significant at the 5% level.

Box 5W

The Unrelated t-test

Select this when you have **interval scores**, when you're sets **approximate normal distribution** and are **similarly dispersed** and you have an **Independent** design. For example, let's say Terry and Geri obtained the data listed below – measured in seconds – from two separate conditions in an Independent design experiment.

Step 1 Arrange the scores in two columns.

Participant	Set A	(A²)	Set B	(B²)
1	2	4	1	1
2	2	4	7	49
3	3	9	2	4
4	5	25	3	9
5	6	36	3	9
6	7	49	4	16
7	8	64	4	16
8	8	64	7	49
9	9	81	7	49
10	9	81	6	36
11	10	100	6	36
12	10	100	6	36
13	10	100	8	64
14	11	121	5	25
15	11	121	8	64
16	12	144	10	100
17	12	144	11	121
18	13	169	9	81
19	15	225	5	25
20	16	256	13	169
Totals	**179**	**1897**	**125**	**959**

Step 2 Count the number of scores in each set to find NA and NB, then add NA to NB to find N: 20 +20 = 40, so $N = 40$

Step 3 Multiply NA by NB to find $NANB$, then divide the outcome of *Step 2* by $NANB$: 40 ÷ 400 = 0.1

Step 4 Total the scores in Set A: Set A total = 179

Step 5 Square all the scores in Set A, then total all the squares. See the table in *Step 1*.

Step 6 Square the outcome of *Step 4*, then divide the outcome by NA: $(179^2 ÷ 20) = (32,041 ÷ 20) = 1602.05$

Step 7 Subtract the outcome of *Step 6* from the outcome of *Step 5*: 1897 – 1602.1 = 294.9

Step 8 Total the scores in Set B: Set B total = 125.

Box 5W (continued)

Step 9 Square all the scores in Set *B*, then total all the squares. See the table in *Step 1*.

Step 10 Square the outcome of *Step 8*, then divide the outcome by *NB*: $(125^2 \div 20 (= (15{,}625 \div 20) = 781.3$

Step 11 Subtract the outcome of *Step 10* from the outcome of *Step 9*: $959 - 781.3 = 177.7$

Step 12 Add the outcome of *Step 7* to the outcome of *Step 11*: $294.9 + 177.7 = 472.6$

Step 13 Calculate $N - 2$ to find *df* (degrees of freedom – this is a mathematical concept related to the number of observations that are contained in your data): $40 - 2 = 38$ *df* = 38

Step 14 Divide the outcome of *Step 12* by *df*, then multiply the outcome by the outcome of *Step 3*: $(472.6 \div 38) \times 0.1 = 1.24$

Step 15 Find the square root of the outcome of *Step 14*: $\sqrt{1.24} = 1.1$

Step 16 Find the means of Sets *A* and *B*, then subtract the smaller from the larger.
(Set *A* mean is $179 \div 20 = 9$) – (Set *B* mean is $125 \div 20 = 6.3$) = 2.7

Step 17 Divide the outcome of *Step 16* by the outcome of *Step 15* to find *t*: $2.7 \div 1.1 = 2.5$, so *t* = 2.5

Step 18 Look in the table in **Appendix 11** to see if the result is significant at the 5% level. In our example, *t* exceeds 2.021 for a two-tailed hypothesis, so the result is significant at the 5% level.

Box 5X

Three steps to take before calculating correlation co-efficients

Take these steps when you've conducted a **correlational study**, you have **paired sets of scores** for two variables and you want to find out if the positive or negative correlation between them is significant at the 5% level. These three steps will enable you to select the appropriate co-efficient calculation for your data (you have two to choose from and these are featured in **Boxes 5Y** and **5Z**). For the moment, let's use an example to clarify things. Let's say you're correlating 'the number of cinemas in six towns' (*Variable A*) with 'the number of recorded incidents of assault in those towns' (*Variable B*). You predict a positive correlation, where 'number of cinemas' and 'number of incidents' will rise and fall together. Here are your scores.

	Town 1	Town 2	Town 3	Town 4	Town 5	Town 6
Variable A (cinemas)	12	13	14	15	17	18
Variable B (assaults)	61	67	70	80	84	88

Step 1 Arrange your two sets of data in a **scattergram**. This is the name given to **a graph for showing the strength of the correlation between two sets of scores**. The vertical axis of a scattergram measures *Variable A*, the horizontal axis measures *Variable B*. **S1** below is a scattergram for the data in our example.

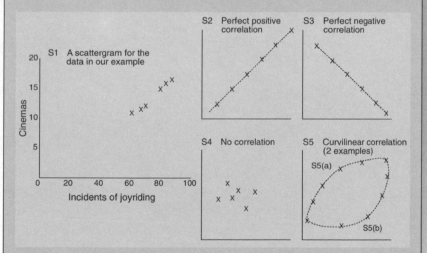

Step 2 Ask yourself 'What "shape" does my scattergram have?' Is it most similar to **S2**, **S3**, **S4** or **S5**?

S2 Perfect positive correlation
S3 Perfect negative correlation
S4 No correlation
S5 Curvilinear Correlation

If it's similar to **S2** or **S3**, go to *Step 3*. If it's similar to **S4** it's safe to conclude that your correlation is not significant at the 5% level. There's no correlation between your sets of scores. Quit your calculations here. If your scattergram is

→

Box 5X (continued)

similar to **S5** your scores are not really appropriate for either of the two methods for calculating correlation co-efficients (just to qualify this a little: a **slight** curve in your scattergram is permissible if you're using the Spearman's rho [coming up below], though the Pearson product-moment [coming up below] certainly won't tolerate a curved shape in your scattergram – it needs to be 'linear'). A shape like those in **S5** means you've found a 'curvilinear' relationship between your two sets of scores, which is certainly an interesting finding in itself when it's presented in the form of a scattergram. But any further tests of correlation will probably give a misleading co-efficient for your data. Quit your calculations here. As for our example, **S1** is similar to **S2** so we'll press ahead to *Step 3*.

Step 3   Ask yourself 'What level of measurement does my study use?' There's a guide to 'levels of measurement' earlier in this chapter. If you're using the **interval** level, work out your correlation coefficient using the **Pearson product-moment correlation**, which you'll find in **Box 5Y** below). For **ordinal** data, use the **Spearman's rho** to work out your correlation co-efficient, which is in **Box 5Z**. Both of these calculations will tell you the significance of your coefficient at the 5% level, though Pearson's product-moment is regarded as the more powerful of the two, being a parametric test.

Box 5Y

Pearson's product-moment calculation

Select this when you have paired sets of scores at the interval level of measurement and when the shape of your scattergram approximates **S2** or **S3** in **Box 5X**
(in other words, when your scores have a linear, rather than curved, distribution).
For our example, we'll use the scores from the 'cinema' study, which is
described in **Box 5X**.

Step 1   Arrange your scores into a table, as follows.

	Column A *Variable A* score	Column B A^2	Column C *Variable B* score	Column D B^2	Column E $A \times B$
Town 1	12	144	61	3721	732
Town 2	13	169	67	4489	871
Town 3	14	196	70	4900	980
Town 4	15	225	80	6400	1200
Town 5	17	289	84	7056	1428
Town 6	18	324	88	7744	1584
Totals	**89**	**1347**	**450**	**34,310**	**6795**

Step 2   Count the number of paired sets, to find N: $N = 6$

Step 3   Calculate *Column B* total × N: $1374 \times 6 = 8082$

Step 4   Square the *Column A* total: $892 = 7921$

Step 5   Subtract the outcome of *Step 4* from the outcome of *Step 3*:
$8082 - 7921 = 161$

Step 6   Calculate *Column D* total × N: $34,310 (6 = 205,860$

Step 7   Square the *Column C* total: $450^2 = 202,500$

Step 8   Subtract the outcome of *Step 7* from the outcome of *Step 6*:
$205,860 - 202,500 = 3360$

Step 9   Multiply the outcome of *Step 8* by the outcome of *Step 5*:
$3360 \times 161 = 540,960$

Step 10   Find the square root of the outcome of *Step 9*: $\sqrt{540,960} = 735.5$

Step 11   Multiply the *Column E* total by N: $6795 \times 6 = 40,770$

Step 12   Multiply the *Column A* total by the *Column C* total: $89 \times 450 = 40,050$

Step 13   Subtract the outcome of *Step 12* from the outcome of *Step 11*. Don't
worry if the outcome is negative. $40,770 - 40,050 = 720$

Step 14   Divide the outcome of *Step 13* by the outcome of *Step 10*, to find r:
$720 \div 735.5 = 0.98$ $r = 0.98$

Step 15   Look in the table in **Appendix 12** to see if the result is significant at
the 5% level. In our example, r is greater than 0.729 for a one-tailed hypothesis, so the result is significant at the 5% level.

Box 5Z

Spearman's rho calculation for working out correlation co-efficients

Select this when you have **paired** sets of scores at the **ordinal** level of measurement and when the shape of your scattergram approximates to **S2** or **S3** in **Box 5X** (in other words, when your scores have a linear, rather than curved, distribution). For our example we'll use the rank values of the scores from a study in which 'the number of cinemas in each of six towns' (*Variable A*) is correlated with 'the number of points that town's biggest women's football team has amassed in the present season (*Variable B*).

Step 1 Arrange your scores into a table, as follows

	Column A Var'ble A score	Column B Var'ble B score	Column C Rank A	Column D Rank B	Column E Rank A – Rank B	Column F (Rank A – Rank B)²
Town 1	12	61	1	6	–5	25
Town 2	13	58	2	5	–3	9
Town 3	14	53	3	3.5	–0.5	0.25
Town 4	15	53	4	3.5	0.5	0.25
Town 5	17	50	5	2	3	9
Town 6	18	1	6	1	5	25

Total 68.5

Step 2 Count the number of paired sets, to find N: $N = 6$

Step 3 Calculate $(N \times N \times N) - N$: $(6 \times 6 \times 6) - 6 = 210$

Step 4 Multiply the *Column F* total by 6 (always use 6, irrespective of the value of N): $68.5 \times 6 = 411$

Step 5 Divide the outcome of *Step 4* by the outcome of *Step 3*: $411 \div 210 = 1.96$

Step 6 Subtract the outcome of *Step 5* from 1 to find rho: $1 - 1.96 = -0.96$, so rho = –0.96

Step 7 Look in the table in **Appendix 13** to see if the result is significant at the 5% level. In our example, rho exceeds 0.886 for a two tailed hypothesis, so the result is significant at the 5% level.the 5% level. In our example, U does not exceed 23 for a two-tailed hypothesis, so the result is significant at the 5% level.

And ANOVA thing: Introducing ANOVA – inferential analyses for more complex research designs

To conclude this section on inferential statistics it may be useful to explain what happens, statistically speaking, when research designs get a little more complicated. You'll have noticed that all the examples referred to in this chapter deal with studies that have one independent variable and two conditions of that variable; for example, the influence of gender (*IV*) on response time (*DV*) in an emergency situation. It has two conditions (male and female) of that single independent variable. Yet in the real world of psychological research, research designs are often more complex. It is common to design **studies with more than two conditions of an independent variable** – known as **multi-level designs**. It is also common to design **studies with more than one independent variable** – known as **multi-factorial designs**.

Multi-level (more than two conditions) and multi-factorial (more than one *IV*) designs are rarely used by students who are relatively new to psychology, so this introduction to them (and to the statistical procedures they require) is fairly fleeting. However, for those who intend to study the subject at a higher level, it is worth knowing something about the inferential analysis of such designs. A key statistical tool for carrying out such analyses is known as **ANOVA – Analysis Of Variance**. The term ANOVA refers to **a group of statistical procedures for making simultaneous comparisons between two or more means**. In other words, they help you to draw inferences about the statistical significance of experiments that have either more than two levels of a single *IV*, or more than one *IV*.

To put this into context, let's look at a couple of examples of such multi-level and multi-factorial studies.

> **A multi-level design** (more than two conditions for a single *IV*):
> Say you decide to investigate the influence of religious belief on the helpfulness of bystanders in an emergency situation. But instead of simply having two conditions of religiosity ('religious' and 'non-religious') you have three conditions, each one comprising participants from different religions. Would Catholics, Hindus or Jains be quickest to offer help?

A design like this, as represented in Table 5.1, requires us to compare the mean scores of three conditions of participants, rather than just two.

Religion	Catholic	Hindu	Jain
Mean reaction times (secs.)	17	15	21

Table 5.1   An experiment to assess the influence of religiosity on mean reaction times in emergency situations

A multi-factorial design (more than one *IV*):

Imagine I decide to set up a multi-factorial study on bystander behaviour. You'll recall the study by Terry and Geri (earlier in this chapter) which investigated the relationship between gender (*IV*) and response time (*DV*). This new study incorporates an additional *IV* of religious belief. Would people who describe themselves as 'having a religious belief' be more likely to offer help in an emergency situation? I want to answer this question, as well as to collect new data on the relationship between gender and helpfulness.

This type of study is known as a 2 × 2 design, and effectively involves the running of two experiments for the price of one. The design structure allows the researcher to gauge the effect of each separate independent variable (gender and religious belief) on the *DV*, as well as to assess any *interaction* between the *IV*s. Before pursuing this idea of interaction, let's take a look at the basic design structure of the experiment. As Table 5.2 shows, the study enables me to investigate both gender and religiosity as factors influencing helpfulness. In some cases the results of multi-factorial experiments can reveal quite surprising *interactions* between IVs. In this (fictitious) sample, for example, it appears that whilst females were quicker to offer help overall, the presence of religious belief appeared to override these gender differences.

	Religious	Non-religious
Male	15	21
Female	15	16

Table 5.2 A 2 × 2 experiment to assess the influence of religiosity and gender on mean reaction times in emergency situations. Times, in seconds, are indicated in cells.

Such **interaction effects** are characterised by situations in which **the effect of one variable** (like gender) **changes under different conditions of another variable** (like religiosity).

Formulas and software for doing ANOVA calculations are beyond the scope of this text, but are widely available in more advanced texts which deal exclusively with statistics for social science.

Bonus Box

Using Inferential Statistics: A–T of terms to remember

ANOVA (Analysis of Variance) is a group of statistical procedures for making simultaneous comparisons between two or more means.

Inferential statistics demonstrate that a change in the value of a dependent variable (*DV*) can be confidently attributed to a change in the value of an independent variable (*IV*), rather than to chance, random variation.

Inferential tests enable you to *infer*, from the data you've collected in your study, whether or not your results are significant at the 5% level.

Interval data is presented as scores on a scale with equal units.

Levels of measurement (Interval, Ordinal and Nominal) are different ways of quantifying behaviour and presenting research data.

Nominal data is presented in separate, discrete groups.

Null hypotheses are predictions of no difference between two sets of scores on a particular variable.

One-tailed hypotheses specify the direction in which an *IV* will influence a *DV*.

Ordinal data are presented in rank order.

Research hypothesis predicts a difference between two sets of scores on a particular variable.

The 5% significance level is a *set* 'level of doubt' that researchers conventionally operate at when they reject null hypotheses.

Two-tailed hypotheses predict that an *IV* will influence a *DV*, but the direction of influence is left unspecified.

Type one errors are made when a researcher rejects null hypotheses that should be accepted.

Type two errors are made when a researcher accepts null hypotheses that should be rejected.

6 What Can I Do with a Psychology Degree?

This final chapter invites you to consider what the future holds for the proud owner of an undergraduate degree in psychology. As you will learn, the choices really are diverse and considerable. A variety of job and career prospects beckon, as do opportunities for further study. Perhaps the most encouraging thing of all is that according to both academics and industrialists, psychology graduates are in demand not just because of everything they know about psychology, but because of the transferable skills they've picked up whilst finding it all out.

● Geoffrey Beattie is watching you

Geoffrey Beattie has used his psychology degree wisely. A graduate of Trinity College, Cambridge, Professor Beattie (to give him his full title) has carved out a double life for himself in both academia and popular culture. Wearing his professorial hat Beattie has carried out research that has made a major contribution to our understanding of the interplay between non-verbal communication and speech (Beattie, 1983). In rather more down-market headgear he has made psychological insights that have reached a much wider audience. He is the resident psychologist in Channel 4 TV's *Big Brother* House.

Beattie is living proof of the diverse employment potential of a degree in psychology. As he himself wrote in the *Guardian* newspaper, whilst clinical psychology remains the most popular choice for Britain's psychology graduates, even those graduates who do not pursue such career routes are still eminently employable in other fields. This is because all psychology degrees instil potential employees with a heady mix of transferable skills.

> All psychology degrees involve training in statistics, all require the writing of essays, dissertations and projects. Psychology graduates are therefore numerate and literate. They can evaluate evidence, they can conduct empirical studies, they can write reports, they can present their findings in seminars and lectures. *Guardian*, 28 May 2002

In other words, psychology graduates are clever so-and-sos. Employers themselves are perfectly aware of the employability of psychology graduates. The Council for Industry and Higher Education (CIHE) seeks to help the business community to fathom which university courses are likely to produce the most employable, innovative graduates. They regularly publish profiles of graduates from different degree courses so that employers know what they're getting when they invite them for interview. In their guidelines to employers (set out after consultation with universities and government departments) they specify that the particular strengths of psychology graduates include the abilities to

- recognise the role of various perspectives and research methods in trying to understand human behaviour;
- generate hypotheses and formulate research questions;
- generate quantitative and qualitative data;
- present findings and generate conclusions;
- generate and communicate evidence based arguments and tailor these to the appropriate audience;
- analyse complex statistical data sets and draw appropriate conclusions as to their significance;
- work in teams and be sensitive to the needs and abilities of others.

No wonder trainees in our subject are so coveted by industry.

The same document (CIHE, 2004) emphasises the fact that with a psychology degree under your belt you're in possession of several transferable skills which are of generalised use to a range of businesses and industries. Numeracy, communication, teamwork, critical thinking and independent learning are all mentioned in this context. Armed with an array of skills then, it is hardly surprising that psychology graduates pop up in teaching, in the media, marketing, IT, social services and various government agencies.

There is further support for the view that a degree in psychology, apart from being intrinsically interesting, is a sensible career move. Each year AGCAS (Association of Graduate Careers Advisory Service – a collaboration between universities and government) conducts a survey to find out what graduates are doing six months after leaving university. Admittedly, some of them might still be recovering from exam stress, or they may be travelling or still considering what to do next. Nevertheless the data provide a guide to the merits of graduating in various disciplines, psychology included. As **Box 6A** shows, employment rates for psychology students are high and there's a good level of stability over the two years covered.

Let's take a closer look at two of the groups covered in the AGCAS survey. Crudely speaking, I refer here to those who have taken 'jobs' and those who are pursuing longer-term progression routes into careers. First, for those in jobs after 6 months in the real world, we might ask – *What kind of employment have they found?* Secondly, for those undertaking further training, we might ask – *What kind of career path have they chosen?* The figures in Table 6.1 address these two questions in turn.

The category 'professional and technical' in the table includes numerous occupations which are not obviously associated with psychology; architects, town planners, librarians, scientific technicians, draughtspersons, quantity surveyors, shipping and

Box 6A

What are psychology graduates doing 6 months after leaving university?

	2004 graduates	2003 graduates
In UK employment (includes full-time and part-time)	57.4%	58.7%
In overseas employment	1.3%	1.2%
Working and studying	11.2%	10.2%
Studying in the UK for a higher degree	7.7%	7.5%
Studying in the UK for a teaching qualification	4.1%	4.8%
Undertaking other further study or training in the UK	3.7%	3.2%
Undertaking further study or training overseas	0.1%	0.2%
Not available for employment, study or training	6.0%	5.9%
Believed to be unemployed	5.4%	6.2%
Other	3.0%	2.2%

Source: AGCAS 2004 and 2005; *What Graduates Do.*

aircraft officers, air traffic controllers, legal associate professionals, social welfare associate professionals, clergy. Such diversity in pathways only reinforces the attractiveness of the transferable skills which are on offer following the achievement of a psychology degree.

Table 6.1 Psychology graduates with jobs 6 months after graduating	
Professional and technical	17.4%
Childcare related	16.2%
Clerical and secretarial	14.6%
Retail and catering	11.4%
Commercial, industrial or public sector managerial	9.9%
Business and finance	6.1%
Teaching	3.3%
Nursing	2.8%

Source: AGCAS 2004; *What Graduates Do.*

Psychology graduates taking higher degrees or further training 6 months after graduating

Just under half of psychology graduates continue their studies, either on a full-time or on a part-time basis. Within this group a wide range of career pathways is open. Ultimately, 15–20% of psychology graduates become professional or chartered psychologists. As to what branch of psychology they train in, the most popular options are outlined in **Box 6B**, along with some extra information about the training process and the nature of the professions involved. Broadly speaking, we can consider those who pursue their studies in psychology in two groups. First, those who study for a PhD. Second, those who train to be chartered psychologists.

● The PhD route

Evidently there has been a growth and flourishing of professional doctorate (PhD) qualifications in various fields of psychology in recent years. So much so, in fact, that psychology is now the third most popular doctoral subject area (UK Graduate Programme, 2006) at UK universities. For the record, 7.6% of all PhDs are in psychology (behind Clinical Medicine [8.2%] and Chemistry [7.7%]). Of course, not all psychology doctorates are professional or vocational. Many are undertaken with a view to pursuing a particular research interest. Even so, attaining a PhD in any psychology-related area will greatly enhance your employment prospects. Indeed, in 2004, 77.8% of social scientists who attained their PhD in 2003 were working in the UK, with only 2% unemployed (UK Grad. Programme, 2006).

● The Chartered Psychologist route

Clearly there are many routes open to psychology students, and many of these lead into chartered psychologist status. In future then when you say you want to be a 'psychologist', you should really supplement this claim by specifying what kind of psychologist you want to be. **Box 6B** offers a detailed guide to the most popular routes into chartered psychologist status, as well as some tips on how to embark on those routes. Once you've decided on the direction you want to take it's time for the real planning to begin. Where will you train, and how long for? Five or six years' accumulation of expertise and knowledge in one of psychology's specialisms may be a passport to a challenging and rewarding career. Who knows, you may even become the next *Big Brother* psychologist.

Postgraduate career paths for psychology graduates (or how to become a psychologist)

Careers for psychology graduates	What do they do?	After achieving my BPS accredited* psychology degree (preferably with a 2:i) how do I become one?**
Clinical	Usually work in hospitals and health centres; aim to reduce anxiety, depression, relationship problems, learning disabilities, child and family problems and serious mental illness. Assess clients using psychometric tests, interviews and direct observation which may lead to therapy or counselling.	Professional training is via the postgraduate, 3-year full-time Doctorate in Clinical Psychology. Enables you to become an employee of the NHS as a trainee Clinical Psychologist. Apply via the Clearing House for Postgraduate Training Courses in Clinical Psychology. Accredited Doctorates are listed on the BPS website.
Counselling	Apply psychological theory and research to therapeutic practice. Effective practice requires a high level of self-awareness, skills and knowledge, especially in terms of personal and interpersonal dynamics. Entails assessment of mental health needs and risk, as well as psychometric testing, implementing of therapy, writing reports and researching. Work in industry, commerce, prisons, education.	There are two routes to train, both involving 3 years full-time or equivalent part-time: (1) Qualification in Counselling Psychology (QCP); (2) take the independent route, which means building up your own training to fulfil the requirements of the QCP. Post-graduate QCPs are offered at various UK universities, which are listed on the BPS website. Apply direct to the universities.
Educational	Address the problems of young people, such as learning difficulties, social or emotional problems. Try to enhance learning and inform teachers about social factors affecting performance. Involves report writing and negotiating the allocation of special educational assistance. Most are LEA employees and work in schools, colleges and nurseries. Some are independent or private consultants.	Do a 3-year, full-time, post-graduate training course leading to a Doctorate in Educational Psychology, which provides academic and practical experience. These are offered at numerous UK universities.

Box 6B (continued)

Forensic	Deal with psychological aspects of law and crime by applying psychology to criminal investigations in order to help us understand criminal behaviour. Involves implementing treatment programmes, modifying offender behaviour, providing research evidence to support practice, prisoner profiling, giving evidence in court, advising parole boards, crime analysis. Main UK employer is the prison service, though they can also work in the health service (rehabilitation units, secure hospitals), the social service (police service, young offenders units, probation service), or privately as consultants.	An MSc in Forensic Psychology (1 year full-time or 2 years part-time). These are widely offered at UK universities. Afterwards you'll need 2 years' practical experience, supervised by a chartered forensic psychologist. During supervision you'll also complete the Diploma in Forensic Psychology.
Health	Use psychology to improve people's attitudes, behaviour and thinking about health and illness. Try to prevent damaging behaviours (smoking, drug abuse, poor diet), encourage exercise, healthy eating, self- examination, health-related cognitions. Try to explain and predict health and illness behaviours. Work in hospitals, universities and health authorities, liaising with GPs and organisations outside the health care system.	Do an MSc in Health Psychology, then complete 2 years' supervision with a chartered health psychologist, which is assessed by the Division of Health Psychology. The process takes 3 years full-time, or the equivalent part-time.
Neuro-psychology	Try to understand the relationship between brain and behaviour, leading to the treatment and rehabilitation of people with brain injury or other neurological disease. Address various neurological problems, like traumatic brain injury, stroke, tumours and degenerative diseases. Requires clinical skills and knowledge of the broad range of mental health problems, as well as specialist knowledge in the neurosciences. Work with neurosurgeons, neurologists and allied disciplines, usually in a regional neurosciences centre. Can also be expert witnesses in court.	You'll need a postgraduate qualification that gives eligibility for becoming registered as a chartered psychologist. This training may be in the fields of clinical or educational psychology. Following this, there'll be a 2- year part-time accredited course in neuropsychology, which you can do at a handful of UK universities.

Box 6B (continued)

Occupational	Deal with people at work, specifically looking at how people and groups operate in working environments. Try to raise the performance of both individual and institution, and to improve job satisfaction. May draw on issues of ergonomics, personnel and time management. Can be an advisory, pedagogical, technical or administrative role. Work in large companies, government and public bodies. Civil service is one of the main employers.	An MSc in Occupational Psychology, then 2-years' supervision and practice under the supervision of a chartered occupational psychologist. MSc. courses are plentiful at UK universities. This is assessed by the Division of Occupational Psychology (DOP). In all it takes 3-years' full-time, or equivalent part-time.
Sport & exercise	Work with participants at amateur and elite levels, helping athletes prepare for competition and deal with psychological demands of their chosen discipline. Offer referees counselling, advise coaches on how to build successful teams, as well as working with the athletes themselves. Work in a range of sporting settings. Mostly they combine consultancy work, teaching and research. Some have full-time positions with professional or national teams.	You need at least 3-years' post-graduate training, full-time. This would include a post-graduate qualification in Sport and Exercise Psychology. These are fairly new qualifications. The end aim of such a qualification is to achieve membership of the Division of Sport and Exercise Psychologists (DPES – see their website for updates, as this is a new and growing pathway). An alternative route, for the moment at least, includes 5-years' full-time (or part time equivalent) successful service delivery involving the practice of Sport and/or Exercise psychology at a consultancy level.
Teaching	Some psychology teachers have already qualified in one of the above applied areas. University lecturers also do research, extending the subject by gathering evidence and publishing articles. Most schools and sixth-forms also now offer psychology as a subject at GCSE, IB, AS and A2 levels. Work in universities, colleges and schools.	For all teaching of psychology a BPS accredited psychology degree is mandatory, followed by a Masters and usually a PhD in your preferred area of research if you want to teach at university. To teach at an FE college or a school, the degree should be supplemented by a relevant Post-Graduate Certificate in Education (PGCE).

* Most, though not all, UK psychology degrees are BPS accredited. Check the BPS website for a full list of accredited courses.
** All of these career pathways assume the achievement of a BPS accredited psychology degree, and therefore GBR (Graduate Basis for Registration) status with the BPS. However, for graduates without a psychology degree, many UK universities do offer psychology conversion courses with an alternative route into GBR status.

Appendix 1
Tribe: a short history of a contentious word

The word 'tribe' has several, mostly negative, connotations. It originated in ancient Rome where it was used to refer to the original inhabitants of the city (Reader, 1997). Meanwhile 20th-century psychology textbooks usually set the word 'tribe' in an African context. There are plenty of ethnic groups living in close proximity to one another outside Africa, yet they are seldom referred to as tribes in the classic psychological literature. Conflicts between neighbouring non-African groups are more likely to be referred to as ethnic or religious, rather than tribal in nature.

Chambers Dictionary defines a tribe as

> A division of a nation or people for political purposes.

No necessarily African connotation here then. Rather, it is a generic term which usually refers to groups that are organised along kinship lines and associated with a particular region. Historically though, the label 'tribal' has been derisive. It has described societies which are deemed to be at a pre-civilised stage of development. Tribes have generally been seen as pre-industrial and pre-literate (Marshall, 1998). This derogatory view may stem from the way in which the word was used in colonial Africa. In the late 19th century it was common for British colonial forces to apply 'tribal' labels to groups which seldom saw themselves as discrete, unified social units (Zulu, Xhosa, Maasai). As one Zambian remarked,

> My people were not Soli until 1937 when the Bwana D.C. told us we were.
> cited in Reader (1997, p. 610)

It seems then that the word 'tribe' may be more an invention of colonial authorities who perceived various groups as being (i) discrete units and (ii) at war with each other, when actually the reality was more complex. Arguably, the *African Tribe* may be less a product of African history, more a product of the colonial imagination.

Appendix 2
Random number table

*To find **random numbers**, use this table.*

```
19 90 70 99 00 20 21 14 68 86 14 52 41 52 48 87 63 93 95 17 11 29 01 95 80
65 97 38 20 46 85 43 01 72 73 03 37 18 39 11 08 61 74 51 69 89 74 39 82 15
51 67 11 52 49 59 97 50 99 52 18 16 36 78 86 08 52 85 08 40 87 80 61 65 31
17 95 70 45 80 72 68 49 29 31 56 80 30 19 44 89 85 84 46 06 59 73 19 85 23
63 52 52 01 41 88 02 84 27 83 78 35 34 08 72 42 29 72 23 19 66 56 45 65 79
60 61 97 22 61 49 64 92 85 44 01 64 18 39 96 16 40 12 89 88 50 14 49 81 06
98 99 46 50 47 12 83 11 41 16 63 14 52 32 52 25 58 19 68 70 77 02 54 00 52
76 38 03 29 63 79 44 61 40 15 86 63 59 80 02 14 53 40 65 39 27 31 58 50 28
53 05 70 53 30 38 30 06 38 21 01 47 59 38 00 14 47 47 07 26 54 96 87 53 32
02 87 40 41 45 47 24 49 57 74 22 13 88 83 34 32 25 43 62 17 10 97 11 69 84
35 14 97 35 33 68 95 23 92 35 56 54 29 56 93 87 02 22 57 51 61 09 43 95 06
94 51 33 41 67 13 79 93 37 55 14 44 99 81 07 39 77 32 77 09 85 52 05 30 62
91 51 80 32 44 09 61 87 25 21 13 80 55 62 54 28 06 24 25 93 16 71 13 59 78
65 09 29 75 63 20 44 90 32 64 53 89 74 60 41 97 67 63 99 61 46 38 03 93 22
20 71 53 20 25 73 37 32 04 05 56 07 93 89 30 69 30 16 09 05 88 69 58 28 99
01 82 77 45 12 07 10 63 76 35 19 48 56 27 44 87 03 04 79 88 08 13 13 85 51
53 43 37 15 26 92 38 70 96 92 82 11 08 95 97 52 06 79 79 45 82 63 18 27 44
11 39 03 34 25 99 53 93 61 28 88 12 57 21 77 52 70 05 48 34 56 65 05 61 86
40 36 40 96 76 93 86 52 77 65 99 82 93 24 98 15 33 59 05 28 22 87 26 07 47
99 63 22 32 98 18 46 23 34 27 43 11 71 99 31 85 13 99 24 44 49 18 09 79 49
58 24 82 03 47 24 53 63 94 09 74 54 13 26 94 41 10 76 47 91 44 04 95 49 66
47 83 51 62 74 22 06 34 72 52 04 32 92 08 09 82 21 15 65 20 33 29 94 71 11
23 05 47 47 25 07 16 39 33 66 18 55 63 77 09 98 56 10 56 79 77 21 30 27 12
69 81 21 99 21 29 70 83 63 51 70 47 14 54 36 99 74 20 52 36 87 09 41 15 09
35 07 44 75 47 57 90 12 02 07 54 96 09 11 06 23 47 37 17 31 54 08 01 88 63
55 34 57 72 69 33 35 72 67 47 82 80 84 25 39 77 34 55 45 70 08 18 27 38 90
69 66 92 19 09 49 41 31 06 70 05 98 90 07 35 42 38 06 45 18 64 84 73 31 65
90 92 10 70 80 65 19 69 02 83 67 72 16 42 79 60 75 86 90 68 24 64 19 35 51
86 96 98 29 06 92 09 84 38 76 63 49 30 21 30 22 00 27 69 85 29 81 94 78 70
74 16 32 23 02 98 77 87 68 07 66 39 67 98 60 91 51 67 62 44 40 98 05 93 78
39 60 04 59 81 00 41 86 79 79 47 53 53 38 09 68 47 22 00 20 35 55 31 51 51
15 91 29 12 03 57 99 99 90 37 75 91 12 81 19 36 63 32 08 58 37 40 13 68 97
90 49 22 23 62 12 59 52 57 02 55 65 79 78 07 22 07 90 47 03 28 14 11 30 79
98 60 16 03 03 31 51 10 96 46 54 34 81 85 35 92 06 88 07 77 56 11 50 81 69
39 41 88 92 10 96 11 83 44 80 03 92 18 66 75 34 68 35 48 77 33 42 40 90 60
16 95 86 70 75 85 47 04 66 08 00 83 26 91 03 34 72 57 59 13 82 43 80 46 15
52 53 37 97 15 72 82 32 99 90 06 66 24 12 27 63 95 73 76 63 89 73 44 99 05
56 61 87 39 12 91 36 74 43 53 13 29 54 19 28 30 82 13 54 00 78 45 63 98 35
21 94 47 90 12 77 53 84 46 47 85 72 13 49 21 31 91 18 95 58 24 16 74 11 53
23 32 65 41 18 37 27 47 39 19 65 65 80 39 07 84 83 70 07 48 53 21 40 06 71
00 83 63 22 55 34 18 04 52 35 99 01 30 98 64 56 27 09 24 86 61 85 53 83 45
87 64 81 07 83 11 20 99 45 18 45 76 08 64 27 48 13 93 55 34 18 37 79 49 90
20 69 22 40 98 27 37 83 28 71 69 62 03 42 73 00 06 41 41 74 45 89 09 39 84
40 23 72 51 39 10 65 81 92 59 73 42 37 11 61 58 76 17 14 97 04 76 62 16 17
73 96 53 97 86 59 71 74 17 32 64 63 91 08 25 27 55 10 24 19 23 71 82 13 74
38 26 61 70 04 33 73 99 19 87 95 60 78 46 75 26 72 39 27 67 53 77 57 68 93
48 67 26 43 18 87 14 77 43 96 99 17 43 48 76 43 00 65 98 50 45 60 33 01 07
55 03 36 67 68 72 87 08 62 40 24 62 01 61 16 16 06 10 89 20 23 21 34 74 97
44 10 13 85 57 73 96 07 94 52 19 59 50 88 92 09 65 90 77 47 25 76 16 19 33
95 06 79 88 54 79 96 23 53 10 48 03 45 15 22 65 39 07 16 29 45 33 02 43 70
68 15 54 35 02 42 35 48 96 32 95 33 95 22 00 18 74 72 00 18 22 85 61 68 90
58 42 36 72 24 58 37 52 18 51 90 84 60 79 80 24 36 59 87 38 67 80 43 79 33
95 67 47 29 83 94 69 40 06 07 46 40 62 98 82 54 97 20 56 95 27 62 50 96 72
98 57 07 23 69 65 95 39 69 58 20 31 89 03 43 38 46 82 68 72 33 78 80 87 15
56 69 47 07 41 90 22 91 07 12 71 59 73 05 50 08 22 23 71 77 13 13 91 08 99
```

Source: F. C. Powell, Cambridge Mathematical and Statistical Tables (Cambridge: Cambridge University Press, 1976), p. 55. Reproduced by permission of the publisher.

Appendix 3
Z-scores table

To find out what proportion of scores lies between your score and the mean score, or what proportion of scores is higher or lower than yours, use this table. For example, for a score with a z-value of 1.5 (or –1.5), 43.32% of the scores in the set separate it from the mean. Equally, for a score with a z-value of 1.55 (or –1.55), 43.94% of scores separate it from the mean.

z	0.00	0.01	0.02	0.03	0.04	0.05	0.06	0.07	0.08	0.09
0.0	00.00	00.40	00.80	01.20	01.60	01.99	02.39	02.79	03.19	03.59
0.1	03.98	04.38	04.78	05.17	05.57	05.96	06.36	06.75	07.14	07.53
0.2	07.93	08.32	08.71	09.10	09.48	09.87	10.26	10.64	11.03	11.41
0.3	11.79	12.17	12.55	12.93	13.31	13.68	14.06	14.43	14.80	15.17
0.4	15.54	15.91	16.28	16.64	17.00	17.36	17.72	18.08	18.44	18.79
0.5	19.15	19.50	19.85	20.19	20.54	20.88	21.23	21.57	21.90	22.24
0.6	22.57	22.91	23.24	23.57	23.89	24.22	24.54	24.86	25.17	25.49
0.7	25.80	26.11	26.42	26.73	27.04	27.34	27.64	27.94	28.23	28.52
0.8	28.81	29.10	29.39	29.67	29.95	30.23	30.51	30.78	31.06	31.33
0.9	31.59	31.86	32.12	32.38	32.64	32.89	33.15	33.40	33.65	33.89
1.0	34.13	34.38	34.61	34.85	35.08	35.31	35.54	35.77	35.99	36.21
1.1	36.43	36.65	36.86	37.08	37.29	37.49	37.70	37.90	38.10	38.30
1.2	38.49	38.69	38.88	39.07	39.25	39.44	39.62	39.80	39.97	40.15
1.3	40.32	40.49	40.66	40.82	40.99	41.15	41.31	41.47	41.62	41.77
1.4	41.92	42.07	42.22	42.36	42.51	42.65	42.79	42.92	43.06	43.19
1.5	43.32	43.45	43.57	43.70	43.82	43.94	44.06	44.18	44.29	44.41
1.6	44.52	44.63	44.74	44.84	44.95	45.05	45.15	45.25	45.35	45.45
1.7	45.54	45.64	45.73	45.82	45.91	45.99	46.08	46.16	46.25	46.33
1.8	46.41	46.49	46.56	46.64	46.71	46.78	46.86	46.93	46.99	47.06
1.9	47.13	47.19	47.26	47.32	47.38	47.44	47.50	47.56	47.61	47.67
2.0	47.72	47.78	47.83	47.88	47.93	47.98	48.03	48.08	48.12	48.17
2.1	48.21	48.26	48.30	48.34	48.38	48.42	48.46	48.50	48.54	48.57
2.2	48.61	48.64	48.68	48.71	48.75	48.78	48.81	48.84	48.87	48.90
2.3	48.93	48.96	48.98	49.01	49.04	49.06	49.09	49.11	49.13	49.16
2.4	49.18	49.20	49.22	49.25	49.27	49.29	49.31	49.32	49.34	49.36
2.5	49.38	49.40	49.41	49.43	49.45	49.46	49.48	49.49	49.51	49.52
2.6	49.53	49.55	49.56	49.57	49.59	49.60	49.61	49.62	49.63	49.64
2.7	49.65	49.66	49.67	49.68	49.69	49.70	49.71	49.72	49.73	49.74
2.8	49.74	49.75	49.76	49.77	49.77	49.78	49.79	49.79	49.80	49.81
2.9	49.81	49.82	49.82	49.83	49.84	49.84	49.85	49.85	49.86	49.86
3.0	49.87	49.87	49.87	49.88	49.88	49.89	49.89	49.89	49.90	49.90

Source: F. C Powell, *Cambridge Mathematical and Statistical Tables*, (Cambridge University Press, 1976), page 71. Reproduced by permission of the publisher.

Appendix 4
Test of goodness of fit

To find out if a given set of scores approximates to the ideal, normally distributed set, use this **goodness of fit test**. To begin the test, say you have a set of scores plotted on a histogram as follows:

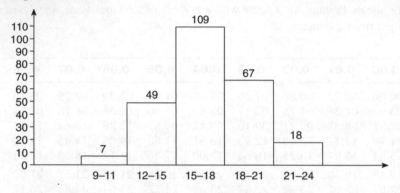

There are 250 scores in this set. The mean value for the set is 17 and standard deviation (SD) is 2.7. Here's how to carry out a **goodness of fit test** on this set of scores.

Step 1   Work out the 'predicted' histogram frequencies as though the set was normally distributed. Do this by working out the 'predicted' proportion of scores lying in each interval along the horizontal axis of the histogram.

In our example, the first interval lies between the values 9 and 12.
9 is $(17 - 9) \div 2.7$ SDs $= 2.96$ SDs away from the mean value.
12 is $(17 - 12) \div 2.7$ SDs $= 1.85$ SDs away from the mean.

The 'predicted' proportion of scores between 9 and 12 is $49.85 - 46.78 = 3\%$ (to the nearest %). These values are taken from the table in **Appendix 3**, using procedures described in **Appendix 3**. Now, repeating this calculation for all the intervals along the horizontal axis: 20% of scores lie between 12 and 15, 41% lie between 15 and 18, 29% lie between 18 and 21 and 7% lie between 21 and 24, 3% lie between 9 and 11.

Step 2   Work out the 'predicted' frequency of scores in each interval. Do this by multiplying the proportions found in *Step 1* by *N* (the total number of scores).

In our example, the outcomes of these calculations, in ascending order, are as follows:
7.5 (between 9 and 12), 50 (12 to 15), 102.5 (15 to 18), 72.5 (18 to 21), 17.5 (21 to 24).

Step 3   For each interval, work out:
(the observed frequency – the 'predicted' frequency)^2 ÷ (the 'predicted' frequency).
In our example, these calculations are:
$(7 – 7.5)^2 ÷ 7.5$, $(49 – 50)^2 ÷ 50$, $(109 – 102.5)^2 ÷ 102.5$, $(67 – 72.5)^2 ÷ 72.5$,
$(18 – 17.5)^2 ÷ 17.5$, which yields the values 0.033, 0.02, 0.412, 0.417, 0.014.

Step 4   Work out the sum of the outcomes of *Step 3* to find *D*.
In our example, $D = 0.033 + 0.02 + 0.412 + 0.417 + 0.014$, so $D = 0.896$.

Step 5   Count the number of intervals along the horizontal axis of your histogram to
find *k*. Subtract 3 from the value of *k*, to find *df* (degrees of freedom).
In our example, $k = 5$, and so $df = 2$.

Step 6   Look up the critical value of χ^2 in the table below for the corresponding *df*
value. For there to be a significant difference between the actual distribution and
the normal model at the 95% level, *D* must be greater than the value in the table.

In our example, *D*, 0.896, is less than the critical value in the table, 4.605, so we
can assume a normal model at the 95% level.

df	critical value of χ^2
1	2.706
2	4.605
3	6.251
4	7.779
5	9.236
6	10.64
7	12.02
8	13.36
9	14.68
10	15.99
11	17.28
12	18.55
13	19.81
14	21.06
15	22.31
16	23.54
17	24.77
18	25.99
19	27.2
20	28.41

Source: F. C. Powell, *Cambridge Mathematical and Statistical Tables* (1976), p. 73.
Reproduced with permission from Cambridge University Press.

Appendix 5
Ranking sets of scores

Ranking a set of scores involves assigning every value in a set a 'rank score'. In other words, putting them in order from first to last. It's the convention to give the smallest value the rank of 1 and the largest value the rank of N, N being equal to the number of values in a set. Generally it's a straightforward procedure, with minor complications where you have more values that appear in a set more than once. *Steps 3* and *4* below should straighten out some of these complications. Here's how you'd rank this set:

1, 3, 4, 4, 6, 6, 6, 7, 7, 7, 7, 9

Step 1   Arrange the set in a column, with the smallest value at the head, the largest at the foot.

scores	preliminary rank scores	final rank scores
1	(1)	**(1)**
3	(2)	**(2)**
4	(3)	**(3.5)**
4	(4)	**(3.5)**
6	(5)	**(6)**
6	(6)	**(6)**
6	(7)	**(6)**
7	(8)	**(9.5)**
7	(9)	**(9.5)**
7	(10)	**(9.5)**
7	(11)	**(9.5)**
9	(12)	**(12)**

Step 2   Allocate **preliminary rank scores**. Do this by giving the top value a score of 1, the next value down a score of 2, and so on until you reach the bottom value, which gets a score of N; N being equal to the number of values in the set. In *Step 1*, preliminary rank scores are shown in the middle column, in brackets.

Step 3   Look for **tied values**. Do this by casting your eye down the set to see if any values appear more than once. In our example there are three tied values: 4 (appearing twice), 6 (appearing three times) and 7 (appearing four times). If your set has no tied values, accept your preliminary rank scores as final rank scores. If your set does have ties, go to *Step 4*.

Step 4   Allocate **final rank scores**. Do this by giving each tied value the 'middle preliminary rank score' for that tie. So for example, for the tied value of 6 (whose three preliminary rank scores are 5, 6 and 7) the middle preliminary rank score is 6. Therefore all these three values take the final rank score of 6. For the tied value of 4, whose preliminary rank scores are 3 and 4, there is no middle preliminary rank score, so these two values take a final rank score that's half way between the two preliminary rank scores. So they take the final rank score of 3.5. It's worth noting that whenever there's a tie between an even number of values the final rank scores will always be 'something and a half'. In *Step 1*, final rank scores are shown in the right-hand column, in bold type.

Appendix 6
The F-test

Testing for similarity of dispersion between two sets of scores calls for what's known as the **F-test**, or Variance Ratio test. Use the F-test when you have two sets of scores at the interval level of measurement. Here's how you'd do an F-test on *Sets A* and *B*, shown below.

	Set A	Set B	Set A^2	Set B^2
	2	4	4	16
	3	5	9	25
	4	5	16	25
	4	6	16	36
	5	6	25	36
	5	7	25	49
	5	7	25	49
	6	8	36	64
	7	10	49	100
	9	11	81	121
Totals	**50**	**69**	**286**	**521**

Step 1   Calculate the mean values for *Set A* and *Set B*:
   Set A mean = (2 + 3 + 4 + 4 + 5 + 5 + 5 + 6 + 7 + 9) ÷ 10 = 5. *Set A* mean = 5
   Set B mean = (4 + 5 + 5 + 6 + 6 + 7 + 7 + 8 + 10 + 11) ÷ 10 = 6.9. *Set B* mean = 6.9

Step 2   Square the *Set A* total, then divide   Square the *Set B* total, then divide
      by N_A $50^2 ÷ 10 = 250$ by N_B $69^2 ÷ 10 = 476.1$

Step 3   Subtract the outcomes of *Step 2* from the *Set A^2* and *Set B^2* totals
   286 – 250 = 36   521 – 476.1 = 44.9

Step 4   Divide the outcomes of *Step 3* by N – 1 to find the Variance for *Sets A* and *B*
   36 ÷ 9 = 4   *Variance A* = 4   44.9 ÷ 9 = 4.99   *Variance B* = 4.99

Step 5   Divide the larger Variance by the smaller, to find *F*
   4.99 ÷ 4 = 1.3   F = 1.3

Step 6   To find out if there is similarity of dispersion between the two sets of scores, use the table below; find the appropriate intersecting value of *F* as follows. Look along **Row N** until you reach the value of *N* – 1 for the set of scores with the larger *Variance*. Next, look down **Column N** until you reach the value of *N* – ! for the set of scores with the smaller *Variance*. If your value for *F* is **smaller than** the appropriate intersecting value of F, you can conclude (with 95% certainty) that there is similarity of dispersion between your two sets.

Row N

	1	2	3	4	5	6	7	8	9	10	12	15	20	24	30	40	60	120	∞
1	648	800	864	900	922	937	948	957	963	969	977	985	993	997	1001	1006	1010	1014	1018
2	38.51	39.00	39.16	39.25	39.30	39.33	39.36	39.37	39.39	39.40	39.42	39.43	39.45	39.46	39.46	39.47	39.48	39.49	39.50
3	17.44	16.04	15.44	15.10	14.88	14.74	14.62	14.54	14.47	14.42	14.34	14.25	14.17	14.12	14.08	14.04	13.99	13.95	13.90
4	12.22	10.65	9.98	9.60	9.36	9.20	9.07	8.98	8.90	8.84	8.75	8.66	8.56	8.51	8.46	8.41	8.36	8.31	8.26
5	10.01	8.43	7.76	7.39	7.15	6.98	6.85	6.76	6.68	6.62	6.52	6.43	6.33	6.28	6.23	6.18	6.12	6.07	6.02
6	8.81	7.26	6.60	6.23	5.99	5.82	5.70	5.60	5.52	5.46	5.37	5.27	5.17	5.12	5.07	5.01	4.96	4.90	4.85
7	8.07	6.54	5.89	5.52	5.29	5.12	4.99	4.90	4.82	4.76	4.67	4.57	4.47	4.42	4.36	4.31	4.25	4.20	4.14
8	7.57	6.06	5.42	5.05	4.82	4.65	4.53	4.43	4.36	4.30	4.20	4.10	4.00	3.95	3.89	3.84	3.78	3.73	3.67
9	7.21	5.71	5.08	4.72	4.48	4.32	4.20	4.10	4.03	3.96	3.87	3.77	3.67	3.61	3.56	3.51	3.45	3.39	3.33
10	6.94	5.46	4.83	4.47	4.24	4.07	3.95	3.85	3.78	3.72	3.62	3.52	3.42	3.37	3.31	3.26	3.20	3.14	3.08
12	6.55	5.10	4.47	4.12	3.89	3.73	3.61	3.51	3.44	3.37	3.28	3.18	3.07	3.02	2.96	2.91	2.85	2.79	2.72
15	6.20	4.76	4.15	3.80	3.58	3.41	3.29	3.20	3.12	3.06	2.96	2.86	2.76	2.70	2.64	2.58	2.52	2.46	2.40
20	5.87	4.46	3.86	3.51	3.29	3.13	3.01	2.91	2.84	2.77	2.68	2.57	2.46	2.41	2.35	2.29	2.22	2.16	2.09
24	5.72	4.32	3.72	3.38	3.15	2.99	2.87	2.78	2.70	2.64	2.54	2.44	2.33	2.27	2.21	2.15	2.08	2.01	1.94
30	5.57	4.18	3.59	3.25	3.03	2.87	2.75	2.65	2.57	2.51	2.41	2.31	2.20	2.14	2.07	2.01	1.94	1.87	1.79
40	5.42	4.05	3.46	3.13	2.90	2.74	2.62	2.53	2.45	2.39	2.29	2.18	2.07	2.01	1.94	1.88	1.80	1.72	1.64
60	5.29	3.93	3.34	3.01	2.79	2.63	2.51	2.41	2.33	2.27	2.17	2.06	1.94	1.88	1.82	1.74	1.67	1.58	1.48
120	5.15	3.80	3.23	2.89	2.67	2.52	2.39	2.30	2.22	2.16	2.05	1.94	1.82	1.76	1.69	1.61	1.53	1.43	1.31
∞	5.02	3.69	3.12	2.79	2.57	2.41	2.29	2.19	2.11	2.05	1.94	1.83	1.71	1.64	1.57	1.48	1.39	1.27	1.00

Appendix 7
Sign test table

To find out if the result of your **Sign test** is significant at the 5% level, consult the table below. To be significant at the 5% level, your value of S must be **equal to or less than** the value in the table, for the appropriate value of N.

N	For a two-tailed hypothesis	For a one-tailed hypothesis
5	–	0
6	0	0
7	0	0
8	0	1
9	1	1
10	1	1
11	1	2
12	2	2
13	2	3
14	2	3
15	3	3
16	3	4
17	4	4
18	4	5
19	4	5
20	5	5
25	7	7
30	9	10
35	11	12

Source: Frances Clegg, *Simple Statistics*, (1983), p. 163. Reproduced with permission from Cambridge University Press.

If your value of S is **equal to or less than** the value shown, you can reject your null hypothesis and declare your result significant at the 5% level.

Appendix 8
Chi-square test table

To find out if the result of your **Chi-square test** is significant at the 5% level, consult the table below. To be significant at the 5% level, your value of χ^2 must be **equal to or more than** the value in the table.

For a two-tailed hypothesis	For a one-tailed hypothesis
3.841	2.706

Source: F. C. Powell, *Cambridge Mathematical and Statistical Tables* (1976), p. 73. Reproduced with permission from Cambridge University Press.

If your value of χ^2 is **equal to or more than** the value in the table you can reject your null hypothesis and declare your result significant at the 5% level. This table should only be used where your data is set out in a simple 2×2 table in *Step 1* of the calculation. More complex versions of this test use a different version of this inferential test – the 'Complex Chi-square'.

Appendix 9
Wilcoxon test table

To find out if the result of your **Wilcoxon test** is significant at the 5% level, consult the table below. To be significant at the 5% level your value of '*T*' must be **equal to or less than** the value in the table.

N	For a two-tailed hypothesis	For a one-tailed hypothesis
5	–	1
6	1	2
7	2	4
8	4	6
9	6	8
10	8	11
11	11	14
12	14	17
13	17	21
14	21	26
15	25	30
16	30	36
17	35	41
18	40	47
19	46	54
20	52	60
21	59	68
22	66	75
23	73	83
24	81	92
25	90	101
26	98	110
27	107	120
28	117	130
29	127	141
30	137	152
31	148	163
32	159	175
33	171	188
34	183	201
35	195	214
36	208	228
37	222	242

N	For a two-tailed hypothesis	For a one-tailed hypothesis
38	235	256
39	250	271
40	264	287
41	279	303
42	295	319
43	311	336
44	327	353
45	343	371
46	361	389
47	379	408
48	397	427
49	415	446
50	434	466

If your value of 'T' is **equal to or less than** the value in the table you can reject your null hypothesis and declare your result significant at the 5% level.

Appendix 10
Mann–Whitney U-test table

To find out if your value for **Mann–Whitney U-test** is significant at the 5% level, use the table below. To be significant your value of U **must not exceed** the value in the table for the appropriate value of NA and NB. Note that the values in the table apply to **two-tailed hypotheses** at the 5% significance level.

NB values

NA \ NB	1	2	3	4	5	6	7	8	9	10	11	12	13	14	15	16	17	18	19	20
1	–	–	–	–	–	–	–	–	–	–	–	–	–	–	–	–	–	–	–	–
2	–	–	–	–	–	–	–	0	0	0	0	1	1	1	1	1	2	2	2	2
3	–	–	–	–	0	1	1	2	2	3	3	4	4	5	5	6	6	7	7	8
4	–	–	–	0	1	2	3	4	4	5	6	7	8	9	10	11	11	12	13	14
5	–	–	0	1	2	3	5	6	7	8	9	11	12	13	14	15	17	18	19	20
6	–	–	1	2	3	5	6	8	10	11	13	14	16	17	19	21	22	24	25	27
7	–	–	1	3	5	6	8	10	12	14	16	18	20	22	24	26	28	30	32	34
8	–	0	2	4	6	8	10	13	15	17	19	22	24	26	29	31	34	36	38	41
9	–	0	2	4	7	10	12	15	17	20	23	26	28	31	34	37	39	42	45	48
10	–	0	3	5	8	11	14	17	20	23	26	29	33	36	39	42	45	48	52	55
11	–	0	3	6	9	13	16	19	23	26	30	33	37	40	44	47	51	55	58	62
12	–	1	4	7	11	14	18	22	26	29	33	37	41	45	49	53	57	61	65	69
13	–	1	4	8	12	16	20	24	28	33	37	41	45	50	54	59	63	67	72	76
14	–	1	5	9	13	17	22	26	31	36	40	45	50	55	59	64	69	74	78	83
15	–	1	5	10	14	19	24	29	34	39	44	49	54	59	64	70	75	80	85	90
16	–	1	6	11	15	21	26	31	37	42	47	53	59	64	70	75	81	86	92	98
17	–	2	6	11	17	22	28	34	39	45	51	57	63	69	75	81	87	93	99	105
18	–	2	7	12	18	24	30	36	42	48	55	61	67	74	80	86	93	99	106	112
19	–	2	7	13	19	25	32	38	45	52	58	65	72	78	85	92	99	106	113	119
20	–	2	8	14	20	27	34	41	48	55	62	69	76	83	90	98	105	112	119	127

(Left axis: NA values)

Source: J. G. Snodgrass, The Number Game, table C.7 (1978). Reproduced with permission of Oxford University Press.

If your value of U is **less than** the value in the table for the appropriate values of NA and NB, reject your null hypothesis and declare your result significant at the 5% level.

Appendix 11
t-test table

To find out if the result of your **t-test** is significant at the 5% level, consult this table. To be significant at the 5% level, your value of 't' must be **equal to or more than** the value in the table. If the 't' value for the precise df you're using isn't included use the nearest possible value. So if $df = 38$, use $df = 40$. If your value of 't' is **equal to or more than** the value in the table, reject your null hypothesis and declare your result significant at the 5% level.

df	For a two-tailed hypothesis	For one-tailed hypothesis
1	12.71	6.314
2	4.303	2.920
3	3.182	2.353
4	2.776	2.132
5	2.571	2.015
6	2.447	1.943
7	2.365	1.895
8	2.306	1.860
9	2.262	1.833
10	2.228	1.812
11	2.201	1.796
12	2.179	1.782
13	2.160	1.771
14	2.145	1.761
15	2.131	1.753
16	2.120	1.746
17	2.110	1.740
18	2.101	1.734
19	2.093	1.729
20	2.086	1.725
21	2.080	1.721
22	2.074	1.717
23	2.069	1.714
24	2.064	1.711
25	2.060	1.708
26	2.056	1.706
27	2.052	1.703
28	2.048	1.701
29	2.045	1.699
30	2.042	1.697

df	For a two-tailed hypothesis	For one-tailed hypothesis
40	2.021	1.684
60	2	1.671
120	1.980	1.658
240	1.960	1.645

Source: F. C. Powell, *Cambridge Mathematical and Statistical Tables* (1976), p. 72. Reproduced with permission from Cambridge University Press.

Appendix 12
Pearson's product-moment table

To find out if the result of your **Pearson's product-moment calculation** is significant at the 5% level, consult the table below. For significance at the 5% level, your value of 'r' must be **equal to or more than** the one in the table.

$N - 2$	For a two-tailed hypothesis	For a one-tailed hypothesis
2	0.95	0.9
3	0.878	0.805
4	0.811	0.729
5	0.754	0.669
6	0.707	0.621
7	0.666	0.582
8	0.632	0.549
9	0.602	0.521
10	0.576	0.497
11	0.553	0.476
12	0.532	0.457
13	0.514	0.441
14	0.497	0.426
15	0.482	0.412
16	0.468	0.4
17	0.456	0.389
18	0.444	0.378
19	0.433	0.369
20	0.423	0.36
25	0.381	0.323
30	0.349	0.296
35	0.325	0.275
40	0.304	0.257
45	0.288	0.243
50	0.273	0.231
60	0.25	0.211
70	0.232	0.195
80	0.217	0.183
90	0.205	0.173
100	0.195	0.164

Source: F. C. Powell, *Cambridge Mathematical and Statistical Tables* (1976), p. 69. Reproduced with permission from Cambridge University Press.

If your value of 'r' is **equal to or more than** the one in the table for the appropriate value of $N - 2$, reject your null hypothesis and declare your result significant at the 5% level.

Appendix 13
Spearman's rho table

To find out if the result of your Spearman's rho calculation is significant at the 5% level, consult this table. For significance at the 5% level your value of rho must be **equal to or more than** the one in the table for the appropriate value of N (the number of pairs of scores). If you have a negative rho value, treat it as though it were positive when using the table, though remember that it will indicate an inverse correlation.

N	For a two-tailed hypothesis	For a one-tailed hypothesis
5	1	0.9
6	0.886	0.829
7	0.786	0.714
8	0.738	0.643
9	0.683	0.6
10	0.648	0.564
12	0.591	0.506
14	0.544	0.456
16	0.506	0.425
18	0.475	0.399
20	0.45	0.377
22	0.428	0.359
24	0.409	0.343
26	0.392	0.329
28	0.377	0.317
30	0.364	0.306

Source: J. G. Snodgrass, *The Number Game*, table C.7 (1978). Reproduced with permission of Oxford University Press.

If your value of rho is **equal to or more than** the appropriate value in the table, reject your null hypothesis and declare your result significant at the 5% level.

References

AGCAS (2004, 2005), *What Graduates Do: Graduate Prospects* (London: HMSO).

Allports, A. (1954), *The Nature of Prejudice* (Reading, MA: Addison-Wesley).

American Psychiatric Association (1980), *Diagnostic and Statistical Manual of Mental Disorders*, 3rd edn (Washington, DC: American Psychiatric Association).

Bales, R. (1958), 'Task Roles and Social Roles in Problem-solving Groups', in E. Maccoby (ed.) *Readings in Social Psychology*, 3rd edn (New York: Holt, Rinehart and Winston).

Banyard, P. (1998), *Applying Psychology to Health* (London: Hodder and Stoughton).

Banyard, P. and Grayson, A. (1996), *Introducing Psychological Research* (London: Macmillan).

Beattie, G. (1983), *Talk: An Analysis of Speech and Non-Verbal Behaviour in Conversation* (Milton Keynes: Open University Press).

Beattie, G. (1989), *All Talk: Why it's Important to Watch your Words and Everything Else You Say* (London: Weidenfeld & Nicolson).

Beatie, G. (2002), 'Head Counts – Psychology is More than a Mental Decoder, says *Big Brother*'s Psychologist, Geoffrey Beatie', *Guardian*, 28 May 2002.

Bell, J. (1989), *Doing your Research Project* (Milton Keynes: Open University Press).

Bell, P., Fisher, J., Baum, A. and Greene, T. (1996), *Environmental Psychology* (New York: Harcourt Brace).

Bhugra, D. et al. (1997), 'Incidence and Outcome of Schizophrenia in Whites, African-Caribbeans and Asians in London', *Psychological Medicine,* 27: 791–8.

Bilton, T. et al. (1996), *Introductory Sociology*, 3rd edn (Basingstoke: Macmillan).

British Psychological Society (1985), 'Guidelines for the Use of Animals in Research', *Bulletin of the BPS*, 38: 289–91.

British Psychological Society (1995), *Ethical Principles for Conducting Research with Human Participants* (Leicester: British Psychological Society).

British Psychology Society: www.bps.org.uk/careers (25 October 2006).

Burton, A. et al. (1999), 'Face Recognition in Poor Quality Video: Evidence from Security Surveillance', *Psychological Science*, vol. 10, 243–8.

Buzan T. (1995), *Use Your Head* (London: BBC Books).

Carbo, R., Dunn, R. and Dunn, K. (1986), *Teaching Students through their Individual Learning Styles* (Englewood Cliffs, NJ: Prentice-Hall).

Caspi, A. et al. (2000), *Childhood Personality and the Prediction of Life-course Patterns* (Dunedin Multi-Disciplinary Health and Development Research Unit, Dunedin, Otago University).

CIHE (2004), *Employability Profiles: Graduate Prospects* (London: Council for Industry and Higher Education Publications).

CIHE (2006), *Degrees of Skill: Student Employability Profiles: A Guide for Employers* (Council for Industry and Higher Education Publications).

Clegg, F. (1983), *Simple Statistics* (Cambridge: Cambridge University Press).

Clegg, F. (1990), *Simple Statistics* (Cambridge: Cambridge University Press).

Coleman, J. (1990), *Foundations of Social Theory* (Cambridge, MA: Harvard University Press).

Coolican, H. (1996), *Introduction to Research Methods and Statistics in Psychology* (London: Hodder).

Coolican, H. (1999), *Research Methods and Statistics in Psychology*, 3rd edn (London: Hodder).

Cunliffe, J. (1983), *Postman Pat's Foggy Day* (London: André Deutsch).

de Castro, J. and de Castro, E. (1989), 'Spontaneous meal patterns in humans', cited in Sommer, B. and Sommer, R., *A Practical Guide to Behavioural Research* (Oxford: Oxford University Press).

Dunn, R., Dunn, K. and Price, G. (1985), *Learning Styles Inventory* (Lawrence, Kansas: Price Systems).

Dyer, C. (1995), *Beginning Research in Psychology* (Oxford: Blackwell).

Elliot, B. (1987), *A Class Divided* (Yale, CT: Yale University Press).

Entwistle, N. (1981), *Styles of Learning and Teaching* (Chichester: Wiley).

Erikson, E. (1980), *Identity and the Life Cycle* (New York: W. W. Norton).

Fernando, S. (2002), *Mental Health, Race and Culture* (Basingstoke: Palgrave Macmillan).

Festinger and Carlsmith (1957), *A Theory of Cognitive Dissonance* (Evanston, Ill.: Row Peterson).

Finnigan, D. (1992), *The Complete Juggler* (Bath: Butterfingers).

Folkman, S. et al. (1987), 'Age differences in stress and coping processes' *Psychology and Aging* 2: 171–340.

Foster, J. and Parker, I. (1995), *Carrying out Investigations in Psychology* (Leicester: BPS Books).

Freud, S. (1909), 'Analysis of a Phobia of a Five-Year Old Boy', in *Pelican Freud Library* (1977), vol. 8, *Case Histories 1*, pp 169–306.

Gross R. D. (1994), *Key Studies in Psychology* (London: Hodder & Stoughton).

Gross, R. D. (1997), *Psychology: The Science of Mind and Behaviour* (London: Hodder & Stoughton)

Gross, R. and McIlveen, R. (1999), *Perspectives in Psychology* (London: Hodder & Stoughton)

Harrison, G. et al. (1997), 'Increased Incidents of Psychiatric Disorders in Migrants from the Caribbean to the UK', *Psychological Medicine*, 27: 799–806.

Haworth, J. (ed.) (1996), *Psychological Research: Innovative Methods and Strategies* (London: Routledge).

Heffernan, T. (2000), *A Student's Guide to Studying Psychology* (Hove: Psychology Press).

Hiatt L. R. (1996), *Arguments about Aboriginals* (Cambridge: Cambridge University Press).

Higher Education Statistics Agency (2006), *What Do Graduates Do?* (London: Graduate Prospects).

Homans, G. C. (1974), *Social Behaviour: Its Elementary Forms*, 2nd edn (New York: Harcourt Brace Janovich).

Izard, C. et al. (1993), 'Stability of Emotional Experiences and Their Relations to Traits of Personality', *Journal of Personality and Social Psychology*, 64: 847–60.

Koestler, A. (1970), *The Ghost in the Machine* (London: Pan).

Lapiere, R. (1934), 'Attitudes vs. Actions', *Social Forces*, 13: 230–7.

Latane, B. and Darley, J. (1970) *The Unrespondent Bystander* (New York: Appleton-Century-Croft.

Leff, J. (1977) 'International Variations in the Diagnosis of Psychiatric Illness', *British Journal of Psychiatry*, 131: 329–38.

Loring, M. and Powell, B. (1988), 'Gender, Race and DSM-III: A Study of the Objectivity of Psychiatric Diagnostic Behaviour', *Journal of Health and Social Behaviour*, 29: 1–22.

Malim, T. and Birch, A. (1988), *Introductory Psychology* (Basingstoke: Macmillan).

Malinowski, B. (1950, 1922), *Argonauts of the Western Pacific* (London: Routledge and Kegan Paul, 1950; 1st edition 1922).

Markey, P. and Kurtz, J. (2006), 'Increasing Acquaintanceship and Complementarity of Behavioral Styles and Personality Traits Among College Roommates', *Personality and Social Psychology Bulletin*, vol. 32, no. 7: 907–16.

Marshall, A. (1988), *Sociology: Oxford Dictionary* (Oxford: Oxford University Press).

May, T. (1993), *Social Research* (Buckingham: Open University Press).

Meyer, P. (1970), *Introductory Probability and Statistical Applications*, 2nd edn (Reading, MA: Addison-Wesley).

Meyerowitz , B. E. and Chaiken, S. (1987), 'The Effect of Message Framing on Breast Self-examination Attitudes, Intentions and Behaviour', *Journal of Personality and Social Psychology*, 52: 500–10.

Middlemist, R., Knowles, E. and Matter, C. (1976) 'Personal Space Invasions in the Lavatory', *Journal of Personality and Social Psychology*, 35: 122–44.

Milgram, S. (1963), 'Behavioural Study of Obedience', *Journal of Abnormal and Social Psychology*, 67: 371–8.

Moghaddam, F. (2005), 'The Staircase to Terrorism: a Psychological Exploration', *American Psychologist*, 60(2): 191–69.

Mumford, A. (1993), 'Putting Learning Styles to Work: an Integrated Approach', *Journal of European Industrial Training*, 17(10): 3–9.

Niens, U., Cairns, E. amd Hewstone, M. (2003), *Contact and Conflict in Northern Ireland* (Coleraine: University of Ulster).

Peng, K. and Nisbett, R. (1999), 'Culture, Dialectics and Reasoning about Contradiction', *American Psychologist*, 54(9): 741–54.

Powell, F. (1976), *Cambridge Mathematical and Statistical Tables* (Cambridge: Cambridge University Press).

Reader, J. (1997) *Africa: A Biography* (London: Penguin).

Riding, R. J. (1991), *Cognitive Styles Analysis* (Birmingham: Learning and Training Technology).

Riding, R. and Cheemal, I. (1991), 'Cognitive Styles: an Overview', *Educational Psychology*, 11(3 and 4): 193–215.

Rose, C. (1986), *Accelerated Learning* (Aylesbury: Accelerated Learning Systems).

Rosenhan, D. (1973), 'On Being Sane in Insane Places', *Science*, 179: 250–8.

Sacks, O. (1985), *The Man Who Mistook His Wife for a Hat* (London: Picador).

Sadler-Smith E. (1996), 'Learning Styles: a Holistic Approach', *Journal of European Industrial Training*, 20(7): 29–36.

Sherif, C. et al. (1956) 'Experiments in Group Conflict', *Scientific American*, 195: 54–8.

Snodgrass, J. (1978), *The Numbers Game* (Oxford: Oxford University Press).

Sommer, B. and Sommer, R. (1991), *A Practical Guide to Behavioural Research* (Oxford: Oxford University Press).

Strachey, J. (1976), *The Standard Edition of the Complete Psychological Works of Sigmund Freud*, vol. 13 (London: Hogarth Press).

Tomkinson, B. (1999), *Learning in Style* (Manchester: Enterprise Centre for Learning and Curriculum Innovation, UMIST).

Triplett, N. (1898), 'Dynamogenic Factors in Pace-making and Competition', *American Journal of Psychometry*, 9: 507–33.

Tronick, E. and Morelli, G. (1992), 'The Efe Forager Infant and Toddler's Pattern of Social Relationships', *Developmental Psychology*, 28(4): 568–77.

Wadely, A. (1999), *Ethics in Psychological Research and Practice* (Leicester: BPS).

Witkin, H. (1959) 'Perceptions of the Upright', *Scientific American*, 200: 50–6.

World Health Organisation (1974), *International Pilot Study of Schizophrenia* (Geneva: WHO).

Wolpe, J. and Rachman, S. (1960), 'Psychoanalytic Evidence: a Critique Based on Freud's Case of Little Hans', *Journal of Nervous and Mental Disease*, 131: 135–45.

Zimbardo, P. (1988), *Psychology and Life*, 12th edn (Glenview, Ill.: Scott Forseman).

Websites

What Do Graduates Do? (25 October 20066) www.prospects.ac.uk

What do PhDs do? (1 November 2006) www.grad.ac.uk

Index